Best Practices in Online Teaching and Learning Across Academic Disciplines

BEST PRACTICES IN ONLINE TEACHING AND LEARNING ACROSS ACADEMIC DISCIPLINES

ROSS C. ALEXANDER, PH.D.
EDITOR

George Mason
University Press

Fairfax, Virginia

Best Practices in Online Teaching and Learning Across Academic Disciplines
Editor: Ross C. Alexander

George Mason University Press
4400 University Drive, MS 2FL
Fairfax, VA 22030

Copyright 2017 George Mason University Press

ISBN: 978-1-942695-08-0
(trade paper)

ISBN: 978-1-942695-09-7
(Ebook)

Book layout by Emily L. Cole, George Mason University Press

First Edition

Published in the United States of America

Contents

Acknowledgements

The editor and contributors wish to acknowledge and thank several people and organizations who have supported the writing and publication of this volume. First, we would like to thank our dedicated students, who never cease to impress us. They are an absolute pleasure to teach. Second, we commend our friends and families for their sustained and continued support of our creative activities, including this one. Third, we thank Indiana University East, which has generously supported all of us as faculty members, teachers, scholars, and researchers during a time when support of faculty members at many colleges and universities is decreasing. Finally, we recognize and thank John Warren and Emily Cole of George Mason University Press for their advice, support, and assistance in the publication of this work.

Ross C. Alexander, Ph.D.
March 2017

INTRODUCTION

ROSS C. ALEXANDER, PH.D.

This volume is a collaborative effort among 42 current and former faculty members, teachers, scholars, researchers, and administrators at Indiana University East, all of whom possess a wealth of experience and credentialing in online teaching and learning and instructional design. Indiana University East is a regional campus of Indiana University that has been a leader and innovator in online education for over 10 years. IU East offers a wide array of diverse and nationally ranked online programs and certificates at the graduate and undergraduate levels in a variety of disciplines, in addition to scores of individual online courses in over 25 disciplines, serving as the leader in online education for the entirety of Indiana University. Over 50% of all credit hours generated at IU East are derived from online education and the institution boasts students from 47 states, the District of Columbia, and over 15 foreign countries.

The prevailing purpose of this volume is to communicate effective, practical, innovative, and engaging best practices and approaches in online teaching and instructional design that can assist university faculty members and teachers, course designers and developers, and administrators invested and involved in online education. The authors are uniquely positioned and qualified to provide this information and advice due to their extensive, collective online teaching experience; course and curricula instructional design and development success; administrative experience in facilitating and growing online programs; and research and publication record in the area of online teaching and learning. All participating and contributing authors have been teaching and developing online courses for many years and in many cases dozens of courses in each role. In addition to the above-mentioned qualifications in the world of online teaching and learning, the authors are experts in their respective academic disciplines, boasting strong records of scholarship and publications in top journals and, in many cases, books published by academic presses. Additionally, several chapter authors have a strong record of applied research and industry experience that is especially relevant to their respective chapters.

Importantly, the authors are seasoned classroom teachers in the traditional sense and are therefore qualified to compare and contrast face-to-face, traditional teaching pedagogies and techniques with those associated with online teaching and learning, providing a richer context for the reader. The vast majority of authors have been teaching and serving as university faculty members for many, many years, even decades in some cases, and range in faculty rank from instructor through full professor. Many have administrative appointments as program coordinators, department chairs, associate deans, and deans. Finally, with regard to training and credentialing, all 42 authors have earned Quality Matters Level One certification; most have completed Level Two certification; and many have earned additional QM certifications beyond Level Two. Additionally, many authors have earned myriad online teaching and learning certifications through various institutions and universities. Please refer to the extensive "author biographies" at the end of the book for more information on the experience and credentials of the 42 authors

THEMES AND STRUCTURE

This book engages a wide audience of readers, scholars, teachers, faculty members, instructional designers, and academic administrators because it highlights best practices and strategies in a diversity of academic disciplines. The chapters purposefully vary somewhat with regard to structure and content, but three themes provide unity:

1. A discussion and analysis of best practices in online teaching and pedagogical approaches in each relevant chapter discipline, sub-disciplines, and multiple courses;

2. A discussion of best practices and strategies in instructional design and delivery in each relevant chapter discipline, sub-disciplines, and multiple courses; and

3. An analysis and overview of innovative, specific, applicable, and practical teaching and engagement tools, strategies, and techniques that have proven useful and successful and that can be integrated and utilized by faculty members and instructional designers.

As mentioned above, the authors possess demonstrated experience and success in online teaching and instructional design in a diversity of disciplines, many of which are not typically associated with online teaching and learning on a mass scale. This book will highlight many of the more "traditional" disciplines as well as those "non-traditional" disciplines throughout the social sciences, humanities, natural sciences, education, nursing, and business administration.

PART ONE: HUMANITIES AND SOCIAL SCIENCES

The first section of the book is the largest and contains 11 chapters in several disciplines that collectively comprise the "Humanities and Social Sciences." These chapters describe and highlight innovations, best practices, and approaches in online teaching and instructional design in the disciplines and areas of: Communication Studies; Composition and Writing; English; Political Science; Criminal Justice; Psychology; World Languages (Spanish and French); History; Fine Arts (Drawing); Sociology, Anthropology, and Geography; and Philosophy. The three common, prevailing themes of the book tie these chapters together while showcasing the disciplinary and instructional nuances and approaches of each. Three chapters in particular—chapters three, seven, and nine, dealing with composition, foreign languages, and drawing—may be of particular interest as they showcase disciplines that one may not typically associate with online teaching and learning, but are effectively taught using approaches and techniques described here.

PART TWO: NATURAL SCIENCES AND MATHEMATICS

The second section of the book contains two chapters in disciplines that are grouped within the "Natural Sciences and Mathematics:" Biological Sciences and Mathematics. These disciplines may not typically be associated with online teaching and learning across the academy, but as evidenced by the content, approaches, and lessons described in both chapters, students can be engaged effectively and substantively in this modality in these disciplines. Of particular interest for readers may be the description of how students complete lab work in both disciplines, utilizing innovative strategies and techniques that, in addition to being more cost effective for students and institutions, also allow faculty members more flexibility and options to engage students. Many times, as the authors indicate, laboratory instruction is superior in the online environment versus the traditional, face-to-face environment for many reasons.

PART THREE: PROFESSIONAL PROGRAMS

The third and final section of the book contains chapters addressing the disciplines of Education; Economics and Finance; and Nursing, grouped together here and often across the academy as "Professional Programs." A common theme among these three chapters, in addition to the three prevailing themes of the entire book, is a description and overview of how students in pre-professional disciplines (future teachers, nurses, and business leaders) are engaged and supported in the online environment. Online programs in Nursing, Business Administration, and Education are relatively common at the graduate level and have been successful for many years. However, similar programs at the undergraduate level are less common, and are highlighted in detail here in these chapters.

The literature, scholars, and authors of this volume contend that an effective and engaging online course is one that is both well-taught and well-designed. As such, this book addresses, discusses, and prescribes best practices and techniques for a marriage or integration of these two important and complementary pillars of online education. There is a purposeful and intentional variation in structure among the chapters, although all are focused on the three prevailing themes. We hope some degree of variation allows for a more engaging read and also highlights disciplinary and pedagogical distinctions. Finally, we do not endeavor to have a monopoly on answers or approaches for online teaching and learning, only a wealth of experience and knowledge that we hope can prove helpful to other teachers, scholars, instructional designers, and even students. We hope you enjoy the book!

PART ONE • **Humanities and Social Sciences**

1

COMMUNICATION STUDIES

Fostering Effective Communication in Online Courses

ROSALIE S. ALDRICH, PH.D.

RENEE KAUFMANN, PH.D.

NATALIA RYBAS, PH.D.

INTRODUCTION

Online courses have become a standard and expected delivery method of instruction at most higher education institutions. Additionally, research supports the idea that online instruction is conducive to student learning; however, according to data from the National Communication Association (2013), Communication courses offered online are still relatively rare. Out of the 801 Communication programs searched, only 151 (16%) offered online courses for fall 2013. This suggests that providing a framework for the construction and delivery of online Communication courses is beneficial. Therefore, the goal of this chapter is to examine effective communication practices while teaching communication in an online environment. Effective communication in instructional settings is a process in which students and faculty negotiate knowledge construction, develop and manage relationships, and influence each other, all of which contribute to learning in online courses. The chapter starts with a description of guiding communication theories for online learning. The rest of the chapter examines how faculty-student interactions and student-student interactions can foster effective communication in online courses in the Communication discipline.

ONLINE LEARNING THEORETICAL FRAMEWORKS

Using theory as a guide to make strategic and informed design and delivery decisions is beneficial when creating and teaching an online course. The key is to consider what communication variables would most benefit the interaction and students' learning. Much of the work done by instructional communication scholars focuses on communication variables that impact students learning outcomes in the face-to-face and online classrooms. The following theories (i.e., Instructional Beliefs Model and Online Collaborative Learning Theory) provide a framework for us as we make communicative choices for the design and delivery of our online communication courses as well as how we approach communication with our students.

When considering what contributes to a student's academic self-efficacy (i.e., instructional beliefs) and the impact on learning outcomes in an online course, the Instructional Beliefs Model (IBM; Weber, Martin, & Myers, 2011) provides a theoretical framework that includes the instructor, students, and course. Weber and colleagues posit three first-order factors that influence a student's instructional belief: instructor behaviors, student characteristics, and course structure. Considering how behaviors as an instructor influence the student's learning is important but so is considering how the course structure and students' characteristics impact the overall perception as well is just as important according to IBM.

Harasim (2012) concurs and suggests that in an online course the instructor should foster instructor-student collaboration and communication in the course. Online Collaborative Learning Theory (OCL) posits students engage in conversation to collaborate and solve content related problems or participate in relationship-building discussions. Harasim outlines three principles for OCL: idea generating, idea organizing, and lastly, intellectual convergence. When designing one's course, considering the technology the students will use to achieve the collaboration goals and how the assignment will promote discussion about the content is a central focus for OCL.

Both IBM and OCL promote the use of communication and collaboration from the students and instructor. Strategically using the online course tools to design these opportunities is part of the challenge when delivering an online course. Relying on OCL's three principles of idea generating, idea organizing, and lastly, intellectual convergence in designing assignments will promote opportunities for communication and collaboration. Employing specific instructor behaviors as well as designing a course structure that supports student communication and collaboration will also aid in building the perception of academic efficacy (i.e., instructional belief) for the content.

EFFECTIVE FACULTY-STUDENT COMMUNICATION

This section focuses on how professors in Communication Studies foster effective communication in Communication courses online. Effective communication in the context of online courses heavily depends on what instructors do: producing the content, performing their identities, interacting with students about the subject matter of the course, and building relationships with students. As courses progress, instructors interact with students about the subject matter of the course and about students themselves. Such multiple layers of interaction produced by the professor occur heavily at the design stages of the course, when faculty create courses, and then when the courses are running.

Research suggests that many variables contribute to effective faculty-student communication within the online environment. Some of the more studied and supported variables include instructor credibility (Finn, Schrodt, Witt, Elledge, Jernberg, & Larson, 2009; Myers, 2001; Schrodt & Witt, 2006), instructor clarity (Limperos, Buckner, Kaufmann, & Frisby, 2014), classroom climate (Kaufmann, Sellnow, & Frisby, 2015), social presence (Clark & Feldon, 2005; Collison et al., 2000; Cox, Carr, & Hall, 2004), and immediacy (Witt, Schrodt, & Turman, 2010).

Instructor credibility reflects students' attitudes toward the instructor as a source of communication (Schrodt, Witt, Turman, Myers, & Kodiane, 2009), and includes three dimensions: 1) competence on a subject matter

(McCroskey, 1998), 2) character, which includes trustworthiness (Frymier & Thompson, 1992), and 3) caring (McCroskey, 1998). Credibility is often viewed as an important variable affecting the instructor-student relationship (Myers, 2001) and student learning (Chesebro & McCroskey, 2001; Tibbles et al., 2008).

Two strategies we have found to be quite impactful in our classes at communicating instructor credibility include: 1) discussing our research interests and experiences as they relate to the course content and 2) creating a welcome video, which includes personal details, research interests and their relations to the course. Discussing one's previous and current research as it relates to the content shows students that the educator is actively engaged in creating knowledge. This strategy allows students to see how faculty work with the course concepts as well as build his or her ethos as an expert in the field. A well-executed welcome video can introduce an instructor to the class and allows the instructor to discuss his or her credentials, topic expertise, and passion for the course. A welcome video also provides an opportunity to express concerns for the student's success in the course. This strategy creates immediacy between the student and the instructor, which is important when building a rapport with the students (Frisby & Housley Gaffney, 2015).

In addition to producing their own personas, faculty communicate with students through interacting with them about the course content. Thus, instructor clarity is a vital part of the teaching and learning interchange. Instructor clarity is the ability to effectively communicate knowledge, both verbally and nonverbally, to facilitate student learning (Chesebro & McCroskey, 1998). Clarity is demonstrated by avoiding the use of vague or ambiguous statements (Sidelinger & McCroskey, 1997) as well as providing materials that are organized and easy to navigate (Chesebro, 2003). Instructor clarity is important to students (Frymier & Houser, 2000) and impacts their motivation in the course and communication satisfaction (Myers, Goodboy, & Members of COMM 600, 2014).

One strategy we have found helpful with clarifying the content is to send a message at the beginning of each week regarding the topic and tasks that will be covered. We refer to this as a "weekly module update." This strategy allows the instructor to go more in-depth with that specific week's assignments, readings, and even the lectures for the week. We encourage instructors to create videos discussing the "update" and post as an announcement via the learning management system that has highlighted or bulleted information points for the students.

In fact, Limperos and colleagues (2014) found that students achieve higher learning outcomes via audio and text PowerPoints due to the clarity it provides them. For us, this allows for verbal extensions of the material. We are able to embed personal examples and apply the material in relevant ways to better serve the students' understanding of the content. In doing so, the slides are not overwhelmed with text, and students can grasp the key points while listening to our applied explanations. Kaufmann and colleagues (2015) also report that when students have access to clear directions for both technology and assignments, they perceive course clarity and positive course climate.

Other strategies we use to increase instructor clarity include:

1. Providing step-by-step instructions (for assignments and technology) with clear assessment rubrics.
2. Creating weekly to-do lists and organizing materials to aid learning as well as activities to complete.
3. Providing in-depth examples.
4. Offering exemplars or models from previous students.
5. Creating a question and answer discussion post for students to ask questions about the course to the instructor and their peers.

During the semester, faculty not only build their own personas and communicate course content, but they also communicate with students about the students themselves. This suggests that perceived classroom climate is an important factor to effective instructor-student communication. Classroom climate is defined as a student's "perceived connection, rapport, or affinity" that occurs between the instructor and the students in the course (Kaufmann, Sellnow, & Frisby, 2015, p. 1). Instructor behaviors, like humor and self-disclosure largely influence if students perceive the classroom climate as supportive or defensive (Gibb, 1961). Kaufmann, et al. (2015) note that if instructors present themselves online as available or supportive such communication is an indicator for a positive classroom climate. Positive and supportive climates are associated with student learning (Worley, Titsworth, Worley, & Cornett-DeVito, 2007), students liking the course (Rosenfeld, 1983), and increased students' motivation to communicate with their instructors (Myers & Claus, 2012).

Another important variable related to effective communication with students is social presence. Social presence, defined by Biocca, Harms, and Burgoon (2003), "as the sense of being together with another, including primitive responses to social cues, simulations of other minds, and automatically generated models of the intentionality of others" (p. 458). In an online setting Kehrwald (2008) suggests that presence is conveyed through the messages sent and how those messages are interpreted by others. Students become more involved in an online discussion when the instructor creates patterns of timely participation, feedback, and support.

In addition to classroom climate and social presence, the impact of immediacy on student outcomes in the classroom (Andersen, 1979; Mehrabian, 1971) is essential. Immediacy refers to the degree of closeness that exists between communicators and is recognized as a strong contributor to student learning (Witt, et al., 2010; Witt, Wheeless, & Allen, 2004), student motivation (Christophel, 1990), and student satisfaction (Arbaugh, 2001). Some immediacy behaviors include: asking students questions, smiling, and praising student work (Gorham, 1988; Richmond, Gorham, & McCroskey, 1987). Employing immediacy behaviors in the online classroom help to decrease the psychological distance (e.g., communication gap) due to the physical separation between the instructor and learner (Baker, 2010).

In our online courses, communication is a key factor to building climate, social presence, and immediacy. As Kaufmann and colleagues (2015) have found, creating opportunities to communicate with the students either via a virtual office or with feedback help boost the perception of positive climate. Temporal dynamics, or timing, deserve a special attention in the discussion of instructor communication, and many of the strategies include an idea of time as a marker of effective communication. According to Walther's (2009) review of research about nonverbal communication in mediated contexts, chronemics convey important meanings about the person who sends messages, produces online content, and initiates communication. We strategically rely on time—timely and timed communication—to create a course flow, build relations with students, and produce one's presence in the course space. This can be achieved asynchronously or synchronously. We encourage our students to employ multiple modalities (e.g., discussion board post with a video response or email with a written response) in order to gain different verbal and nonverbal responses.

Some of our strategies to create a positive communication climate, social presence, and immediacy include:

1. Making regular (weekly or biweekly) announcements.
2. Setting times to meet with students (e.g., by phone, chat, video conference, or on campus).
3. Responding to students with messages of support and understanding.
4. Providing feedback on assignments.
5. Strategically participating in discussion forums or other public spaces.
6. Responding to students' messages within a short time frame.

EFFECTIVE STUDENT-STUDENT COMMUNICATION

As mentioned in the above section, classroom climate is related to many student learning behaviors and outcomes; however, much of the research is largely focused on the instructor's actions. Myers (1995) argues, "For the student, climate may be affected by the need to establish and defend personal worth and social stability in the eyes of both instructors and peers" (p. 193). Thus, student-student communication and relationships contribute to overall classroom climate and are positively related to student learning (Johnson, 2009; Prisbell, Dwyer, Carlson, Bingham, & Cruz, 2009; Russo & Benson, 2003).

In addition to positively impacting learning, research indicates that students desire positive peer communication (Anderson & Carta-Falsa, 2002). Developing relationships with online peers may be challenging if there is a limited opportunity to engage with one another. Johnson (2009) suggests, one way to increase students' comfort with interacting with peers online is to provide students with ongoing opportunities to collaborate. "Collaborative learning uses small groups of learners in the instruction encouraging them to maximize their own learning and each other's learning. Collaborative learning engages learners in knowledge sharing, inspiring each other, depending upon each other, and applying active social interaction in a small group" (Tu,

2004, p. 12). In addition to increasing student comfort, research indicates that collaborative learning contributes to clarifying ideas (Cox et al., 2004), understanding material, developing critical thinking skills, and retaining learning (Garrison, Anderson, & Archer, 2001). Clearly, one way to promote learning in the online classroom is through collaboration (Tsai, 2013).

There are a range of asynchronous (e.g., discussion forums) and synchronous (e.g., Skype, Zoom) tools available to encourage collaboration between students (Bradshaw & Hinton, 2004). Online discussions are a commonly used tool to encourage collaborative learning. Research suggests there are multiple benefits of effective discussions in online classes, such as promoting understanding (Carr, Cox, Eden, & Hanslo, 2004), allowing students to prepare thoughtful and reflective posts (Meyer, 2003), gaining deep cognitive learning (Akyol & Garrison, 2011), and empowering and engaging the learner (Salter & Conneely, 2015). For these reasons, we include discussions in our online classes.

In order to ensure high-quality interactions, it is essential for instructors to have clear expectations and criteria regarding discussion posts (Jackson, 2010). One author developed a discussion rubric with the criteria of frequency of posts, contribution to community of learning, interaction with the course material, and professionalism. The rubric describes in detail what is needed to receive full credit in each category as well as the time line for the discussion (i.e., initial response to prompts due Thursdays, two responses to peers due Sundays). In addition to the rubric, a short instructional video was created detailing the expectations while providing additional tips and suggestions. Finally, the instructor provides personal and detailed feedback to each student about his or her posts as well as suggestions for improvement on future discussions. This strategy appears to work, as the students generally respond positively in course evaluations (both about the classroom environment and course discussions) and oftentimes even state they desired more discussion opportunities.

There are various ways to organize discussions in online courses. Students in pairs or small groups can complete a synchronous conversation (over phone or video conference) and submit a report at the end of the week. Discussion prompts focusing on comparing personal experiences as well as focusing on solving problems may be more effective for such conversations. The synchronous discussions provide multiple layers of engagement with the course content: when students prepare for the conversation, when they actually do the conversation, and when they compose a report.

For asynchronous versions of discussions, there are multiple creative options as well. An alternative to discussions within a fixed group, students can change discussion forums (or discussion rooms). In such a setting, faculty suggest three or more situations or questions, and students respond to at least two of the suggested questions. This approach provides a variety of discussion settings and helps both students and faculty maintain freshness in their dialogue. Another way to organize conversations in groups is to assign roles to individual students who can take roles of discussion initiator, curator, or closer. The initiator creates a beginning for a conversation in the form of a series of questions, a case, or an initial post, to which other group members should respond. The curator keeps the conversation going by providing clarifying questions, suggesting alternative views, and making supportive remarks. The closer finalizes the conversation by providing a summary of the talk and identifying gaps or errors. These roles can be assigned as a package to one student in a group, or to different students. When students approach a discussion in a role, the students craft their responses in ways that keep their conversation going, for example, the students may address specific details in peers' posts or examine areas in-depth.

Beyond discussions, we encourage student-student communication in the following ways:

1. Requiring peer review of presentations, papers, and other assignments.
2. Placing students in smaller discussion groups.
3. Assigning group work, such as projects, role plays.
4. Creating a class or group Wiki pages where everyone contributes throughout the semester.
5. Using chatrooms within the learning management system.
6. Using social media sites like Facebook, Twitter, Flickr.
7. Sharing proposals, reports, and other student work in the public spaces in LMS.

One of the authors uses a unique "buddy" system, which requires students to find "buddy groups" of three or four students, or the instructor can assign buddy groups. The use of pairs presents problems as there always seems to be one pair that has issues. For example, one student does not respond or participate, causing unnecessary stress and angst for the other student. When there are more than two people working together, if one person does not participate, the other two or three are not at a complete standstill and can move forward with the assigned task. There are also problems coordinating schedules and focusing the project when more than four people are in a buddy group.

Throughout the semester, buddy tasks are assigned, such as completing a worksheet over a difficult chapter or working together on a presentation. It is important to note that if the buddy system is to work effectively, the students must be told in advance so they have time to coordinate their schedules. When buddy groups are used to complete an assignment, such as a worksheet, the students are given the following instructions: 1) Touch base with your group, EARLY, to develop a strategy for working together to complete the assignment (do NOT complete separate sections and compile them together, this generally results in a poor grade). Help each other understand and learn the material. 2) It is recommended that everyone complete the assignment to the best of his or her ability individually, and then set up a 30-minute to 1-hour meeting to discuss your responses. You can use Zoom, Skype, Google Hangouts, etc. 3) If having an actual meeting is unrealistic due to scheduling issues, then decide on a way to communicate as a group (e.g., "Buddy Discussions" set up in the learning management system, through email, Facebook Messages, etc.). 4) Have one member of your group submit this document with your group responses. 5) If your group indicates that you did not participate in a meaningful way, you will receive a zero for this assignment. The buddy system has been successful at helping them connect with other students in the course and increasing understanding of difficult concepts. Research supports that group interactions where multiple perspectives are shared results in effective learning and student satisfaction (Sher, 2009).

CONCLUSION

In conclusion, considering the communicative behaviors that instructors and students engage in within the online course is fruitful for the online course climate and learning outcomes for the students. In this chapter, we explained the importance of effective communication practices while teaching in an online environment. We suggest faculty think about their communication goals, for themselves and their students, before teaching their next online course. We encourage them to plan assignments, interactions, and even class policies around those communication goals for a successful online course experience.

REFERENCES

Akyol, Z., & Garrison, D. R. (2011). Understanding cognitive presence in an online and blended community of inquiry: Assessing outcomes and processes for deep approaches to learning. *British Journal of Educational Technology, 42*, 233–250. doi: 10.1111/j.1467-8535.2009.01029.x

Andersen, J. F. (1979). Teacher immediacy as a predictor of teaching effectiveness. In D. Nimmo (Ed.), *Communication Yearbook, 3* (pp. 543–559). New Brunswick, NJ: Transaction Books.

Anderson, L. E., & Carta-Falsa, J. (2002). Factors that make faculty and student relationships effective. *College Teaching, 50*, 134–138.

Arbaugh, J. B. (2001). How instructor immediacy behaviors affect student satisfaction and learning in web-based courses. *Business and Professional Communication Quarterly, 64*, 42–54. doi: 10.1177/108056990106400405

Baker, C. (2010). The impact of instructor immediacy and presence for online student affective learning, cognition, and motivation. *The Journal of Educators Online, 7*(1), 1–30.

Biocca, F., Harms, C., & Burgoon, J. K. (2003). Toward a more robust theory and measure of social presence: Review and suggested criteria. *Presence, 12*(5), 456–480. doi: 10.162/105474603322761270

Bradshaw, J., & Hinton, L. (2004). Benefits of an online discussion list in a traditional distance education course, *Turkish Online Journal of Distance Education-TOJDE, 5*, 1–9.

Carr, T., Cox, G., Eden, A., & Hanslo, M. (2004). From peripheral to full participation in a blended trade bargaining simulation. *British Journal of Educational Technology, 35*(2), 197–211.

Chesebro, J. L. (2003). Effects of teacher clarity and nonverbal immediacy on student learning, receiver apprehension, and affect. *Communication Education, 52*, 135–147.

Chesebro, J. L., & McCroskey, J. C. (1998). The relationship between teacher clarity and immediacy and students' experiences of state receiver apprehension when listening to teachers. *Communication Quarterly, 46*, 446–455. doi: 10.1080=01463379809370114

Chesebro, J. L., & McCroskey, J. C. (2001). The relationship of teacher clarity and immediacy with student state receiver apprehension, affect, and cognitive learning. *Communication Education, 50*(1), 59–68.

Christophel, D. M. (1990). The relationships among teacher immediacy behaviors, student motivation, and learning. *Communication Education, 39,* 323–340. doi:10.1080/03634529009378813

Collison, G., Elbaum, B., Haavind, S., & Tinker, R. (2000). *Facilitating online learning: Effective strategies for moderators.* Madison, WI: Atwood Publishing

Cox, G., Carr, T., & Hall, M. (2004). Evaluating the use of synchronous communication in two blended courses. *Journal of Computer Assisted Learning, 20,* 183–193.

Finn, A. N., Schrodt, P. W., Witt, P. L., Elledge, N., Jernberg, K. A., & Larson, L. M. (2009). A meta-analytical review of teacher credibility and its associations with teacher behaviors and student outcomes. *Communication Education, 58,* 516–537.

Frisby, B. N., & Housley Gaffney, A. L. (2015). Understanding the role of instructor rapport in the college classroom. *Communication Research Reports, 32*(4), 340–346. doi: 10.1080/08824096.2015.1089847

Frymier, A. B., & Houser, M. L. (2000). The teacher-student relationship as an interpersonal relationship. *Communication Education, 49,* 207–219.

Frymier, A. & Thompson, C. (1992). Perceived teacher affinity seeking in relation to perceived teacher credibility, *Communication Education, 41,* 388–399.

Garrison, D. R., Anderson, T., & Archer, W. (2001). Critical thinking, cognitive presence, and computer conferencing in distance education. *The American Journal of Distance Education, 15*(1), 7–23.

Gibb, J. R. (1961). Defensive communication. *Journal of Communication, 11,* 141–148.

Gorham, J. (1988). The relationship between verbal teacher immediacy behaviors and student learning. *Communication Education, 37,* 40–53. doi:10.1080/03634528809378702

Harasim, L. (2012) *Learning Theory and Online Technologies New York*/London: Routledge. See more at: http://www.tonybates.ca/2014/07/29/learning-theories-and-online-learning/#sthash.NxJGSvDb.dpuf

Jackson, K. (2010). What value assessment rubrics in shaping students' engagement in asynchronous online discussions? In C. H. Steel, M. J. Keppel, P. Gerbic, & Housego (Eds.), *Proceeding of the 27th Annual Conference of the Australasian Society for Computers in Learning in Tertiary Education* (pp. 454–458). Sydney: Sydney University Press.

Johnson, D. I. (2009). Connected classroom climate: A validity study. *Communication Research Reports, 26*(2), 146–157. doi: 10.1080/08824090902861622

Kaufmann, R., Sellnow, D. D., & Frisby, B. N. (2015). The development and validation of the online learning climate scale (OLCS). *Communication Education,* 1–15.

Kehrwald, B. A. (2008). Understanding social presence in text-based online learning environments. *Distance Education 29,* 1, 89–106.

Limperos, A. M., Buckner, M. M., Kaufmann, R., & Frisby, B. N. (2014). Online teaching and technological affordances: An experimental investigation into the impact of modality and clarity on perceived and actual learning. *Computers & Education, 83,* 1–9.

McCroskey, J. C. (1998). *An introduction to communication in the classroom.* Acton, MA: Tapestry Press.

Mehrabian, A. (1971). *Silent messages.* Belmont, CA: Wadsworth Publishing Company.

Meyer, K. A. (2003). Face-to-face versus threaded discussions: The role of time and higher-order thinking. *JALN, 7*(3), 55–65.

Myers, S. A. (1995). Student perceptions of teacher affinity-seeking and classroom climate. *Communication Research Reports, 12*, 192–199. doi: 10.1080=08824099509362205

Myers, S. A. (2001). Perceived instructor credibility and verbal aggressiveness in the college classroom. *Communication Research Reports, 18*, 354–364.

Myers, S. A., & Claus, C. J. (2012). The relationship between students' motives to communicate with their instructors and classroom environment. *Communication Quarterly, 60*(3), 386–402. doi: 10.1080/01463373.2012.688672

Myers, S. A., Goodboy, A. K., & Members of COMM 600 (2014). College student learning, motivation, and satisfaction as a function of effective instructor communication behaviors. *Southern Communication Journal, 79*, 14–26. doi: 10.1080/1041794X.2013.815266

National Communication Association (2013). *Online communication courses. C-Brief, 3*(2). Retrieved from http://www.natcom.org/uploadedFiles/More_Scholarly_Resources/Data_about_the_Discipline/C-Brief%20June%202013.pdf

Richmond, V. P., Gorham, J. S., & McCroskey, J. C. (1987). The relationship between selected immediacy behaviors and cognitive learning. In M. L. McLaughlin (Ed.), *Communication Yearbook 10* (pp. 574–590). Newbury Park, CA: Sage.

Rosenfeld, L. R. (1983). Communication climate and coping mechanisms in the college classroom. *Communication Education, 32*, 167–174.

Russo, T. & Benson, S. (2003). *Learning with invisible others: Online presence and its relationship to cognitive and affective learning.* Conference paper presented at the International Communication Association annual meeting in San Diego CA, P1–27. doi: ica_proceeding_11822.pdf.

Salter, N. P., & Conneely, M. R. (2015). Structured and unstructured discussion forums as tools for student engagement. *Computers in Human Behavior, 46*, 28–25.

Sher, A. (2009). Assessing the relationship of student–instructor and student–student interaction to student learning and satisfaction in web-based online learning environment. *Journal of Interactive Online Learning, 8*(2), 102–120.

Sidelinger, R. J., & McCroskey, J. C. (1997). Communication correlates of teacher clarity in the college classroom. *Communication Research Reports, 14*, 1–10. doi:10.1080=08824099709388640

Tibbles, D., Richmond, V., McCroskey, J., & Weber, K. (2008). Organizational orientations in an instructional setting. *Communication Education, 57*, 389–407.

Tsai, C. W. (2013). An effective online teaching method: The combination of collaborative learning with initiation and self-regulation learning with feedback. *Behaviour & Information Technology, 32*(7), 712–723. doi: 10.1080/0144929X.2012.667441

Walther, J. B. (2009). Nonverbal dynamics in computer-mediated communication or: (And the net: ('s with you, :) and you :) alone. In V. Manusov & N. Patterson (Eds.), *The SAGE Handbook of Nonverbal Communication* (pp. 461–479). Thousand Oaks, CA: Sage.

Weber, K., Martin, M. M., & Myers, S. A. (2011). The development and testing of the Instructional Beliefs Model. *Communication Education, 60*, 51–74.

Witt, P. L., Schrodt, P., & Turman, P. D. (2010). Instructor immediacy: Creating conditions conducive to classroom learning. In D. L. Fassett & J. T. Warren (Eds.), *The SAGE handbook of instructional communication* (pp. 201–220). Thousand Oaks, CA: Sage.

Witt, P. L., Wheeless, L. R., & Allen, M. (2004). A meta-analytical review of the relationship between teacher immediacy and student learning. *Communication Monographs, 71*, 184–207. doi:10.1080/036452042000228054

Worley, D., Titsworth, S., Worley, D. W., & Cornett-DeVito, M. (2007). Instructional communication competence: Lessons learned from award-winning teachers. *Communication Studies, 58*, 207–222. doi: 10.1080=10510970701341170

2

COMPOSITION AND WRITING

Embedding Success: Supplemental Assistance in Online Writing Instruction

SARAH E. HARRIS, PH.D.

TANYA PERKINS, M.A.

J. MELISSA BLANKENSHIP, M.F.A.

INTRODUCTION

As online instruction has expanded rapidly over the last decade, so has recognition that online students need appropriate support for successful learning. In 2013, the Conference on College Composition and Communication published the Position Statement of Principles and Effective Practices in Online Writing Instruction. Among many pedagogical and institutional recommendations, the statement explicitly acknowledges that "writing instruction that is conducted online requires online support systems" ("Rationale for OWI Principle 13," para. 2). The authors explain that such support should include, among other things, online writing labs, IT assistance and tutors. This position acknowledges that online students need as much support as face-to-face students and perhaps even more, since evidence suggests that many students traditionally considered "at risk" struggle with aspects of online writing coursework. Yet even as the number of online writing students grows, many campuses are, for a variety of reasons, reducing or eliminating basic or remedial writing courses, leading to a much wider range of academic preparedness in students enrolling in online sections of first-year composition. Together, these trends underscore the need to focus on how best to provide supplemental assistance for these students, particularly in online environments.

While best practices for teaching writing online have been studied, there is comparatively little research in best practices for supplemental support in these courses. As part of an ongoing pilot in our writing program to integrate tutoring support in first-year writing (FYW) courses, in Fall semester of 2015 we added graduate-level course assistants (CAs) as embedded instructional support in most FYW courses taught 100% online. Our campus Writing Center also provides both face-to-face and online tutoring services, which adds an additional layer of optional support for students enrolled in online courses that include assigned writing. We believe CAs can act as a bridge to help improve course retention and student success through embedded support. In order to consider which practices were most effective at supporting the "process-oriented elements of writing as well as its social nature" (CCCC, 2013, "Rationale for OWI Principle 13," para. 2), we conducted case study interviews with support providers and faculty engaged with the online writing courses in our pilot program; both our interview results and data from the CA embedded pilot courses indicate that additional online support can improve student success in online courses through opportunities for deepened interactions with both support providers and instructors. Based on the results of our pilot, we recommend three effective practices for developing and sustaining online writing support, including the use of both online writing labs (OWLs) and embedded course support to build effective, reciprocal relationships centered on student writing and student success.

ONLINE STUDENTS AT RISK

The need for support in online courses is real. Numerous studies indicate higher attrition rates for distance course delivery compared to face-to-face (Angelino, Williams, and Natvig, 2007). Xu and Jagger's (2014) broad-based study of 40,000 college students found that academic performance declined overall when students moved from face-to-face to online courses. The most significant decline was among students who might otherwise be at risk of withdrawal or failure even in brick-and-mortar classrooms—students who were younger, non-white, male, and those less academically prepared and with lower GPAs. These findings are particularly troubling in the face of continued expansion of online learning because, as the authors note, they portend worsening education gaps between vulnerable student populations and higher-achieving groups. Thus the need to find effective and timely ways to support online students takes on greater urgency.

Supplemental instruction (SI) is a model of embedded course support focused on courses rather than particular populations of students; it targets courses with high DFW (drop, fail, and withdrawal grade) rates, and thus is well-suited to adaptation for a variety of online classes. SI, while not necessarily a panacea, is widely recognized as an effective support measure within face-to-face learning environments, particularly for freshman and other groups at higher risk for academic difficulty (see Bowles, McCoy, and Bates, 2008; McGuire, 2006; Ning and Downing, 2010; Oja, 2012). However, its use within online environments, particularly with respect to writing instruction, has been less studied. Findings to date suggest challenges to the successful implementation of this kind of support, underscoring the need for further research.

Research focused on traditional tutoring centers and practices points to challenges with the format. Price, Richardson and Jelfs (2007) found that online tutorial support was less effective than face-to-face assistance, a distinction at least partially attributed to communication difficulties, including the "lack of paralinguistic information" including voice tone and other physical cues (p. 18). Hewett's (2010) research into online writing conferences evidences that such supplemental support can be effective without reliance on what she calls the "wink" and "nod," a reference to physical cues, but only with pedagogy designed consciously for the digital environment—helping students learn from "instructional text" as opposed to strictly physical/verbal direction (p. 13). Similarly, Rilling (2005), in discussing the use of online writing support for ESL students, found that well-planned tutor training was critical to successful online dialogue between students and tutors, and that creating effective online support for writing students requires "collaboration, dedication and imagination" (p. 371). Most research on online support has focused on OWLs, rather than embedded tutoring methods similar to SI. Our own campus success with embedded SI support in face-to-face writing classes, however, suggests that embedded support in online courses might help address the communication gap identified in the literature on OWL support.

The student population on our small, regional commuter campus includes a high percentage of first-generation college students who are at higher risk of academic difficulty but may, because of challenges specific to their commute or other circumstances, require online course work. Beginning in fall semester of 2014, we embedded supplemental instruction in face-to-face FYW courses in an effort to increase overall retention in our writing program and in the first year more generally (Harris, 2017). Following the success of that program, in fall semester of 2015 we expanded our support to online courses, piloting embedded CAs in eight sections of our online FYW course offerings. All CAs selected for the pilot program had masters-level coursework in writing studies, and many had previous experience as online CAs for other online courses at the university. CAs were assigned across FYW courses, including courses meeting both the Writing I and Writing II general education requirements on our campus; courses ranged from Reading, Writing and Inquiry I, a 100-level general education course and the first in the general education sequence, to Professional Writing and other 200-level courses meeting the campus requirement for a second general education writing course. Prior to the pilot semester, course instructors and CAs were contacted with a list of guidelines and recommended course practices, and were encouraged to collaborate on resource management and course planning. CAs were then embedded in the pilot sections through the full semester. Additionally, our OWL offered asynchronous tutoring support on an appointment basis, as they do for all courses at our institution.

The immediate goal of the pilot program was to increase student success in these online sections in anticipation of an increase in online offerings the following year (beginning fall 2016). In alignment with a campus-wide emphasis on retention, our program goals include reducing the number of students who would need to repeat the course, as our campus retention data show that students with an overall GPA below 2.0 at the conclusion of their first year of college are at a much higher risk of leaving the university, and writing courses are among the few critical courses into which most first-year students enroll. Initial results of the pilot were promising, with improved overall grade point averages in the pilot sections and an overall reduction in the course DFW rate as compared to online offerings in fall 2014 (see Table 1). Average course grades for students in the CA-embedded sections improved by about one-third of a letter grade, or from a C+/B- to a B-/B on our campus' 12-point grade scale, which accounts for +/- grades.

Table 1

Online FYW Course Grades and Retention Data

	Fall 2014			Fall 2015		
	n	M (SD)	DFW%	n	M (SD)	DFW%
COURSE GRADE	208	7.9 (5)	28.3	155	8.6 (4.5)	21.3

Note. FYW courses require a grade of C or higher to meet prerequisites for the program and most majors; in order to account for the prerequisite requirements, in this instance the DFW percentage calculation also includes C- grades.

Though our program director was pleased with the initial success of the pilot program, we also wanted to place the numbers into context, and to investigate some of the best practices that might lead not only to increased grades or course retention in online courses, but also to deeper learning and improved student engagement. In the semester following the pilot, therefore we conducted a series of qualitative, case study interviews with key stakeholders in online writing instruction and student support: five faculty members teaching online writing courses, two OWL tutors providing online support, and one graduate course assistant who participated in the pilot program. Though our study is necessarily local and limited in scope, it is our hope that readers may find insight in the voices of these participants that they can adapt to their own institutional contexts and purposes. In the remainder of this chapter, we present the major insights and lessons learned from our small pilot program regarding best practices for online student support, emphasizing the value of increased course interaction for student success and the necessity for strong planning, adaptability, and communication in designing strong student support for online writing environments.

Following the pilot semester, we contacted faculty, tutors, and CAs who were engaged with online support for writing courses to request participation in hour-long, open-ended case study interviews. Each of our study's authors conducted one-on-one interviews with designated participants, using a core set of five questions related to teaching and learning as a standard base from which to generate contextual discussion of teaching and learning in the pilot courses. Interviews were then transcribed and reflexively analyzed by all three authors of this study, who looked for key patterns across the range of participant responses, using their own local knowledge as members of the writing program and as writing teachers to help guide analysis of the results.

Generally, we first noted that all instructors interviewed found the presence of a CA in an online class to be helpful; in a teaching environment that necessarily involves a heavy literacy load and "intensive written communication" (CCCC, 2013, "Rationale for OWI Principle 3," para. 1), resources that instructors perceive as helpful to workload management are critical. The range of tasks undertaken by CAs varied widely and included moderating or facilitating online discussion forums, commenting on early drafts, grading smaller assignments, attending to what one instructor called "housekeeping items," answering student emails, holding online office hours in a dedicated chatroom, monitoring student participation and potential problems, and commenting on student blog posts. One instructor, Sue[1], commented that the CA was particularly good at posing questions in the online forums and "pulling the discussion to a...deeper level," thus creating the kind of dynamic communication that research seems to suggest is helpful to online students persisting in their coursework. At least two instructors expressed some uncertainty over what kinds of tasks a CA should undertake or how much student information, such as grades, should be available.

Both the course assistant and the writing tutors interviewed for this study also emphasized the importance of interaction and engaged relationships online. Nancy, who worked as a CA in two writing courses, explained that for her "interaction is the key. There is such a different atmosphere than in the

---

[1]   All participant names are pseudonyms.

classroom where people may be more apt to raise a question.... I think some-times [students] need a little more instruction online." Nancy described being available to students in a chat room to address questions or clarify course terminology, and working to respond to student drafts in discussion forums and through email messages. She thought that sometimes instructor commu-nication was "short," perhaps with simply syllabus or course schedule instruc-tions to read a text, and used her role to address student questions related to those instructions. Much like Nancy, the writing tutors also emphasized relationships and interaction in their interview responses. Amy, for example, discussed at length her efforts to create a "personal touch" with online tutor-ing encounters. This level of proximal intimacy was something she was well-tuned to in her tutoring work prior to taking on online support tutoring, and she explained that this experience helped her develop greater intimacy with online students, stating "I've been most successful as a writing consultant when I really try to engage on an individual basis with each student. I think they need to feel comfortable opening up a dialogue right away with us." Amy reported developing this rapport through the recreation of face-to-face inter-action in an online environment, using inspiring dialogue as foundational to the types of comments she provides on papers in margins and end comments.

Amy explained that she offers "more extensive comments than [she] would if [she] was doing it in person because, in person, you can have that follow-up conversation...hand them the resources in person, when in online, you don't have that option." During her initial consult, she described her initial "reviews [as more like] personal comments and comments on issues" with handouts provided via electronic links, which she embeds in margin comments or in a general comment field. Moreover, she noted that subsequent contact with that student through follow-up e-mails often confirms the importance of these electronic handouts. A common critique of asynchronous tutoring models is that "even though there is potential for students to email additional ques-tions to a previous tutor, the dynamic often is criticized as being a question/answer session instead of a dialogue" (Martinez and Olsen, 2015, p. 192). The opportunity to follow up and create dialogue around resource use and other supplemental services beyond a one-way critique of student work in online support can work to craft ongoing interactions. Embedded course tutors are also well-suited to provide resources and follow-up with students; Nancy also described an ability to point students toward resources as a key component of her work and relationship building in the course, directing students to particular library resources or serving as a bridge to the instructor when students had particular questions.

In order to best foster and develop these interactive, engaged relationships online, interview participants indicate that successful experiences arise from a combination of preparation, collaboration, and an almost organic adaptation of support roles in response to local student needs. In fact, we identified three elements common to those participants who reported the most successful experiences in using support in an online class: (1) advance planning, (2) collaborative and evolving roles, and (3) open communication. Further examination of these three components is useful in understanding how supplemental support, whether through embedded assistance or an OWL, can best be integrated into an online writing course.

ADVANCE PLANNING

The most successful instructors in our pilot program contacted their assigned CA before the semester's start and began actively planning for the CA's role, avoiding leaving it to happenstance or to last-minute prep. Kelly, one of the pilot instructors, reported that "as soon as I knew that I would have a CA in the course, I was given her email and got a hold of her right away," so that planning the CA's activities was integrated into her overall course preparation. In at least two cases, instructors reported that planning was done in collaboration with CAs. Writing tutors also emphasized a need for careful course planning. When asked about ways that instructors and students can make better use of support services in online writing courses, Amy discussed a desire for students to be, at a minimum, strongly encouraged, but preferably required to "be more specific with what kind of assistance" they need. Becky, an online tutor with the writing center who also had experiences with online tutoring for entities outside our campus, believes that a check-off list of specific items and issues for students to complete during the submission process might provide a better focal point for tutors on any particular project. Many students, she reported, "include an assignment sheet or a rubric that the instructor has given [to] them." Both tutors point to a need for instructors to help students plan for interactions with the writing center and to provide students with the context that will help them make the most of their feedback, whether that includes development of specific questions to ask the writing tutors or simply the inclusion of course materials with submissions.

In her role as a CA in the pilot, Nancy reported that though she contacted her instructors at the beginning of the semester, they "didn't really have a plan in mind" for how to integrate her into their courses. So she began by setting up a chat room during dedicated hours to speak with students, but found that the resource was underutilized, leading to an evolution of her role in the course, and pointing to the need for ongoing collaboration and adaptability, in addition to careful planning, as key components of successful support.

COLLABORATIVE AND EVOLVING ROLES

At least three of the five pilot instructors we interviewed approached the CA relationship as a collaboration, with the CAs encouraged to articulate their own goals for the course. Fostering a partnership instead of a hierarchy is consistent with the kind of de-centralized, facilitative environment that many instructors seek to create in both face-to-face and, more challengingly, online contexts. But this didn't mean that the CA's role was static. As Joan noted, "[The CA] eventually wanted to be a teacher so I wanted to give her more freedom, and so her role changed over the course of the semester," evolving from creating her own online discussion forum to holding online office hours and answering student emails. More than one instructor described the CA as a second pair of eyes, not just in terms of reviewing student work and offering feedback, but as a first alert, as someone who can spot when a student begins to struggle and intervene before minor set-backs become major. This worked both ways, however, as Kelly, another instructor, noted: "I would let her know if there were students who needed particular help, and she would let me know, too, what she saw, a trend...that we needed to work on." Hewett (2010) acknowledges the naturalness—almost the inevitability—of this kind of overlap, arguing that where online instruction is involved, "there is good reason to blend the roles of tutor and teacher" (p. 9).

Moreover, the writing tutors also spoke of a need for more of this kind of collaboration—where it is built into the embedded CA/instructor relationship, writing center tutors may feel more separated from what is occurring in any given classroom. Amy suggested "the writing center and instructors should collaborate," particularly when instructors direct particular students or even a full class to use the center, so that tutors can more effectively "navigate" students' complicated feelings about the requirement to seek assistance.

Nancy reported adapting her role in the course in response to student needs once she recognized that her online chat room was being underutilized. She first contacted the course instructors, asking them to remind students of the resource. She then began responding to student drafts in discussions, and ultimately found that she was able to most effectively assist through direct draft feedback and discussion:

> Going back and re-reading [the students'] revisions, they had improved. I try to be pretty clear when I make a suggestion, and if it's not clear and they still come back to me we work on it again, so I think that [...] the revisions were better with the suggestions, they did work on them.

Nancy ultimately expressed feeling "better" at the end of the semester, knowing she was able to help particular students and see their work improve, than she did in the beginning when participation was low. Regular communication and adapting her role to the needs of the students in the course were what allowed her role to evolve and, ultimately, be most effective.

OPEN COMMUNICATION

The strongly collaborative relationship that developed in the most successful instructor/CA teams sprang from regular, often frequent, communication. As Joan said:

> Communication is really important. Not just two way but in all ways, between instructor and student and back and forth between the instructor and the CA...I communicated with [the CA] at least once a week, but some weeks multiple times a day.

Moreover, many of the CAs became a conduit for student communication, with multiple instructors noting that they relied on the CA to field emails "about all the little things [students] feel like they can't email you about," as Joan put it. Nancy reported addressing these kinds of questions when she indicated that occasionally students would enter her chatroom during her scheduled conference hours to ask "hey do you know what we're supposed to be doing," or would seek her out to explain concepts for the reading or assignment terminology; Nancy reported that students in one section found the term intertextuality confusing, so "I kind of had to re-explain it." The presence of the CA in the online environment seemed to encourage students to ask questions like these, questions about which they might not otherwise have felt they could "bother" the instructor. Considered in the light of Price, Richardson and Jelfs' (2007) findings, which implicate communication struggles in the difficulties surrounding online support, such openness may bode well for the efficacy of online learning in this particular context, especially when dialogue remains strong, in turn, between instructor and CA, so that the instructor remains in the loop.

Students may also choose online tutoring for similar pragmatic reasons. Amy suggested that some students "choose the online writing center" because "they're either not on campus very much [or] don't have access to visit in person, or they would prefer not to talk to somebody face-to-face because they're shy or would just prefer to have an online consultation." For these students, the nature of an online tutoring option allows them to seek feedback in a more open-ended environment.

ADMINISTRATIVE CHALLENGES: BUILDING COLLABORATIVE SPACE

Although online tutoring support through the campus writing center has been available to students since 2010[1], because our embedded tutoring support was a pilot program, this was the first time all the interviewed instructors had used an embedded CA in an online writing course. All emerged from

---

1   The administrative home of writing tutoring was moved from a central tutoring hub in academic support services to a stand-alone writing center in the school of Humanities and Social Sciences in January 2010. Online tutoring in writing was developed prior to this date, alongside online tutoring in other content areas.

the semester with a better idea of what they would do differently next time. All agreed that regular communication between instructor and CA was crucial. Four of the five instructors desired better ways to connect students with support services like the CA and the OWL, and to motivate students to make great use of them, citing the need for resources such as online tutorials that could be embedded in the learning management system.

The CA and writing tutors also described a desire for instructors to direct students toward their services, though they were divided in their assessments of how to do so. Nancy suggested that instructors require some course activities involving the CA early in the course, while the writing center tutors expressed some frustration with student attitudes toward required submissions to the writing center. Becky explained that instructor-required submissions created "a hard situation to navigate" for tutors faced with disengaged or frustrated students. This distinction may point to some of the inherent advantages of embedding tutors in online courses; students may be more inclined to accept a course assignment with an embedded support component than a requirement to seek "tutoring" outside the course, which many students see as a remedial or "extra" requirement. As Nancy explained "if [students] don't use it, they don't know" the benefits of tutoring support, and a support system already in place in the course is one they may be less inclined to question. Sue described what she saw as a "disconnect for online students between what they are doing online and the campus," creating a virtual barrier between distance students and available resources; embedded course support can be one way to help bridge that barrier.

However, embedded support also creates new administrative challenges related to the inherently messy crossover between the role of instructors and CAs in a given course. At least two of the interviewed instructors wanted better administrative guidance on using the CAs, including restrictions or limitations that they needed to be aware of when it came to assigning tasks. Nancy also spoke to the need to develop concrete guidelines and resources as the program grows, expressing concerns she had about trying certain strategies or activities for fear of "stepping on toes." She thought at times that "the instructors had this resource and they just didn't really know what to do with me," and though she believed in the end that the instructors she worked with had been satisfied, she expressed a desire for clear boundaries related to the role of the instructor and the CA. As the program develops, it will be critical to add training and other materials that help instructors and CAs set clear goals and boundaries for interactions, and to create a library of sample methods and materials both CAs and instructors can use to plan their course activities.

It is integral to the success of online writing courses that we continue to develop and deepen our infrastructures for student support. We should focus on support experiences that encourage and deepen student interaction, providing multiple possibilities for students to ask questions, work with others, and build relationships around the reading and writing they are doing in our courses. Beth Godbee (2005) argues that we need to look to the innovative opportunities that online support provides to build opportunities for shared composing spaces, moving away from a model where "writers... simply ask questions and wait at their computer terminals for tutors to give directions" (p. 3). Technological tools like video conferencing and document collaboration software provide opportunities to rethink the support relationship and craft support that focuses on the writer over what they are writing. Nancy suggested creating a space for CAs to lead online reading discussions, deepening students' understanding of key course concepts. Other possibilities might include CA facilitation of collaborative projects or other models of composing. As support for online writing continues to develop, we can think past the one-stop-shop of the OWL, and build bridges between our campus support centers, our tutors, our instructors, and our students. Through careful planning, collaboration, and open communication, we can develop robust and innovative opportunities for learning and interaction in online environments that lead not only to increased retention, but also to increased learning and satisfaction for our writing teachers and our students.

REFERENCES

Angelino, L., Williams, F. K., & Natvig, D. (2007). Strategies to engage online students and reduce attrition rates. *The Journal of Educators Online, 4*(2). 1–14.
Bowles, T. J., McCoy, A. C., & Bates, S. (2008). The effect of supplemental instruction on timely graduation. *College Student Journal, 42*(3). 853–859. Retrieved from http://www.projectinnovation.com/college-student-journal.html.
CCCC Committee for Best Practices in Online Writing Instruction. (2013). A position statement of principles and example effective practices for online writing instruction.

Position statement. Retrieved from http://www.ncte.org/cccc/resources/positions/owiprinciples.

Godbee, B. (2005). Community building in online writing centers. *Praxis: A Writing Center Journal*, 2(2). 1–5. Retrieved from http://www.praxisuwc.com/godbee-22.

Harris, S. E. (2017). The kairotic classroom: retention and supplemental instruction in the first year. In B. Brunk-Chavez, H. Estrem, T. Ruecker & D. Shepherd (Eds.), *Retention, persistence, and writing programs*. Logan, UT: Utah State University Press.

Hewett, B. L. (2010). *The online writing conference*. Portsmouth, NH: Boynton/Cook Publishers Inc.

Martinez, D., & Olsen, L. (2015). Online writing labs. In B. L. Hewitt & K. E. DePew (Eds.), *Foundational practices of online writing instruction*. Fort Collins, CO: The WAC Clearinghouse.

McGuire, S. Y. (2006). The impact of supplemental instruction on teaching students how to learn. *New Directions for Teaching and Learning, 106*. Summer 2006. doi: 10.1002/tl.228

Ning, H. K., & Downing, K. (2010). The impact of supplemental instruction on learning competence and academic performance. *Studies in Higher Education, 35*(8). 921–939. doi: 10.1080/03075070903390786.

Oja, M. (2012). Supplemental instruction improves grades but not persistence. *College Student Journal, 46*(2). 344–349. Retrieved from http://www.projectinnovation.com/college-student-journal.html.

Price, L., Richardson, J. T. E., & Jelfs, A. (2012). Face-to-face versus online tutoring support in distance education. *Studies in Higher Education, 32*(1). 1–20. Retrieved from http://www.tandfonline.com.

Rilling, S. (2005). The development of an ESL OWL, or learning how to tutor writing online. *Computers and Composition 22*. 357–374. Retrieved from http://www.sciencedirect.com.

Xu, D., & Jaggers, S. S. (February 2013). Adaptability to online learning: differences across types of students and academic subject areas (CCRC Working Paper No. 54). Retrieved from http://files.eric.ed.gov/fulltext/ED539911.pdf.

3

English
Facilitating Online Learning through Discussions in the English Classroom: Tools for Success and Stumbling Blocks to Avoid

MARGARET THOMAS-EVANS, PH.D.

STEVEN PETERSHEIM, PH.D.

EDWINA HELTON, PH.D.

INTRODUCTION

Building a vibrant learning community is a primary objective for many instructors who teach in a university setting. In a face-to-face classroom, the hubbub of large and small group discussions, small group workshop activities, and partner activities serves as a sign of a successful learning community. In the English classroom, learning that is not simply lecture-based often occurs through conversations about literature and language, about creative projects and research-based projects, about professional writing situations and more. In a face-to-face classroom environment, instructors can see the liveliness of the learning community and can readily recognize and address student confusion when faces cloud in frustration as some wave of conversation leaves them in its wake. How can instructors reinvent this energetic and engaged community of learners effectively in an online learning environment? Our argument is that the community-building crucial to student engagement and success in face-to-face classrooms can also be successfully designed into online learning through a versatile use of online discussions.

Rather than prescribing the best way to encourage learning in all situations, educators would do well to consider the best practices for learning the specific types of content, purpose, and outcomes that apply to their specific courses in online learning as well as the face-to-face classroom environment. In courses in professional writing, language, or literature, the best practices for facilitating learning in a face-to-face setting or an online setting sometimes overlap, but the two types of classrooms create unique situations that must be addressed by careful attention to the classroom environment. In courses across the English discipline and related courses, however, it has been our experience that effective learning is enabled most fully when learning communities are established and encouraged. In online courses, discussion centers are essential to the kind of learning communities we form in language and literature courses.

Tools for building online learning communities that provide situations where learning can be scaffolded include the use of discussion boards or forums, messages between the professor and students, and peer review. While messages sent from professor to students focus on the individuality of the student and professor relationship, differing from office visits or pre/post-class chats only in being written rather than spoken, the use of discussion boards is likely the primary focus for community-building in online courses in professional writing, language, and literature. Thus, most of our attention in this chapter will be devoted to this tool.

Our contention that discussions are essential to online learning in the English discipline proceeds from our conviction that learning is a constructivist process rather than simply a transmission of information. Vygotsky's (1978) theory of child development can readily be adapted to online learning environments. As Vygotsky puts it, the zone of proximal development "is the distance between the actual developmental level as determined by independent problem solving and the level of potential development as determined through problem solving under adult guidance or in collaboration with more capable peers" (p. 86). Furthermore, Vygotsky claims intellectual growth takes place in specific contexts: "human learning presupposes a specific social nature and a process by which children grow into the intellectual life of those around them" (p. 88). While learning may be instinctual in some situations, the kind of learning that happens in a higher education setting usually is not. Instead, the more complex learning that occurs in higher education involves a more deliberate process of building one's understanding. Thus, rather than pushing our students out of the nest of their current knowledge as a mother bird does, effective educators teach students how to organize their learning and build their capacities and understanding in a process of learning that is more than instinctual. Vygotsky's educational model of the zone of proximal development, with its emphasis on the scaffolding that is provided by instructors or peers, provides us with a theoretical framework that helps us to conceptualize how we may help students to bridge the gap between what learners know or understand and what they do not yet know or understand. In the online classroom, instructors serve as mentors and classmates serve as peers to create a collaborative learning environment, and this classroom culture is evident in discussions.

In their multi-year study of online learning communities, Palloff and Pratt (2005) enumerate the following components of an online learning community: 1) People with a shared purpose and common guidelines, 2) Use of online technology, 3) Participation in collaborative and reflective learning, and 4) an atmosphere of social presence. The latter point, which Palloff and Pratt added after observing the interaction of the first three components, suggests that social learning theory has much to offer to the study of online learning communities as well (p. 3). These components of online learning communities apply especially well for discussion building, analysis, and assessment.

Instructor presence and involvement are key to building a successful online learning community. Pollard, Minor and Swanson (2014) argue that "instructor immediacy is essential in the creation of a sense of community." Dunlap and Lowenthal (2014) describe searching for the right balance of social presence using strategies including threaded discussions, personal emails to students, and Twitter; they refer to this as the "quest for the social presence grail" (p. 41). Further, they question how to achieve the right number of discussions, whether they should be all-class or small groups and if the students should have specific tasks to complete. Many studies emphasize the value of discussions for learning in online courses (Blackmon, 2012; Palmer, Holt, & Bray, 2008). Dennen (2005) claims that discussions need to be carefully designed in order for learning to take place and that instructor presence is crucial in developing valuable student discussions. Quality discussion does not simply happen because instructors expect it; the focus of the conversation and the directions to follow must be thoughtfully crafted to achieve the kind of results instructors seek. In the examples that follow, we will outline strategies that may be used successfully to shape the online learning environment in ways that stimulate optimal engagement of learners and instructors alike.

ESTABLISHING SHARED GUIDELINES

While numerous strategies may be enacted to establish shared guidelines in an online classroom community, shared guidelines are especially important for shaping discussions in a meaningful way. Syllabus statements or etiquette guidelines, prompts that require reflective responses to the assignments, and rubrics are three methods we have used successfully to communicate and establish clear and consistent guidelines for the course throughout the entire semester.

A syllabus statement about discussion posts and responses is the most direct and least time-consuming method of setting up shared expectations for discussions. The following example is an actual syllabus statement about discussion responses:

> Your response must in some way <u>extend the conversation</u> begun by the other student. You must do more than tell how horrible or wonderful someone else's ideas are. (Rants and raves receive little to no credit.) Often, you will find it helpful to suggest **additional ideas or questions raised for you by the other student's discussion of the text,** ideas or questions that encourage rereading and deeper thinking about the issues raised by the discussion post.

By ensuring that the emphasis is on extending the conversation rather than simply telling each other whether they are "right" or "wrong," or whether another student agrees or disagrees, this syllabus statement clearly communicates the desire for an ongoing conversation rather than an unrealistic expectation of finding the "right" answer for the kinds of multi-faceted questions often engaged in humanities classrooms. Since this example gives a general description of discussion expectations, it applies to all regular posts and responses throughout the semester. In a literature course, most discussions are centered on the assigned readings for the course in order to allow for the kind of classroom characteristic of highly-engaged face-to-face classrooms. Self-identified introverts have commented that the ability to write their responses rather than speaking allows them the time to formulate their thoughts without responding negatively to the pressure of the moment. Discussions in any English classroom may also be centered on upcoming assignments in the course. When using a syllabus statement such as the one above, any deviations from these expectations can be clearly identified for special assignments.

The etiquette statement or policy is widely touted in online course design as a necessity. Such a statement treats students professionally by building a community of learners without placing undue emphasis on poor student behavior. Sharing expectations of civility in interaction on the discussion board is an absolute necessity for preventing problems with student community-building, the hurt feelings or offense that can derail and disengage a student from learning. By explaining the reason for and purpose of the statement in welcome pages, introductory videos reinforce the etiquette statement. Netiquette sets out guidelines for behavior which include being sensitive to the other student's culture, language, religious and political beliefs. They also recommend avoiding profanity, the use of all capital letters which suggests shouting, avoiding confusing acronyms and in general using correct grammar and spelling ("Sample of Network Etiquette," 2016).

Having a statement is not enough. There are still occasions where someone's buttons are pushed by something a classmate says resulting in a derogatory, "are you kidding me" or "you cannot be serious" prefaced inflammatory statement. Then an announcement reminding students of the etiquette policy could be sent out as a reminder without singling out individual students. However, students generally figure out why the reminder is being sent out which can threaten the delicate balance of the learning community built among students. Helton offers a reminder announcement every three or four weeks to reinforce the effectiveness of the policy in preventing issues. This keeps the policy in mind and may eliminate the need for a potentially damaging response on the discussion board. Students can also be advised to contact the instructor directly if something on the message board is found to be problematic, creating a teachable moment and more pleasant scenarios that preserve a positive community among students.

In our experience, courses with carefully crafted prompts to point students in the direction of academically-engaged conversations or a general prompt that requires them to reflect on assigned course readings work better than completely open-ended prompts. In her technical and professional writing classes, Thomas-Evans assigns specific chapters from the textbooks in her classes each week and rather than give questions to guide the students, she asks them to reflect on the reading and show how it connects to their professional or academic experience as appropriate. She finds students share helpful insights about their experiences. Many of them are working professionals, although some are traditional students with much less workforce exposure. They learn from each other. She prefers that students don't all answer the same professor-directed question; she would rather they respond and generate their own focus and lead the discussion in ways that are meaningful to them.

Another method of establishing clear guidelines is to attach a rubric to discussions. The following rubric gives an example of a rubric developed for literature courses but adaptable to many other types of assignments as well. The focus of the rubric is the students' engagement with a prompt written by the instructor.

Criteria/ Performance	Strong	Satisfactory	Weak
Completes and Develops Post	Posts are completed on time, written as 2–3 paragraphs (not including quotations), and are fully developed. 4 pts	Posts are completed on time and written in paragraphs but not as fully developed as an excellent post. 3 pts	Posts are present but greatly underdeveloped. 2 pts

Addresses Prompt	Posts effectively address and reflect on the prompt. 4 pts	Posts are related to the prompt and engage with the prompt at some level. 3 pts	Posts vaguely allude to the prompt but do not represent an adequate engagement with the prompt. 2 pts
Provides Support	Posts include specific words, phrases, or details from the text/ film as needed to explain a question or issue related to the text. 4 pts	Posts include some support from the text, but the support is somewhat vague or overgeneralized. 3 pts	Some details are provided, but they do not clearly support or explain. 2 pts
Response(s) that Extend(s) Conversation	Responses show some agreement/ disagreement or offer additional conclusions, questions, considerations, etc. that continue the discussion. 5 pts	Responses show some connection to the original post but may only minimally extend the conversation (perhaps offering mostly rants or raves). 3 pts	Responses are simply repetition of points made by others or offer simple unreflective agreement/ disagreement. 2 pts
Uses Correct Grammar and Mechanics	The post and response are written in (almost) completely correct grammar, using (mostly) correct spelling, punctuation, etc. 3 pts	The post and response are written in readable paragraphs, but there may be some errors in grammar or mechanics. 2 pts	The post and/or response contain numerous errors that distract from the reading. 1 pt

By clearly identifying where each part of the grade is coming from, students learn to refer to the rubric whenever they have a question. Since Petersheim instituted rubrics for his discussions, he has noticed a dramatic decrease in student questions about discussion grades. Each of these methods of establishing shared guidelines work in an online classroom, but in his experience a rubric creates the least amount of confusion for students.

Closely related to the practice of establishing common expectations is the practice of creating a shared purpose for each discussion. Instructors can do this through the careful creation of discussion prompts that consistently tie back to the purposes of the course as a whole. We employ numerous strategies that aid in achieving this goal, but two of the most effective strategies in our experience are creating prompts that ask students to connect course readings to course objectives and encouraging students to read discussion prompts before doing the assigned reading or other work.

Creating a prompt that asks students to find links between specific course readings or other assignments and a specific course objective can help to create a shared purpose. Following is an example of how Petersheim enacted this strategy for a slave narrative in a course on nineteenth-century American literature.

Reading: *Incidents in the Life of a Slave Girl* by Harriet Jacobs

Course Objective: to demonstrate an understanding of the ways race and gender influence one's sense of American identity in the nineteenth century

Prompt: How does Harriet Jacobs' slave narrative demonstrate the way race and gender are considered a threat by those in power? In your post, cite at least one specific passage from her text to help you address this question, showing how details from the selected passage(s) engage with some or all of these ideas.

In this example, specific details about the reading are paired with language from an appropriate course objective (race and gender, sense of identity) to create a unique prompt that encourages students to engage with the text. While this approach is particularly useful for courses with extensive reading assignments, it can be adapted successfully to other courses as well. In a writing course, for example, Petersheim has asked students to show their development as a writer (a course objective) by describing their learning about a certain style of expository writing (a course assignment).

The second strategy for creating a shared purpose is simple but raises the degree of student engagement—often dramatically. By reading and commenting on the discussion prompt in a video mini-lecture on the readings, instructors can give students a purpose for reading before they even begin the assigned reading. Enacting this strategy has allowed Petersheim to inspire student interest, connections, and questions about the assigned literary work before becoming familiar with the text itself. When students write their first post and respond to other students, they enter the conversation he has initiated with his prompt, sometimes by quoting what other scholars have said about the text.

DISCUSSIONS AS TOOLS OF COLLABORATIVE LEARNING AND SOCIAL PRESENCE

Discussions provide a unique opportunity for collaborative learning, especially when structured to allow the rich back-and-forth conversations that characterize the best face-to-face classrooms. At the beginning of a course, students often introduce themselves in some way. In our classes, we encourage students also to tell why they are taking the course in order to make introductions themselves a springboard for talking about course content and materials. As discussed, building community in an online writing class is one of the most crucial factors in creating a successful course and a positive experience for students. Through multiple interactions, students must get to know each other and learn to feel comfortable and safe enough to share their work either in whole class discussion forums or in smaller peer groups for review. To achieve this necessary element in online classes, students begin the semester with the typical Introduction Discussion. Here they can tell their classmates whatever they choose to reveal. Thomas-Evans models this activity by starting with her own introduction. She shares information on how long she has worked at her current institution, where she earned her degrees, brief details about her family, and what she enjoys doing to have fun (places she has traveled or would like to travel, books she likes reading, projects she is knitting, TV shows she watches). She tries to show she is a person with normal interests and a family so they can relate to her. Students respond to each other (choosing who to greet) and often to her.

When class begins each semester, Thomas-Evans sees students recognizing each other from previous classes; they wish each other well and share a sense of accomplishment when they are nearing graduation in her senior capstone course. Without ever having met in person, in most cases, they greet each other as friends and this easy camaraderie helps build the class community. Many of them have taken classes with us before and they are not shy about talking about instructors in their introductions—at least the ones who have positive things to say! They freely comment on last semester's classes—ours and others! Other students say it is their first class with a professor or in the program; they are sometimes a bit more timid, but it does not often last long. Even the more reticent students participate. They may not always be quite as involved, but their active presence is noted.

One strategy for shaping discussions as collaborative learning opportunities is to write a prompt that guides students to respond to each other as well as to compose initial posts in response to the instructor's prompt. For example, the previously mentioned prompt about Harriet Jacobs' text only requires students to write a post in response to the instructor's prompt. This prompt could have a part two, with instructions such as this:

> In your responses to other students, evaluate whether the passages they cited help them make their point, and discuss why or why not. You may also wish to suggest additional passages that seem to support or undermine the other student's post, but make sure that your response continues the discussion rather than shutting it down.

This response helps students remember to think about their reading more deeply rather than simply giving knee-jerk reactions to the text. In our experience, students who know their peers will be commenting on their papers expend much greater effort when composing their original posts.

Another strategy for using discussions as collaborative learning is for the instructor to enter the discussions from time to time with the express purpose of pointing out connections between different discussion threads—either between threads going on simultaneously or between a current discussion and a discussion that occurred earlier in the classroom. Such connections can enhance student learning not only by making learning a collaborative effort but also by helping students transfer what they are learning from one instance to another. We are always on the lookout for ways to help students become life-long learners and this simple method is one way of promoting such learning.

Students can also take classroom discussions into the larger blogosphere, using their experience in discussions to guide their discussion on blogs and vice versa. One project in Thomas-Evans' Digital Writing class requires students to create and maintain a blog with a specific topic focus for the semester (they post ten times by specified due dates). She suggests blog platforms to use (and provides directions for those); they can select an alternative platform, but it must be free and accessible to the class without a login. The students all post a link to their blog in a discussion space in the course management system. They are required to read and respond to the blogs of two students in class. She typically lets them either pick two to follow all semester or meander around selecting different ones each time. Unfortunately, this can mean that some students get limited feedback (she responds to them all). For the purposes of grades, she requires them to post in the class discussion rather than reply to the actual blog platform so that she can keep track. This is required work after all. She encourages, but does not require, them to also post their comments directly in the blog platform so the student might develop a following. In the blogs, as they are public/open spaces, some of the students get responses from others not associated with the class. This task makes them consider the importance of writing for a public audience beyond their classmates (a good thing) and forces them to think about being members of a much larger collaborative learning community.

Many collaborative learning strategies also work to create social presence in discussions. Instructor feedback to student discussions may come in the form of responses in the discussions themselves, as noted earlier. However, instructors may also respond by leaving grading comments, using a consistent discussion rubric, or discussing the posts and responses face-to-face or through a video recording.

Group work can also be completed in multiple ways, but discussions provide an effective way of organizing and facilitating group work in an online learning environment. There is a great deal to consider when assigning groups. Thomas-Evans offers students the option to be assigned to a group or have the agency to select their own group. For the first project, students often ask to be assigned. Maybe they are not comfortable picking yet; they may not know each other. When the class gets to later projects, when given the same option, many suggest students they would prefer to work with. If they want to create their own groups, they can set them up through email and chat. The benefit of this method ties in with goals for community-building. Those who arrive in the chat room early find others who are also eager and ready to go. Those who come late are met with other students who follow a similar pattern. Helton finds the natural rhythms of building community enhanced by this practice, allowing students to identify other learners whom they naturally understand and appreciate. The groups form with like-minded orientations to doing group work based on the timing and the encounters of the chat room group formation. Under this method, she has not encountered the typical challenges of group formation such as unbalanced workload, single student dominance, or uncomfortable community environment.

If one person is clearly not fitting in with a group for whatever reason, adjustments should be made to provide all students with the best group experience. Thomas-Evans allows her students to stay in the same group or move. They have often started to get comfortable with their group and want to keep with the known. She negotiates all this with tact and diplomacy, allowing switches but being careful not to hurt anyone's feelings. She does not tell students if people have indicated they do not wish to continue working with a specific student (it happens occasionally, usually because the student has been lax in providing feedback or contributing to the group). She shuffles them a bit, keeps those together who have asked to be together, and moves those who are indifferent as to whom they work with to complete groups as needed. If two or more students tend to over-dominate in class, she might put them together. This works to prevent shyer students from feeling intimidated by those strong voices. The students who are eager post first and end up together because it means they can move at a faster pace without feeling held back by a student who posts later (still on schedule but posting on the last day rather than several days early).

Online learning communities can also be built for peer review, when conducted through discussions rather than simply completed with a partner. Discussions that can be viewed by all students allow students to learn from each other—both by reviewing other students' work and by observing how other students review each other's work. The instructor can be involved in the process by commenting directly on peer reviews that offer exemplary models of peer review or that need further engagement.

Effective peer review is a structured activity. In her upper level professional writing courses, Thomas-Evans' students create their own peer review document. She requires her students to create a user test document. They ask questions about their work to which they want their peers to respond. She offers some guidelines/categories based on the assignment and course. She also provides a sample that she allows them to "borrow" from, but they must modify the questions and add their own. Before they use the user test document, she reviews them. They then tweak it for later projects in the course to shape the questions to fit the task. Creating their own questions requires them to think about what they want to know and what they need to improve.

When they post a draft in their group space for review, they also post the user test sheet to get feedback. Thomas-Evans has found this method to be much more useful than simply creating a user test for the whole class to use because they get much more specific than she could with a one-size-fits-all approach. The students also see why the feedback is then more specific to them. The first time they do this in a class, the students might struggle a bit and feel unsure if they are asking the "right" questions, but a little encouragement and seeing their classmates' user test sheets reassures them they are doing okay. When they repeat the process for later assignments, they know exactly what to do and what questions they need to ask.

DISCUSSIONS AS REFLECTIVE LEARNING

Reflective learning is essential for cultivating students' growth as learners in any classroom, but the online English classroom considers reflection an organic feature of the class rather than simply as a supplement to the learning process.

Students can be encouraged to reflect upon themselves as learners from the moment they enter the classroom. Discussions can aid in this process if students assess their own level of learning and readiness for the course either by responding informally to questions during course introductions or by responding formally to a pre-test or survey they take at the beginning of the course. In his literature courses, Petersheim typically includes a mixture of simple and more difficult questions about literature and about the specific authors or texts they are studying so that students begin to think about learning by recognizing the insights and limits of their learning so far without feeling overwhelmed or bored. Commenting on their current level of learning in discussions allows students to give and receive feedback in order to begin finding points of commonality with instructors and with classmates who will become peers and collaborators who will help to facilitate their learning throughout the course.

Sometime near the middle and again at the end of the course, students can be asked to respond to more specific questions about what they have learned or enjoyed so far in the course. When asking students to reflect on their learning at the end of the course, Petersheim reminds them of the shared purposes of learning in this course. Here is an example of a final reflection prompt that he has used in some of his courses:

> Your final discussion gives you a chance to think about what skills or content you have learned in this course. Return to the course objectives in the syllabus and to the survey you completed at the beginning of this course. Review what you have learned, paying particular attention to any objectives that confused you or any questions that you answered incorrectly when you first took the survey. If what you have learned is not brand new, how do you understand the concept in great depth or detail? Feel free to respond to other students if they mention things about this course and our reading that you had forgotten but find inspiring.

By requiring students to reflect in the discussions, Petersheim typically has found that students celebrate what they have learned rather than venting any frustrations they may have experienced individually. Although he first undertook this method without thinking about its effect on student evaluations, this practice has dramatically reduced the number of seemingly disconnected comments students leave on course evaluations as well. Students remember the way they have engaged over the course of the semester when they are asked to reflect on it in the same manner used throughout the semester—through discussions.

By using discussions as a place for reflection, students learn to become self-assessors. Instructors also benefit from these reflections, whether for designing learning activities for the current course or for future courses. If too infrequent, course reflections may fail to leave a lasting effect on students; if too frequent, course reflections may bog down the learning process by detracting from time to interact with subject content. One method that has proven especially effective in literature classes is as follows: a reflection on a course survey taken at the beginning of a course as a kind of pre-test, one course reflection on the effectiveness or clarity of learning activities at midterm, and a final reflection on the overall learning experience while looking back at the entire duration of the course. If completed in the discussion forum, students can stimulate learning in others and can be reminded of learning that they had forgotten. Using discussions also reduces the number of reflections that do not adequately reflect on the course since less-engaged students can see committed students posting more thoughtful reflections.

DISCUSSION PROBLEMS

Early on in our teaching careers, we learn the great value of the few minutes before class, before a workshop activity, or peer review that students go through a brief period of bonding through griping about the assignment, activity, or class itself. It is a healthy form of community-building where someone starts out with a gripe, others commiserate or build the person up. Good things happen as an outcome. Teachers sit at the front, often pretending not to hear the gripes. Students gripe for five minutes, then dive in to do great work. In beginning online teaching, we experimented with online spaces for such griping to occur. While some of us used a discussion board just for questions and gripes, we found such discussion boards little used, probably because they require more careful online navigation and motivation to go there. Helton suggests shifting to chat rooms for such discussions, an approach that has led to much stronger outcomes that allow students the space for griping but also for constructive peer encouragement.

A perfect recipe for disastrous discussion is providing only brief open-ended question. The open-ended question generally results in responses that skim the surface with little depth or development. The open-ended question tends to result in short responses of a few sentences that do not encourage others to join in the conversation or to extend upon the students' original thoughts. Worse are the responses to the short posts, or the shut down in community that results when students are faced with responding to the few sentences that have little content or depth.

While completely open-ended questions sometimes produce high quality responses for advanced or self-motivated students, many students offer more incisive commentary when given some guidance that requires them to interact with the text rather than simply responding to it. Open-ended questions can result in burnout from students who are not sure what the instructor expects and from instructors who spend excessive amounts of time on assessment.

CONCLUSIONS

The main purpose of discussion centers in the online classroom, of course, is to facilitate discussion. However, discussions boards or forums can be used in a wide variety of ways to facilitate learning in an online environment. Here, some of the back and forth among students and instructors that is found in effective face-to-face settings may be replicated. Students can introduce themselves and respond to each other at the beginning of class, they can reflect on their learning processes, or they can complete other learning activities such as group work or peer review activities. But at the heart of each discussion-based learning environment are those routine interactive discussions completed throughout most of the duration of the course.

Strategies for facilitating discussions as online learning communities begin with the syllabus and end with course reflections. Some components of online learning communities are specific to online learning, just as face-to-face courses have some components specific to face-to-face learning. However, many components of online learning also work well with face-to-face or hybrid classes. Thus, we have occasionally included examples that cross from one environment to the other.

Community-building in the online classroom is possible and contributes to student success in our experiences. By trial and error, reflection, and constant tinkering with online learning tools, strong student community-building is not only possible but crucial to successful learning outcomes. Many of the learning activities outlined here can be conducted by means other than the discussion boards or forums provided by online learning platforms, such as Facebook groups. Discussions, however, provide a unique side of online learning well-suited to the English classroom, related disciplines, and any class that encourages extended critical thinking or interactive learning.

REFERENCES

Blackmon, S. J. (2012). Outcomes of chat and discussion board use in online learning: A research synthesis. *Journal of Educators Online, 9*(2), 1–19. Retrieved from ERIC database.

Dennen, V. P. (2005). From message posting to learning dialogues: Factors affecting learner participation in asynchronous discussion. *Distance Education, 26*(1), 127–148. doi: 10.1080/01587910500081376

Dunlap, J. & Lowenthal, P. (2014). The power of presence: Our quest for the right mix of social presence in online courses. In A. Pina & A. Mizell (Eds.), *Real life distance education: Case studies in practice* (pp. 41–66). Charlotte, NC: Information Age Publishing.

Mooney, M., Southard, S., & Burton C. H. (2014) Shifting from obligatory discourse to rich dialogue: Prompting student interaction in asynchronous threaded discussion postings. *Online Journal of Distance Learning Administration, 17*(1). Retrieved from ERIC database.

Palloff, R., & Pratt, K. (1999), *Building learning communities in cyberspace: Effective strategies for the online classroom.* San Francisco: Jossey-Bass.

Palloff, R., & Pratt, K. (2005). Online learning communities revisited. In *21st Annual Conference on Distance Teaching and Learning* (pp. 1–5). Retrieved December 2015 from http://www.uwex.edu/disted/conference/resource_library/proceedings/05_1801.pdf

Palloff, R., & Pratt, K. (2003), *The virtual student; A profile and guide to working with online learners.* San Francisco: Jossey-Bass.

Palmer, S., Holt D., & Bray, S. (2008). Does the discussion help? The impact of formally assessed online discussion on final student results. *British Journal of Educational Technology, 39*(5), 847–858. doi: 10.1111/j.1467-8535.2007.00780.x

Pollard, H., Minor, M., & Swanson, A. (2014). Instructor social presence within the community of inquiry framework and its impact on classroom community and the learning experience. *Online Journal of Distance Learning Administration, 17*(2). Retrieved from ERIC database.

Sample of network etiquette or 'netiquette.' (2016). In *University of Hawai'i Hilo.* Retrieved January 2016 from http://hilo.hawaii.edu/academics/dl/netetiquette.php

Vygotsky, L. S. (1978). *Mind in society: The development of higher psychological processes.* (M. Cole, V. John-Steiner, S. Scribner, & E. Souberman, Eds.). Cambridge, MA: Harvard University Press.

4

Political Science
Engaging students through Effective Instruction and Course Design in Political Science

CHERA LAFORGE, PH.D.

KRISTOFFER REES, PH.D.

LILIA ALEXANDER, M.P.A.

ROSS C. ALEXANDER, PH.D.

INTRODUCTION

Political science has long considered itself a leader in civic engagement. Our students frequently participate in service learning, civic engagement, simulations, internships, and other forms of experiential learning to bridge what they have learned in the classroom to the actual world of politics and policy. This focus on active learning has been challenged, however, by the growth in online education. For some instructors, online learning is incongruous with the tenets of active learning and experiential learning. In the chapter below, we demonstrate how thoughtful instructors can utilize creative assignments and course design to mimic these experiences in the online classroom, regardless of subfield or the level of the course.

Quality course design is especially important in the online environment. Studies of withdrawn students found that a confusing layout, vague instructions, and unclear faculty expectations can all derail student success and persistence in online courses (Morris & Finnegan, 2008). Furthermore, we know that students who remain in engaged in active learning strategies, regardless of the format of the classroom, are more likely to persist and graduate (Braxton et al, 2000). And, the application of real world problems to the classroom may ensure students are developing the necessary transferrable skills—like critical thinking, written communication, and problem-solving—to gain employment and pursue successful careers after graduation (Shatkin, 2012).

Below, we present recommendations and suggestions for teaching both lower-level general education and upper-level online courses in political science. This includes recommendations for course design, assignment construction, multimedia selection, and rubric and evaluative criteria formation. Throughout the chapter, we pay careful attention to the marriage of superior course design with effective and efficient instruction, as well as the applicability of our courses to the real-world political environment.

AMERICAN POLITICS GENERAL EDUCATION COURSES

Students enroll in introductory American politics for a variety of reasons: It is a common gateway course for students entering into the major, a popular general education elective, and a required class for other disciplines including social work and education. Finally, politically interested students may opt into the course as an elective to become better informed or to "talk about politics" on a regular basis. The incorrect assumption that political science equates to political current events, as well as the diverse backgrounds of enrolled students requires careful attention to course design.

One component of successful online course development is to ensure peer-to-peer interaction (often through forums), which can help build community, support learning, and increase satisfaction (Kolloff, 2011; Swan, 2002). In a climate where political polarization is prevalent, selecting discussion questions that allow for critical thinking and respectful back-and-forth can be difficult. Instructors must also acknowledge online classes are popular because of the flexibility they afford, which prevents synchronous interactions, and prompts must be designed with this in mind (Dutton et al, 2002). One effective discussion assignment in Introduction to American Politics deals with voter turnout, which is a popular topic in contemporary media and for students. After reading the assigned chapter and working through several module tasks, students are required to identify and describe one reason individuals fail to turn out to vote and design a potential reform to overcome that excuse (the discussion prompt is presented in Figure 1 below). These posts are generally due by Friday evening and students are unable to view their classmate's posts until theirs is received.

Figure 1. Increasing Voter Turnout Discussion Forum Prompt

Instructions: Political scientists and pundits have long lamented the low voter turnout displayed by Americans. Compared to other democracies around the world, citizens of the United States turn out at very low rates, which may (or may not) have an effect on the quality of our system. As you can see from Figure 14.1 of your textbook, Americans have not cracked 65 percent turnout in either a presidential or midterm election in decades.

For your forum posting this week, I want you to consider some methods for increasing voter turnout. After reading the textbook for this week, identify one method of increasing voter turnout. Describe your reform in some detail and defend why it would be the best option for increasing voter turnout. This original forum post is due on Friday.

Then, consider what others have posted and respond to one of your fellow classmates, identifying a challenge of their reform. Why might their suggested method of increasing voter turnout hit a snag? How could it be improved? Please be cordial and professional in identifying a shortcoming. The purpose of this exercise is to show why it's so difficult to increase voter turnout in the American system. This forum response is due on Monday.

After the Friday deadline, students have several days to respond to at least one of their classmate's posts and critique potential challenges in instituting the reform and address how the reform can be improved. The assignment shows students the wide variety of reasons, both big and small, for low voter turnout in the United States and highlights the unintended consequences and inherent challenges in reforming the system. It also begins to build a community within the classroom as students read and interact with other posts, even when they may be time zones away.

Another assignment the authors have implemented is the application assignment, which require students to apply what they learned in class in the real world. In the week on media, students are required to watch and access two forms of media, one of which must be the nightly news or a comparable cable news show. The instructor can leverage the online environment, as most news stations allow access to free rebroadcasts and students are generally utilizing online news sources as their second source. The assignment requires they examine the stories covered—including depth and detail—and then compare and contrast the reporting to any other media source. The most important part of the prompt is the application of the course material. Students must identify examples of common media concepts including structural or commercial bias, horse race coverage, shrinking sound bites, or beat journalism. The assignment is successful because it allows students to build media literacy, apply and reinforce learning of course materials, and engage with the real world. With a critical eye towards content and structure, they may also recognize potential biases in their preferred news sources.

These examples demonstrate ways to link political science concepts to real-world examples. Though individual instructors may choose to highlight different outcomes in their own classes, the assignments profiled above build commonly desired, transferrable skills including written communication, critical thinking, and media literacy. These skills are important regardless of the major or motivation for student enrollment.

COMPARATIVE POLITICS AND INTERNATIONAL RELATIONS GENERAL EDUCATION COURSES

This section addresses the online teaching of comparative politics and international relations by identifying best practices in teaching and instructional design. As noted by Pollock and Wilson (2003), the Internet has three pedagogical functions: information, instruction, and communication (561). In the context of teaching courses in comparative politics and international relations, the utility of the Internet can be divided into at least four distinct categories: resources from other academic institutions, resources from non-profit "idea sharing" organizations, reputable news organizations, and governmental and international organizational websites.

Resources from other academic institutions are particularly valuable since they provide the opportunity to bring diverse voices to the online class environment. For example, Yale University hosts *The MacMillan Report*, which "features Yale faculty in international and areas studies and their research" (yale.edu). The interviews on the show, which are published weekly throughout the academic year, address topics of relevance to the comparative politics and international relations classrooms and are usually 15 to 20 minutes long. Moreover, the interviewees include not only Yale faculty, but also influential figures such as UN Secretary General Ban Ki-Moon. The wide range of guests on the show and the accessible format affords the opportunity of including the diverse perspectives and expert content knowledge of these scholars, even on campuses that do not have the budget to bring any one of them to their own campus. Moreover, because Yale leverages YouTube as the storage provider for most of its video resources, it is a straightforward process to embed the videos into module pages in the LMS.

Non-profit "idea-sharing" organizations, such as TED (Technology, Entertainment, and Design) also produce videos (typically with high production values) that can easily be incorporated into online classes. TED Talks are most useful in upper-level classes since topics addressed include poverty, global inequality, human rights, and the challenges of development. However, TED talks like the 2014 talk by Thomas Piketty addressing his book, *Capital in the 21st Century*, can be incorporated into introductory-level classes since they break down important readings and concepts into digestible units. Again, like *The MacMillan Report* interviews discussed above, TED Talks are useful because they tend to be self-contained discussions that run no longer than twenty minutes, which aligns with substantial empirical scholarship content retention (e.g., Bonwell and Eison, 1991). Thus, these resources are well-structured to be an effective part of organizing lessons in comparative politics and international relations. However, many TED talks skew towards the liberal end of the political spectrum, so care must be taken to balance use of these types of resources with other perspectives.

Issues of comparative politics and international affairs are unique in that there are few opportunities to engage in experiential learning outside of the classroom. With the exception of examinations of US foreign policy and some international organizations, most current issues of comparative politics and international relations take place in distant places around the world. The transition of traditional print news media to online formats provides a way to easily incorporate critical analysis of current events into the online classroom. This active learning strategy can directly link current events in international politics to the course learning objectives. Most reputable news organizations that feature extensive coverage of international politics (including *The New York Times*, *The Washington Post*, and *The Guardian*) can be subscribed to by students for a nominal cost, or have monthly quotas for free-to-read articles that are sufficient for the needs of the course.

Official websites of government branches, agencies, and other offices, as well as the corporate websites of international organizations tend to provide a wealth of accessible information on their structure, history, and function. Additionally, as in the case of international organizations such as the United Nations, NATO, or Save the Children, they offer reports and analyses of current and past issues of note. Utilizing these authentic materials allows students to learn firsthand the roles and functions of these institutions. Instructors of introductory level classes in comparative politics may use information on the intricate workings of the parliamentary system of government hosted on the official website of the UK Parliament, for instance. Websites of international organizations also offer information on the history, structure, and function of the institutions. In addition to web-hosted materials, there are also downloadable pamphlets and embeddable videos. Upper division classes can access actual project reports from the United Nations as well as from other humanitarian organizations such as the International Crisis Group, Freedom House, and Transparency International.

Aligning the free resources discussed above to quality course design and appropriate and imaginative assignments is essential for program growth and student satisfaction and retention. Below, several strategies for instructional design of introductory courses in comparative politics are discussed, including selection of course materials, peer-to-peer interaction, and instructor feedback and assessment.

Experimentation over several iterations of an online introduction to comparative politics class indicates that utilizing a course textbook at the general education level results in higher student satisfaction. Using a single textbook rather than an instructor-curated selection of web-based text, audio, and video resources, and academic and other journal articles provides students a perception of structure and balanced reading load that is otherwise absent. This contrasts with upper division courses, where students are more willing to utilize authentic materials, like case studies and project reports. In general, upper division courses in comparative politics and international relations have more opportunity for successful innovation, as is discussed below.

Broadly speaking, courses in comparative politics and international relations do well when developed according to best practices in course design, instructional effectiveness, and interactivity that are applicable to adult-centered online learning environments. For example, discussion boards are a common way of encourage student-student interaction and direct student-instructor interaction in online courses. Active learning and critical thinking skills are particularly developed when discussion forum prompts link theoretical and conceptual material to issues of present day international politics (Grant and Thornton, 2007). Additionally, instructor feedback in online courses in comparative politics and international relations should follow the best practices discussed in Leibold and Schwarz (2015), including frequent, balanced, specific and personalized feedback in a positive tone.

UPPER-LEVEL POLITICAL SCIENCE ELECTIVES

As noted above, upper-level comparative politics and international relations courses allow for greater instructor innovation. The following presents a case study of one such innovative technique—the online simulation. In a face-to-face class, simulations such as Model United Nations are an almost indispensable part of the applied learning process within the discipline. Even though the quantitative attainment of learning outcomes is similar in simulation-based courses and non-simulation-based courses, qualitative evidence suggests simulations increase student perception of learning outcome attainment (Raymond, 2010). In addition to simulations of the decision-making processes of specific international organizations, the practice of using popular games to teach concepts essential to the study of international relations, such as the struggle for power is well documented (e.g., Brynen, 2014). A wide range of simulation activities already exist for face-to-face environments from multi-day, inter-collegiate Model United Nations simulations to more condensed exercises intended for one to two class periods. However, a review of some commonly used in-class activities (including the UN-focused "Palmyra" simulation available from the United States Institute for Peace, the WTO negotiation simulation created by Steagall et al., (2012) and the globalization-related simulation created by Pallister) indicated none of the simulations were directly transferable to an online learning environment.

In a pilot test of a simulation-focused upper division course in international organizations, the simulations proved pedagogically effective and students responded positively. The test course, International Organizations, examined the role of major formal intergovernmental organizations in international politics. Online simulation activities directly addressed the course learning objective that required students to collaboratively respond to contemporary issues of global governance by critically analyzing selected issues, developing theoretically and empirically informed action plans, and judging the effectiveness of potential solutions offered by their peers. This learning objective would be difficult to achieve through other means.

The overarching philosophy for the class involved a focus on critical thinking and decision-making strategies with a major secondary goal for students to experience the difficulties of information-limited, group-mediated decision-making. Such decision-making processes are experienced by diplomats working within international organizations, as well as various other workplaces. Therefore, the existing face-to-face simulations were adapted to the online environment. This process of adaptation was iterative throughout the semester with four different simulations (UN, NATO, EU, and WTO) run. The lessons learned in the implementation of the prior simulations were able to be applied towards the subsequent ones. This feedback loop was essential for maximizing student attainment of learning outcomes.

One major issue lies in the amount of pre-simulation technical information presented. For example, in-person versions of international organization simulations favor relatively skeletal presentations of specific roles with the pedagogical goal of allowing students to discover for themselves the limitations and constraints of their assignment. However, in the first simulation, it was discovered that setting the students loose to self-discover was ineffective at encouraging student engagement with the activity. Therefore, as the simulations progressed, more substantial information about the constraints impacting each student's role was provided. Paradoxically, this increased student involvement, because they would strategize with their group members about how to sidestep these constraints. Post-simulation activities were equally important and required students to critically examine the real-world implications of the simulation process. One of the debrief assignments is shared in the figure shown.

Figure 2. International Organizations Simulation Debriefing Assignment

Instructions: Reflect on the simulation and your role in the negotiation process. In your response, address the following:

The simulation represents one round of what would likely be multi-round trade negotiations. What do you anticipate the outcome of the second round of negotiations would be?
What were the obstacles to creating a set of policies that everyone could agree on?
Who "won" the negotiations, based on your observations? Who lost?
What did you find frustrating about this simulation? Why?
How would you evaluate your own level of participation in this week's simulation activity?

Your response should be approximately 250–500 words or the equivalent of one to two double-spaced letter-sized pages.

Based on the quality of the student self-reports and instructor observation of the discussions, the final simulation surpassed the instructor-set goals for the quality of student interaction and for student-internalization of the real-world difficulties of diplomatic negotiation.

Broadly speaking, teaching asynchronous online courses in comparative politics and international relations should follow the general set of best practices for online teaching that are already in practice. Beyond these best practices, the authors find leveraging the wealth of authentic materials available on the Internet to be important. These resources can involve discussions from world-renowned specialists and academics that would otherwise be inaccessible to learners, to the utilization of the education, informational, and analytical materials published by a variety of governments and international organizations. Finally, political simulations should not be overlooked, despite the challenges in adapting them to the online environment.

Having examined best practices in online instruction and course design in upper-division, major-level comparative politics and international relations courses, this section addresses approaches, strategies, and best practices for major-level, online political science courses in our remaining subfields. Below, we discuss two courses that bridge the sub-disciplines of American politics, political theory, and public administration—American Political Theory and State and Local Government. As noted repeatedly in this chapter, the authors utilize an approach and specific assignments that demonstrate an intentional and direct linkage between effective teaching and learning and effective instructional design (Park and Mills, 2014; Rabe-Hemp, Woolen & Humiston, 2009; Rhoads & Rhoads, 2013; and Tsai, 2013).

American Political Theory traces the development and influence of the foundational documents, writings, essays, and speeches that have formed the "canon" for the American political system. At its outset, the course typically covers in detail the American Colonial period leading up to the controversy surrounding the drafting, debate, and subsequent adoption of the American Constitution in 1789. As such, the Declaration of Independence, Federalist Papers and responses, and the Constitution itself are featured prominently. Similar courses oftentimes devote the entire semester to the Constitutional debate, but the authors utilize a structure that covers roughly 1620 to the present. The course is rich in controversy and debate, addressing such flashpoint topics and controversial periods as: governmental expansion in the early American period, slavery, the Civil War, women's suffrage, socialism, the organized labor movement, civil rights, populism, expansion of US involvement in international affairs, the American feminist movement, issues related to the Cold War and Vietnam War, environmental activism, and even neoconservatism in the late 20th and early 21st centuries, among many others. Due to its debate-centric nature, the course is natural for traditional, face-to-face delivery. So, how can an instructor structure it to be successful in the online environment?

In the experience of the authors, capitalizing upon the debate-centric and active-learning nature of the course is integral for success in the online modality and best facilitates and ensures student learning and engagement (Espasa and Meneses, 2010; Bluic, et al., 2009; and McCarthy & Anderson, 2000). To accomplish this task, the instructor can place students in groups and have them "argue" opposite sides of a particular debate (i.e., Federalists v. Anti-Federalists; abolitionist v. pro-slavery factions; unionists v. secessionists; capitalists v. socialists; isolationists v. internationalists; liberals v. conservatives; industrialists v. environmentalists). Effectively utilizing and integrating technology is vital to the richness and success of the debates and can include narrated PowerPoint or Prezi presentations; formal, recorded video presentations; YouTube clips; interactive media; voice threads, and social media images and videos (among others). The instructor should provide parameters, an evaluative rubric, and requirement for peer-review and feedback, in video and written form. Students tend to have a great deal of fun and generate excitement with these debate assignments, which are an effective and rewarding supplement to written assignments, papers, and tests. Many students have even dressed in period-specific costume or garb when making their presentation videos. These presentations are an effective means of empowering students to have fun, as well as address and learn material that is often challenging, dense, and controversial.

State and Local Government is a popular major-level course in most political science programs. It compares and contrasts the nature, historical development, and structure of myriad and diverse state and local governance structures in the American federal system and covers such topics as state constitutions, state legislatures, governors and executive agencies, state court systems, county and municipal governmental systems, state and local education policy, campaigns and elections, and policymaking at the state and local level. In the experience of the authors, a particular assignment that has effectively reinforced and addressed course learning outcomes and the material—in both traditional and online modalities—has been the "attendance at a public meeting" assessment. In this assignment, students are required to attend a meeting of a state or local public body or agency (i.e., city council, county commission, school board, state legislative subcommittee, judicial proceeding) and then write an analytical essay summarizing and describing the event, its intended audience and purpose, its linkage and relevance to the course and its outcomes, reinforcing and integrating the relevant academic literature, and providing a detailed analysis. It is an effective means of linking theory and practice for the course.

The assignment is more effective and impactful in the online environment for several reasons. First, most public bodies have meetings either recorded or linked to their official website or live-streamed, so students can access and watch the meeting at their convenience, which is beneficial for non-traditional or working students. Second, in the online environment, students can provide links to their chosen meeting with their analysis paper, documenting their "attendance" at the meeting. Third, students can choose from a much more diverse set of meeting options in the online environment, including meetings of public bodies across the nation and even internationally. The authors have had students attend and analyze meetings of several foreign entities and supranational organizations. Fourth, the diversity of meetings and ability to share links of meetings drives discussion and peer feedback. It also makes grading and evaluation simpler and more efficient for the instructor.

The preceding sections of this chapter highlighted best practices, strategies, and techniques for effective teaching, instruction, and course design for undergraduate political science courses. This section will address graduate-level political science courses and curricula, particularly those found in most Master of Public Administration (M.P.A.) programs, as the M.P.A. is perhaps the most common graduate degree found within the discipline of political science. One of this chapter's authors has been teaching and developing courses in various M.P.A. programs since 2003, including over 10 years of experience teaching and designing both "core" and elective courses in the online modality across several LMS platforms.

Unlike other graduate degrees in political science (e.g., M.A., Ph.D., or M.A.I.A.), the M.P.A. is a practitioner-focused degree, geared towards pre-service or in-service public administration and management professionals. While perhaps not as theory-focused or driven as other political science graduate degrees, the M.P.A. is a terminal, professional degree, which focuses on applied lessons, issues, strategies, scenarios, challenges, or cases that may confront current or future public administrators at all levels of government. M.P.A. programs traditionally offer a flexible curriculum and structure in order to appeal to in-service practitioners and professionals, utilizing night, weekend, and residency-type classes and cohort structures for many decades, with much success. Not surprisingly, due to the increasing need and desire of students for flexible degree options, online M.P.A. programs proliferated and have been successfully delivered for 10 to 15 years by many types of universities, serving as models for graduate education in the online environment writ large. According to the Network of Schools of Public Policy, Affairs, and Administration (NASPAA), there are over 40 completely online M.P.A. programs in the United States (NASPAA.org).

A theme of this text and chapter has been that quality and effectiveness in online teaching and learning is best achieved or facilitated by a "marriage" of quality instruction and intentional and deliberate course design (Brinthaupt, et al., 2011; Bolinger and Wasilik, 2009; Kearns, 2012; and LaPrade, Gilpatrick & Perkins, 2014; LaForge, et al., 2015). Similarly, instructors and designers must employ myriad techniques of varying sophistication to effectively engage students—ranging from relatively simple weekly discussions or blogs to research-intensive projects and papers (Hendricks and Bailey, 2014; Portugal, 2015; Raffo, et al., 2015). This strategy is especially relevant to graduate students in M.P.A. programs who are often returning to school after many years working "in the field" and may lack the technological sophistication or familiarity of other, younger students who have taken online, hybrid, blended, or technology-enhanced courses throughout both high school and college. Finally, this quality-focused "marriage" between instruction and design enhances and standardizes the student experience, which can be used as a growth strategy for entire programs (LaForge, et al., 2015; Alexander, 2015), a factor that is always a concern for graduate programs especially, given the amount of competition in the online marketplace.

In the experience of the authors, the "best" online graduate courses in political science, particularly in practitioner-focused M.P.A. courses are those in which theories, readings, and course materials are applied to real-world, practical issues and challenges that face current and future public administrators, using integrated, practical, and varied assignments of all levels of sophistication, difficulty, and intensity. What follows is a description and overview of several of these assignment approaches in three "core" courses found in almost every M.P.A. curriculum: 1) Public Budgeting and Finance, 2) Public Human Resource Management, and 3) Leadership and Organizational Theory.

It is integral that public administrators working in all types of government agencies at all levels of government have a working knowledge of governmental budgeting and financial management processes. As such, Public Budgeting and Finance is a primary component of nearly every M.P.A. curriculum. Due to the technical, overwhelming, and often confusing nature of governmental budgeting, particularly at the federal level, it is important that any online Public Budgeting and Finance course utilize assignments and exercises that transcend levels of government and are universally applicable to situations and realities faced by most public administrators, all of whom are intimately affected by the budget process, usually on a daily basis. Assignments should be practical, applicable, useful, and demonstrate the relevance of the required readings and bodies of literature studied in the course.

One example is the "budget analysis" assignment. In this course, it is imperative that students learn that a budget is simply a plan for government. By examining and deconstructing an actual budget from a real public organization or unit, students can decipher the actual (stated) versus the "hidden" priorities of that particular governmental unit or agency. "Following the money" leads to the truth. The "budget analysis" assignment requires students to access an agency's budget online (preferably the student's agency of employment to maximize relevance), analyze it based upon a set of established criteria using a rubric created by the instructor, write an analysis or summary of findings in a report, share the report and link to the budget with the entire class within the online course, and offer analytical comments on at least two of their classmates' reports, generating a larger discussion of findings. This process and assignment is inordinately smoother and easier in the online versus face-to-face environment due to the ability to link to large, voluminous budgets; ease of discussion and commentary upon reports and analyses of multiple students; use of evaluative and grading rubrics; and timeliness of feedback and discussion—all producing a richer, more substantive, and significant learning experience for students, including those that can utilize that knowledge in their existing agencies. The addition of peer feedback creates an important community of scholars within the classroom and exposes students to budgets from a variety of agencies outside of their existing sphere of knowledge (Sadera et al, 2009).

One of the core competencies, functions, and tasks of public human resources professionals is the drafting, writing, and analysis of job descriptions. Job descriptions provide important information regarding a public agency and determine, in large part, the quality of candidates pursuing and securing jobs within it. As such, writing and understanding accurate, informative, legally compliant, and detailed job descriptions is vital to the success of any public administrator with a human resources function. In Public Human Resources Management, an interactive assignment on job description creation and analysis empowers current and future public administrators to operate effectively. In this assignment, students are required to analyze five job descriptions each for various jobs at the federal, state, and local levels of government (15 total), found online at official federal, state, and municipal websites, using a standard set of evaluative criteria and rubrics (see Figure 3 below for a sample rubric from this assignment). Students write a summative report and analysis, highlighting strengths and weaknesses of each description, offering recommendations for improvement, if necessary. Next, they write an original job description for a fictitious professional position in the public sector (most suitably a position similar to the one they hold), implementing best practices gleaned from their analysis and the materials from the course. They then upload and share their analytical report of the 15 governmental jobs in addition to their original job description to the LMS for peer review and feedback from their classmates and instructor. Again, the online medium makes this entire assignment and review process logistically smoother and easier to facilitate for the instructor, producing a richer learning experience for students.

Figure 3. Job Description Rubric

Public Human Resources Management Grading Rubric **Assignment: Job Description Analysis** **Total Points: 100**					
	A	**B**	**C**	**D**	**F**
# of Job Descriptions 20 points	Exceeds minimum number of required descriptions (15+)	Meets minimum number of required descriptions (15)	12–14 descriptions addressed	10–11 descriptions addressed	Nine or fewer descriptions addressed
Variety of Job Descriptions 20 points	More than five each of federal, state, local descriptions analyzed	At least five each of federal, state, local descriptions analyzed	Four or fewer each of federal, state, local descriptions analyzed	Three or fewer each of federal, state, local descriptions analyzed	Two or fewer each of federal, state, local descriptions analyzed
Quality/ Reliability of Job Descriptions 20 points	All descriptions reliable and trustworthy	Most descriptions reliable and trustworthy	Some descriptions reliable and trustworthy	Few descriptions reliable and trustworthy	Little or no descriptions reliable and trustworthy

Level of Analysis 20 points	Entirety of analysis is detailed, well-written, thorough	Most of analysis is detailed, well-written, thorough	Analysis is inconsistent and lacks sufficient detail throughout	Incomplete, poor writing, lack of detail	Incoherent, poor writing, insufficient depth and detail
APA Format and Citations 20 points	All descriptions are formatted and cited appropriately	There are a few errors in formatting and citations	There are some errors in formatting and citations	There are many errors in formatting and citations	Little or no adherence to APA format

Nearly every M.P.A. program has an organizational theory or leadership course focused heavily upon the theoretical literature in the discipline. Due to its theoretical nature and divergent themes and focus from the other courses in the curriculum, it is often one of the more difficult courses for students and can be one of the more challenging courses to teach. It is vital to choose assignments that bridge the gap between theory and practice and allow students to apply themes from the course to real-world contexts, including those in their organizations. One such assignment the author has found effective in Leadership and Organizational Theory is the "leadership analysis." This assignment allows and empowers students to provide a 360 degree, comprehensive overview and evaluation of the leaders and leadership infrastructure in the organization in which they are currently employed or one with which they are familiar. The assignment utilizes themes and theories studied in the course and in the relevant literature, but applies those theories to specific agency or workplace realities, issues, problems, and solutions. As a significant academic assignment, students are expected to provide a lengthy and thorough analysis in the form of an APA formatted essay, integrating and utilizing a minimum of 15–20 peer-reviewed sources. Over the course of 10 years, the author has found that this is one of the most effective and impactful assignments students in the M.P.A. program will complete, empowering them to better understand the health, state, and future of their organizations and their role within it. In the online environment, it is vital that students be required to offer peer review and feedback and to glean common themes and challenges that transcend all their respective organizations, facilitating rich and profound discussion.

The field of political science is one rich in real-world application and motivations. Face-to-face instruction has long capitalized on pedagogical innovations including service learning, civic engagement, simulations, internships, and other forms of experiential learning. This chapter demonstrates instructors can marry quality instruction and course design to facilitate these activities in the online environment. The application of real-world problems ensures students are developing the necessary transferrable skills to gain employment and pursue meaningful careers after graduation. Students also remain engaged, which can contribute to student retention and persistence. We also show how thoughtful course design and assignment construction can help ease faculty workload and improve instructor satisfaction with online teaching, as well. The use of well-defined rubrics with specific, evaluative criteria can improve the quality of student assignments and streamline grading.

REFERENCES

Alexander, R. C. (2015). Establishing an administrative structure for online programs. *International Journal of Instructional Technology and Distance Learning, 12*(6): 49–56.

Bluic, A. M., Ellis, R., Goodyear, P., & Piggott, L. (2009). Learning through face-to-face and online discussions: Associations between students' conceptions, approaches, and academic performance in political science. *British Journal of Educational Technology, 41*(3), 512–524.

Bollinger, D., & Wasilik, O. (2009). Factors influencing faculty satisfaction with online teaching and learning in higher education. *Distance Education, 30*(1), 103–116.

Braxton, J. M., Milem, J. F., & Sullivan, A. S. (2000). The influence of active learning on the college student departure process: Toward a revision of Tinto's theory. *The Journal of Higher Education, 71*(5), 569–590.

Brinthaupt, T. M., Fisher, L. S., Gardner, J. G., Raffo, D. M., & Woodward, J. B. (2011). What the best online teachers should do. *Journal of Online Learning and Teaching, 7*(4), 515–524.

Brynen, R. (2014). Teaching international relations through popular games, culture and simulations (part 1). *PAXsims.* Retrieved from https://paxsims.wordpress.com/2014/09/07/ teaching-international-relations-through-popular-games-culture-and-simulations-part-1/

Chun, M. (2002). Looking where the light is better: A review of the literature on assessing higher education quality. *Peer Review, 4*(2/3), 16–25.

Dutton, J., Dutton, M., & Perry, J. (2002). How do online students differ from lecture students? *The Journal for Asynchronous Learning Networks, 6*(1), 1–20.

Espasa, A., & Meneses, J. (2010). Analyzing feedback processes in an online teaching and learning environment: An exploratory study. *Higher Education, 59*, 277–292.

Grant, M. R., & Thornton, H. R. (2007). Best practices in undergraduate adult-centered online learning: mechanisms for course design and delivery. *Journal of Online Learning and Teaching, 3*(4), 346–356.

Hendricks, S., & Bailey, S. (2014). What really matters? Technological proficiency in an online course. *Online Journal of Distance Learning Administration, 17*(2).

Kearns, L. (2012). Student assessment in online learning: Challenges and effective practices. *Journal of Online Learning and Teaching, 8*(3), 198–208.

Kolloff, M. (2011). Strategies for effective student/student interaction in online courses. 17th annual conference on distance teaching and learning.

LaForge, C., You, Y., Alexander, R., & Sabine, N. (2015). Online program development as a growth strategy across diverse academic programs. *International Journal of Instructional Technology and Distance Learning, 12*(8), 25–39.

LaPrade, K., Gilpatrick, M., & Perkins, D. (2014). Impact of reflective practice on online teaching performance in higher education. *Journal of Online Learning and Teaching, 10*(4), 625–639.

Leibold, N., & Schwarz, L. M. (2015). The art of giving online feedback. *The Journal of Effective Teaching, 15*(1), 34–46.

McCarthy, J. P., & Anderson, L. (2000). Active learning technique versus traditional teaching styles: Two experiments from history and political science. *Innovative Higher Education, 24*(4), 279–294.

Morris, L. V., & Finnegan, C. L. (2008). Best practices in predicting and encouraging student persistence and achievement online. *Journal of College Student Retention: Research, Theory & Practice, 10*(1), 55–64.

Network of Schools of Public Policy, Affairs, and Administration (NASPAA) website. NASPPA.org (accessed January 18, 2016)

Park, J. Y., & Mills, K. A. (2014). Enhancing interdisciplinary learning with a learning management system. *Journal of Online Learning and Teaching, 10*(2), 299–313.

Pollock, P. H., & Wilson., B. M. (2002). Evaluating the impact of internet teaching: Preliminary evidence from American national government classes. *PS: Political Science and Politics, 35*(3), 561–566.

Portugal, L. M. (2015). Work ethic, characteristics, attributes, and traits of successful online faculty. *Online Journal of Distance Learning Administration, 18*(1).

Puzziferro, M., & Shelton, K. (2008). A model for developing high-quality online courses: Integrating a systems approach with learning theory. *Journal of Asynchronous Learning Networks, 12*(3–4), 119–136.

Rabe-Hemp, C., Woollen, S., & Humiston, G. S. (2009). A comparative analysis of student engagement, learning, and satisfaction in lecture hall and online learning settings. *The Quarterly Review of Distance Education, 10*(2), 207–218.

Raffo, D. M., Brinthaupt, T. M., Gardner, J. G., & Fisher, L. S. (2015). Balancing online teaching activities: Strategies for optimizing efficiency and effectiveness. *Online Journal of Distance Learning Administration, 18*(1).

Raymond, C. (2010). Do role-playing simulations generate measurable and meaningful outcomes? A simulation's effect on exam scores and teaching evaluations. *Faculty & Staff Articles & Papers* 22. Salve Regina. Retrieved from: http://digitalcommons.sale.edu/fac_staff_pub/22.

Rhoads, J., & Rhoads, R. (2013). The complexity of online discussion. *Journal of Online Learning and Teaching, 9*(1), 68–78.

Sadera, W. A., Robertson, J., Song, L., & Midon, M. N. (2009). The role of community in online learning success. *MERLOT Journal of Online Learning and Teaching, 5*(2), 277–284.

Shatkin, L. (2012, August 1). Transferable skills with the biggest payoff [Web log post]. Retrieved from http://www.careerlaboratory.blogspot.com/2012/08/transferable-skills-with-biggest-payoff.html

Steagall, J. W., Jares, T. E., & Gallo, A. (2012). Teaching real-world political economy: simulating a WTO negotiation. *Journal of Teaching in International Business, 23*(1), 46–58.

Sunal, D. W., Sunal, C. S., Odell, M. R., & Sundberg, C. A. (2003). Research-supported best practices for developing online learning. *The Journal of Interactive Online Learning, 2*(1), 1–40.

Swan, K. (2002). Building learning communities in online courses: The importance of interaction. *Education, Communication & Information, 2*(1), 23–49.

The MacMillan Report (n.d.) *Yale University.* Retrieved from http://www.yale.edu/printer/bulletin/htmlfiles/macmillan/the-macmillan-report.html

Tsai, C. (2013). An effective online teaching method: The combination of collaborative learning with initiation and self-regulation learning with feedback. B*ehaviour & Information Technology, 32*(7), 712–723.

United States Institute of Peace (2003). Simulation on the case of Palmyra. Retrieved from http://www.usip.org/publications/the-case-palmyra

5

CRIMINAL JUSTICE
Calming, Critical Thinking, and Case Studies:
The Politics, Pitfalls, and Practical Solutions for
Teaching Criminal Justice in an Online Environment

STEPHANIE N. WHITEHEAD, PH.D.

M. MICHAUX PARKER, PH.D.

INTRODUCTION

Teaching criminal justice in an online environment presents instructors with many unique opportunities and challenges. While every field of inquiry has its own online pedagogical challenges, criminal justice can be particularly problematic in terms of content and student expectations. Criminal justice students are exposed to a variety of sensitive, politically charged, and controversial topics. Topics such as domestic violence, gangs, sexual assault, and drug use all carry the potential to evoke emotionally and politically laden responses from students. Moreover, criminal justice students all too often enter the classroom expecting a practitioner-based curriculum. These assumptions and expectations present many challenges to criminal justice instructors and can be exacerbated by pedagogical parameters in the online environment.

In this chapter, we discuss several strategies to effectively counter pedagogical concerns in the virtual criminal justice classroom. We begin by offering a brief overview of the pedagogical challenges instructors face given student anxieties and expectations in criminal justice courses. Next, we discuss ways to ease students' anxieties and fears in the online classroom. Of particular focus is ensuring "ease of use" for students by using a modular approach to structure and organize online courses. We then focus on the importance a dialogic conversational approach to course discussions as a way to assist students' attainment of critical thinking skills and as a tool for demythologizing students' knowledge of crime and criminality. The final section centers on the use of cases studies to counter students' understandings of the relevancy of material for their future careers.

CRIMINAL JUSTICE STUDENTS IN THE ONLINE CLASSROOM

Our approach to online learning has developed largely in response to the nature of the field of criminal justice and the students this major attracts. Students too often enter criminal justice classrooms with strong opinions about topics well before they enter the field of study. While most students have little experience with the criminal justice system, all have had some exposure to mass media depictions of crime and criminal justice. As Durham (1992) notes,

> Largely as a result of the attention accorded to crime- and justice-related issues by the print and electronic media, American students generally come to the university fully equipped with a set of perceptions about crime and justice. The perceptions often are at considerable variance with reality, and not surprisingly, the judgments based upon these perceptions are often equally lacking in sensibility (p. 46).

Students thus enter the classroom with many mythological understandings of why people engage in criminal behavior and how the criminal justice system operates (or should operate) (Farnworth, Longmire, and West, 1998). Students (particularly in introductory courses) are not yet prepared to grasp the complexity of crime and so come into classes with beliefs and ideas that too readily simplify the reality of criminal justice (Bjerregaard and Lord, 2004).

Students are often frustrated when introduced to the field from a social science framework—a framework that challenges the mythologies of crime and justice. This can make it difficult to move students towards the higher-level thinking skills required to understand the cultural, social, and political factors that influence crime and criminality. While some students enter the classroom prepared for challenges to their prior knowledge, there are many who become uncomfortable when faced with information that confronts their systems of belief and prior knowledge. Given that students often come into courses with predetermined ideas about criminal justice phenomenon, they can experience an incredible sense of frustration when those ideas and beliefs are tested.

Students also enter the field of criminal justice with expectations of a practice-based curriculum (e.g., learning specific techniques for investigating crimes, for example) (Mackey and Courtright, 2000). Traditionally, criminal justice has been a discipline in which practitioners are not required to hold a college degree. Even the few positions that do require a college degree do not require credentialing specifically in the field of criminal justice. Criminal justice students thus often struggle with the necessity of completing a degree and are easily frustrated when presented with abstract concepts that do not seem to apply to their future careers.

A necessary aspect of any criminal justice curriculum is thus to create a learning environment that pushes students to understand the complexities of the criminal justice system and its practices, and to help them become more conscious of the emotionally laden, immediate reactions they bring to criminal justice issues and topics. Moreover, we must do so in a context that makes material explicitly relevant. As such, our role as instructors is to help guide students as they journey through the often uncomfortable, and anxiety-producing, process of recognizing their habits of thought, the consequences of mythological thinking, and how what they learn relates to their future careers in the field.

Managing students' anxieties and frustrations is a concern in all course delivery methods, but can be particularly challenging in the online environment. Online learning is fraught with pedagogical challenges including a sense of disconnection from instructors and material, the lack of discussions that occur in "real time," and the increased potential for miscommunication. Each of these concerns can heighten students' frustration in the online classroom. Crafting courses, materials, and assignments that inspire meaningful engagement for criminal justice students thus demands that we work to make online learning environments and instructional materials relevant through explicit career connections, critical thinking exercises, and in ways attuned to the anxieties of our online students.

MANAGING ANXIETY THROUGH COURSE STRUCTURE

Research demonstrates that one of the most important factors affecting students learning in an online environment is the organization and structure of the course (Shank, 2010). To be successful, students must be able to easily access course material and to effortlessly navigate through the course site. In online courses lacking proper organization, students can spend more time focusing on finding material and learning new technologies as opposed to learning the material. This can create a sense of anxiety among online students, which distracts them from the cognitive work they could otherwise invest in their learning. This is perhaps particularly important in courses where students are easily frustrated with course content and with material they perceive to be professionally irrelevant.

We have faced this issue quite often in our online courses. When students cannot easily find material, or we ask them to use tools with which they are not familiar, they send messages or make comments in evaluations demonstrating their sense of panic and unease. The time it takes students to search for course materials, or to learn new tools, is much better utilized working on assignments for the course. Moreover, the frustration with course structure can quickly bleed into already existing frustrations with course content and materials. Thus, a logical and consistent structure that allows students to focus solely on course material is tantamount to successful student learning (Anderson, 2008).

Our online learning platform, Canvas, has several tools available to help develop a consistent and intuitive structure within our courses. In our online courses, we are proponents of a modular approach to the online environment. Modules allow instructors to break up (or "chunk") content into specific sections and helps students clearly flow through the course. Using this approach allows students to move sequentially from module to module. Each module is arranged thematically, according to a field-related topic, and contains sections that offer specific information related to each overall theme. Figure 1 offers an example of modules developed for an introductory criminal justice course.

Figure 1

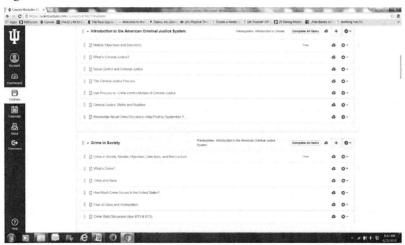

The organizing framework is to develop one module for each topic traditionally covered in introductory criminal justice courses (e.g., History of the Criminal Justice System; Police in America; Corrections in America). Each module contains sections where students are exposed to key concepts of each individual section. In short, the arrangement of modules serves as an outline to the content of the course. Sixteen modules were developed for this course, with each module corresponding to the number of weeks in a semester, so students work on one module per week in a full-term semester (in summer sessions, students will work on two modules per week).

Each module follows a consistent structure beginning with an introduction to the topic. The introduction reminds students of information that is also found in the syllabus—the reading for the week and assignment due dates. Specific learning objectives are also listed for each module offering students an explicit guide for the knowledge they should gain at the end of each module. Figure 2 offers example of this format.

Figure 2

Module Mini-Lecture (click below):

Module 3: Crime and Society

It may take a view minutes to download this file. If you have trouble viewing it you might need to update your flash player. If you still have trouble, please contact me ASAP. These mini-lectures are important for helping you understand the major themes of the modules and directions for assignments

If you are having trouble with the link above, you can also find the mini lecture at this link.

Module 3: Crime and Society

For this module you will read:

Chapter 2 (Pollock)

By the end of this module you will be able to:

• Distinguish between a social definition and a legal definition of crime, and summarize the problems with each.

• Explain why crime and delinquency statistics are unreliable.

• Identify the two major sources of crime statistics in the United States.

• Describe the principal finding of the national crime victimization surveys.

• Summarize the general finding of self-report crime surveys.

• Identify the costs of crime.

• Describe the extent of fear of crime in the United States and the characteristics of people most likely to fear crime.

• List the characteristics of people who are the most likely and the least likely to be victims of crime.

Each section of a module further introduces students to particular aspects of the topic. For instance, in the module devoted to criminological theory, specific sections were developed for each framework discussed in the textbook. Figure 3 offers an example from a module created to introduce students to criminological theory.

Figure 3

▼ ✓ Module 4: Explaining Crime and Criminal Behavior (2/2 - 2/8)
  ▪ Module Objectives, Directions, and Mini-Lecture
  ▪ What is Criminological Theory?
  ▪ Classical and Neoclassical Approaches
  ▪ Positivist Approaches
  ▪ Critical Approaches
  ▪ Special Topic: Mental Illness and Crime
  ▪ Exam I (Due February 8th)

In each of the sections, a mix of text and media are used to engage students in the topic and to supplement the textbook readings. An example is shown in Figure 4.

Figure 4

Given the unreliability of official statistics and the inability to uncover the 'dark figure of crime' it is almost impossible to measure the true extent of crime and criminality in the United States.

The following video discusses in more detail problems and issues with measuring crime and suggests some ways to better measure crime. This discussion is based on a global perspective of crime and crime statistics, but are also applicable to the United States.

TEDxCroatia - Jennifer Flaten - Measuring Nations Crime

Statistics about crime and delinquency are probably the most unreliable and most difficult of all social statistics. This is due to several factors:

−Behavior may be wrongly labeled (a robbery might be labeled a simple theft)
−Crimes go undetected (victimless crimes might not be detected by the police)
−Crimes are sometimes not reported to police
(a victim might be afraid to report a crime)
−Crimes may be inaccurately recorded by police or not recorded at all.
−Statistics do not include the dark figure of crime.

The two major sources of crime statistics in the United States are the uniform crime reports (UCR) compiled by the FBI and the national crime victimization surveys (NCVS) compiled by the Bureau of Justice Statistics.

The national crime victimization surveys (NCVS) produce different results from the FBI's uniform crime reports (UCR). The NCVS generally show more crimes committed than the UCR since it can identify crimes that victims fail to report to the police.

Self-report crime surveys show that the amount of hidden crime in the United States is enormous; more than 90% of all Americans have committed crimes for which they could have been sentenced. How many of you have sped over the speed limit, but were not caught? How many of you used illegal drugs, but were never reported?

Again, there are several reasons why crime and delinquency statistics are unreliable. These include:

*First, some behaviors are labeled criminal by one observer but not by another.
*Second, a large proportion of crimes are undetected.

Comments from our students speak to the importance of structure and organization in easing frustrations and anxieties with online learning. We frequently receive high marks in course evaluations on questions related to course organization. Students also frequently remark how the ease of use contributed to a safe and engaging learning environment. Using this approach has also resulted in fewer complaints about finding material and in fewer messages displaying a sense of frustration with course structure.

CRITICAL THINKING AND DIALOGIC CONVERSATIONS

Interactive classroom discussions remain a primary pedagogical tool to assist students in the development of higher-order thinking skills (Bean, 2011). Interactive discussions provide many opportunities for students to practice the skills needed to learn how to question, assess evidence and claims, problem solve, and to construct and clearly communicate knowledge. These skills are particularly important for helping students learn ways to demythologize their existing knowledge about the criminal justice system. We have found that engaging in conversations about course material, and their ideas and beliefs about the material, better prepares students to deconstruct ideas and knowledge about criminal justice concepts and ideas.

An essential feature of our approach to student learning in criminal justice is thus the necessity for dialogic conversations between students and instructors. A dialogic conversational model is different from other discussion-based methods that tend to be managed in the form of monologue style lecture and answer sessions. Instead, this model allows for the immediacy of a natural conversation style—a method that opens the opportunity for students to capture and reflect on habits of thought leading to simplifying concepts and thus from recognizing the deeper meanings of criminal justice phenomenon (Jackson, 2008). By engaging in cumulation, or "building carefully on what is said and chaining individual utterances and ideas into coherent lines of inquiry" during discussions, dialogic conversations create opportunities where students learn to make connections between prior knowledge and beliefs, current materials, and their own learning process (Skidmore, 2006, pg. 506).

The use of dialogic conversational approaches can be problematic in the online environment. The lack of immediate interaction and the inability to engage in the spontaneity of utterances during conversations are all concerns when managing discussions in the online classroom. Moreover, the potential for miscommunication can further enhance anxieties and frustration with controversial and sensitive material. While often misunderstood as solely applying to spoken discussion, dialogic conversations can occur in any communicative medium, including written assignments. A dialogic conversation model also requires instructors be attuned to the affective dynamics of student learning by being aware of emotional reactions to course material—a pedagogical concern that is particularly problematic in criminal justice courses.

In online courses, dialogic conversations can be recreated in a number of ways.

First, and perhaps most importantly, instructors must become active participants in classroom discussions. Instructors must be present to intervene in discussions that become heated, to point out errors in reasoning, or to help students make connections to other course material. Figure 5 offers one example of how instructors might interact with students by engaging in discussions.

Figure 5

Word Count: (70)
Forum Assignments / Helping Prisoner's Adjust / Re: Week 12 Forum (Nov 16, 2013 8:54 AM) **Grade | [display in conversation]**

I think you all raise an important notion of "hesitancy". I think as a society we are so focused on "risk assessment" that we don't try a lot of things out of fear. We know most people in prison are non-violent offenders, but we focus programs and particularly release on those that are most violent which sets everyone up for failure. Just some food for thought this morning...

Word Count: (109)
Forum Assignments / Helping Prisoner's Adjust / Re: Adjusting to Life Outside the Bars (Nov 16, 2013 8:52 AM) **Grade | [display in conversation]**

You all have some great ideas here. I do like the idea of a "bankruptcy" system. However, I wonder how that would really play out? I can imagine a situation where that happens, someone's record is deleted, then you have the one or two individuals who re-offend, then there would be public outrage that it was tried. This has happened with many programs - it works for most, but you have one or two that it does not work for and they pull the entire program. I'm just speculating based on history, but it does raise interesting questions for the problems with attempts to fix the issue.

Word Count: (5)
Forum Assignments / Midterm Check In / Re: check-in (Oct 14, 2013 10:26 AM) **Grade | [display in conversation]**

I couldn't agree more!

Word Count: (66)
Forum Assignments / Midterm Check In / Re: Check In (Oct 14, 2013 6:53 AM) **Grade | [display in conversation]**

Also, I think I responded to you about this in another post - be sure to contact our Center for teaching and learning about your technical issues. That is precisely why they are there and they are fantastic at what they do. You can reach them at eaonline@iue.edu or 765-973-8300. They are more than happy to assist you all with anything you need.

In this example, the instructor highlighted some areas of concern in the discussion and pointed to areas of agreement. The instructor was also present to assist students with difficulties using course technologies. Instructors can also engage in discussions with students using feedback on assignments or requiring students to engage in formal peer reviews with other students, both of which lead to valuable conversations about course material.

Being an active participant in conversations also allows instructors to set the tone for discussions. By modeling professional behavior and "netiquette," instructors can intervene if discussions become heated. Actively participating allows instructors many opportunities to teach students appropriate ways for managing differences in opinions, how to handle criticism, and to offer critiques of others' work. Students will undoubtedly need these skills in their professional careers. Online, dialogic conversations have the potential to offer a safe space for students to practice these and other communicative competencies.

MANAGING CAREER DISCONNECTION THROUGH CASE STUDIES

Many criminal justice students find it difficult to engage with material that seems to lack a direct impact on their future careers. The first strategy in addressing this problem is to draw explicit connections between academic lessons learned and future career demands. These explicit connections will inevitability needed in almost every aspect of the online course. Drawing explicit career connections may appear relatively simple and should be part of all criminal justice courses. However, maintaining student engagement in subjects such as statistics and research methods is often quite difficult.

As Sundt (2010) observes, few courses in the criminal justice curriculum evoke more anxiety and resistance to learning than research methods. In her research, Sundt (2010) finds that,

> Students often struggle to understand the relevance of research methods to their education and career goals, complain that the topic is tedious and difficult, and approach the course with a minimum of enthusiasm and more than a little dread (pg. 266).

This could equally apply to students experience with statistics. The two subjects are traditionally viewed as more demanding and difficult for undergraduate students due to the large degree of abstract concepts and what students perceive to be a lack of relevance. Addressing the issue of relevance can be even more acute in the online environment. Online students are primarily non-traditional students, many whom work in their field of study. These students can grow particularly frustrated in courses they feel are irrelevant to their existing careers. For these reasons, it is important for instructors to challenge criminal justice students by creating opportunities to ensure students understand the significance of the subject matter to their existing or future careers.

There are several ways to challenge students' assumptions about the usefulness of assignments in each of these courses. One example is when students are required to properly cite references in written assignments. This is one task that students learn in all research methods courses. Criminal justice majors appear to immediately grasp the idea that, without proper evidence, it is impossible to make a case in criminal trials. When discussing the need to properly cite references, an effective strategy is thus to explain that giving proper attribution for the student's work is great preparation for documenting evidence in future criminal cases. This is the type of explicit career connection that can be used to assist students in developing habits that will make them better in their respective jobs.

Perhaps the most valuable tool to ensure explicit career connections in criminal justice courses is the use of active learning assignments (Robinson, 2000; Williams and Robinson, 2004). As Robinson (2000) notes,

> [Active learning] activities address the second reason that active learning strategies are important in criminal justice. Jobs obtained by criminal justice graduates require them to work well with others and to develop good communication skills. Active learning strategies assist in developing these needed skills. Active learning strategies encourage group work, as well as speaking and writing skills. For example, in a debate, students can be encouraged or required to argue one side and then to actively listen to other students; then they can fairly and accurately summarize the main points of the other side verbally or in writing.

> Logically, such activities prepare students to use these skills in the real world upon graduation. This may make them better police officers, better attorneys, better probation officers, better counselors, and so forth. (pg. 69).

The use of case studies is one active learning strategy instructors can use to foster student engagement and increase critical thinking in online courses. By using cases that involve real-world situations, students can gain a better understanding of the linkage between abstract concepts and the skills needed for employment.

Case studies are often better suited to making career connections than other traditional written assignments. Traditional forms of questioning (e.g., essay questions, research papers) do not necessarily promote the problem solving skills required in criminal justice careers. Essay questions, for example, can be useful when requiring students to describe course content. However, they do not necessarily promote critical thinking and may seem one-dimensional and irrelevant to students. Figure 6 shows one example of a traditional approach to student questioning.

Figure 6. Traditional Essay Question

"Using Nazi Research Data"

Q: What are the ethical implications of using Nazi research data in contemporary research?

A: There are many ethical issues that come into play when discussing the Nazi research. Some of the types of ethical problems that come into play when discussing the Nazi research include harm, voluntary participation, analysis/reporting, and, but not limited to, legal liability (Parker, 2015). First of all, the types of harm that were endured are unfathomable. Physical harm, psychological harm, harm to the participant, and even harm to third parties were all endured during these experiments (Parker, 2015). I think it goes without saying that the victims of Nazi research experienced all these different types of harm.

There are even issues with voluntary consent. There was no consent given to the Nazi researchers from their prisoners, and if they did receive consent, it is unlikely that consent was given without the fear of reprisal if it was refused (Parker, 2015). There are also no formal documentations of the Nazi research (Cohen, 2010). This is a problem especially when discussing whether the Nazi research data should be used in today's society. Because there are no formal records of the positive or negative outcomes of the research, it is hard to determine what actions of the researchers were effective, and which researchers were ineffective (Babbie, 69: 2010).

All of these reasons, plus many more, all indicate that the Nazi research was unethical. Understanding and coming to terms with the fact that the Nazi research was conducted unethically is one thing, but using the data for knowledge is another. I agree that everything about the research is unethical, but it is still research, and it is at our disposal. I do not think that using the Nazi research data will give other "scientists" the thought that they can still conduct illegal and unethical research practices. I agree with the idea that the use of the data would give purpose to all of those who suffered and died through the Nazi research conduct (Cohen, 2010).

References
Babbie, Earl (2010). The practice of social research. Belmont, CA: Wadsworth, Cengage Learning. Print
Cohen, Baruch C (2010). Jewish law articles: the ethics of using medical data from Nazi experiments. Retrieved from http://www.jlaw.com/Articles/NaziMedEx.html
Parker, M. (2015). Research ethics: Chapter 3. [PowerPoint slides]. Retrieved from https://oncourse.iu.edu/portal/site/

Using several different case study formats are an effective way to make a variety of connections for students. Criminal justice students have a variety of career options, including graduate school. Therefore, it is incredibly important to ensure that case studies include scenarios from a variety of different employment and educational sources. Figure 7 displays one example of a simple case study from early discussions in a 200-level undergraduate research methods course. The case study in Figure 7 requires students to apply their knowledge of research design in order to identify the errors in a fictional research proposal. In order to identify the multiple errors, the student must cognitively realign the research design elements that should fit together and then orient them to the overall goal of the project. For example, students must reconcile the discontinuity between using a cross-sectional time dimension with a study designed to examine exam failure over a four-year period, the inappropriate selection of the university as the unit of analysis to study individual students' exam failure and the use of idiographic focus for a Social Science research study.

Students are tasked with the responsibility of correcting the methodology in order to produce a viable research design. This added component provides the student an opportunity to exercise critical thinking in constructing a solution to the case study. The case study in Figure 7 is effective in promoting critical thinking and problem solving and will certainly be seen as relevant for students planning to attend graduate school.

Figure 7. Basic Unstructured Case Study

"Dr. Lind's Research Proposal"

You are a graduate assistant for Dr. H. M. Lind. Dr. Lind has written a research proposal to study exam failure at the local university. Dr. Lind is interested in explaining the relationship between insufficient sleep and student exam failure over the course of a student's four-year matriculation. The unit of analysis for the study is the university as an organization. Dr. Lind intends to use a cross-sectional time dimension for the study. During his explanation of the study, Dr. Lind assured the university board that the study will have complete anonymity and be very significant to the scientific community because of the study's idiographic focus. Dr. Lind has asked you to proofread his proposal. What are the research design problems with Dr. Lind's proposal? Please explain how Dr. Lind might fix these errors.

Figure 8 displays another example of a case study from an undergraduate statistics course. The student is required to read the short case study and to be prepared to answer questions about the information presented. In order to answer the question, the student must complete some basic computations and identify notation error in the case study. The major difference in Figure 3 is that there are structured individual questions to which the student must respond as opposed to open-ended case study analyses found in Figure 8. These structured analyses can also be useful for acclimating undergraduate students to the process of analyzing case studies. The case study in Figure 8 is considered a hybrid structure because it requires some minor computation, but computation is not the primary goal of the case study. In short, this case study blends the features of a traditional essay by asking students to identify and define abstract concepts, yet also offers the opportunity to apply those concepts to a real-life scenario.

Figure 8. Hybrid Structure Case Study

"Warden Lind's Report"

You are a new correctional officer with the state prison system. Your facility is undergoing an investigation about fraudulent reporting. Your supervisor has just learned that you have a degree in criminal justice and wants you to examine the following information from the Warden's report to the investigating committee. Examine the following information and recalculate the data as is necessary. Be prepared to discuss the Warden's report.

"During the 2014 year, inmate assaults were not problematic. There were only a small frequency of inmate assaults (F= 481) compared to the total number of prison incidents (n= 1,120). Inmate assaults comprised approximately 10% of all the prison incidents. The only thing concerning the prison staff is the number of assaults on gang members (N= 21). Gang assaults continue to rise as a sub-sample of the overall assaults. The proportion of gang assaults was 2.345 in the general population."

Q1: How many notational errors are in Warden Lind's report?
Q2: Should the prison officials be concerned about gang assaults?
Q3: What percent of the prison incidents are inmate assaults?
Q4: What is the proportion of gang assaults?
Q5: Can you support the Warden's report in its current state?

For students, this case study makes several connections to the criminal justice field by asking students to identify potential problems they may encounter in a correctional facility. It also provides the opportunity for students to better understand why the need for empirical evidence is important in identifying potential issues and possible solutions.

The case studies displayed in Figure 9 and Figure 10 can be classified as computational case studies as they require students to complete statistical computation as its primary function. It is important to note that computational case studies should also involve a secondary function requiring the student to make a decision about their completed analysis. It is the application of the "derived solution" that benefits the critical thinking process.

Computational case studies are considered to be more advanced than basic case studies due to the introduction of dross data. Dross data is data that is meaningless to the analytical questions at hand. Examples of the introduction of dross data can be found in Figure 9 and Figure 10. The discussion of candidate B's "lush hair" and his alumni status from "Purdue University" in Figure 9 serves to help the student develop the ability to disregard dross data and focus on the data pertinent to the analysis. The case study in Figure 10 contains politically-oriented dross data—a feature that helps students critically evaluate the politically motivated assumptions often made in criminal justice policies and practices.

Figure 9. Computational Case Study

"Hiring the New Warden"

After Warden Lind's disastrous report on inmate assault, the state correctional committee in Ohio wanted to avoid this type of embarrassment in its hiring of a new warden. The search has been narrowed down to two candidates. Most of the committee members are in favor of hiring candidate B because they are impressed with the two (2) perfect scores on the hiring exams. Additionally, several committee members have commented on his "wonderfully lush head of hair". Another committee member commented that "anyone who went to Purdue University would surely make a great addition to the team." Below you will find the scores of the two candidates. Analyze the data and be prepared to select a candidate. Please show your work and explain your selection.

Candidate-A: 86, 85, 90, 87, 89
Candidate-B: 100, 62, 43, 95, 100

Figure 10. Computational Case Study

"Prison Distributions"

Below you will find three data distributions of data collected from a local prison. There are some concerns about rehabilitation programs, staffing, and the overall safety of the facility. The staff researcher for the prison has claimed that the inmate population is highly homogeneic based on the inmates' ages and number of arrests. The staff researcher is personally offended that anyone would dare question his analysis. You have been warned by several coworkers that the staff researcher is the nephew of the governor and the governor is very protective of his nephew. Additionally, the staff researcher claims that the inmates do not pose a threat to staff because they are relatively non-serious offenders. Compute a univariate data analysis (Mean, Median, Mode, and Standard deviation) for each distribution. Be prepared to support or refute the claims of the staff researcher.

Using these types of case studies allow instructors to assess students' reactions to a variety of situational variables simply by changing dross element within the scenario. As future criminal justice professionals, students will be in positions that require them to distinguish between information that is either relevant or irrelevant to a case. Case studies, such as those used in the examples above, offer the opportunity for students to practice this skill in a way that immerses them in the context of real-life scenarios.

CONCLUSION

Teaching criminal justice in the online environment can be a rewarding experience for both instructors and students. In criminal justice, our students plan to become police officers, probation officers, and lawyers. As future actors in organizations that represent what is arguably the most powerful mechanism of formal social control, criminal justice instructors have a special reasonability in ensuring our students have the critical thinking and problem-solving skills required of professionals in the field. This requires that instructors carefully develop online courses aligned with the best practices in online learning and attuned to the needs of our students.

In this chapter, we addressed some of the pedagogical issues instructors face in online criminal justice courses and offered practical strategies they can use to address these concerns. Student course evaluations and peer reviews of our courses indicate the effectiveness of these strategies for managing student's anxieties and expectations in criminal justice courses. Strategies such as using modules to structure and organize courses, developing dialogic conversational style discussions, and integrating case studies are all simple and straightforward practices instructors can incorporate into any online criminal justice course.

REFERENCES

Bean, J. (2011). *Engaging ideas: The professor's guide to integrating writing, critical thinking, and active learning in the classroom.* Jossey-Bass: San Francisco, CA.

Bjerregaard, B., & Lord, V. (2004). An examination of the ethical and value orientations of criminal justice students. *Police Quarterly, 7*(2), 262–284.

Durham, A. (1992). Observations on the future of criminal justice education: Legitimating the discipline and serving the general university population. *Journal of Criminal Justice Education,* 3(1), 35–52.

Farnworth, M., Longmire, D. R., & West, V. M. (1998). College students' views on criminal justice. *Journal of Criminal Justice Education,* 9(1), 39–57.

Jackson, L. (2008). Dialogic pedagogy for social justice: A critical examination. *Studies in Philosophy and Education,* 27(2-3), 137–148.

Ko, S., & Rossen, S. (2010). *Teaching online: A practical guide.* 3rd edition. Routledge.

Mackey, D. A., & Courtright, K. E. (2000). Assessing punitiveness among college students: A comparison of criminal justice majors with other majors. *The Justice Professional, 12,* 423–441.

Robinson, M. (2000). Using active learning in criminal justice: Twenty-five examples. *Journal of Criminal Justice Education,* 11(1), 65–78.

Shank, P. (2010). The importance of intuitive navigation in online course design. In Robert Kelly, (Ed.) *Online course design: Thirteen strategies for teaching in a web-based distance learning environment* (Online Classroom Newsletter), pp. 20–21. Madison, Wisconsin: Magna Publications Inc.

Sundt, J. (2010). Overcoming student resistance to learning research methods: An approach based on decoding disciplinary thinking. *Journal of Criminal Justice Education,* 21(3), 266–284.

Williams, E. J., & Robinson, M. B. (2004). Ideology and criminal justice: Suggestions for a pedagogical model. *Journal of Criminal Justice Education,* 15(2), 373–392.

6

PSYCHOLOGY

Student Misconceptions of Psychology: Steps for Helping Online Students Toward a Scientific Understanding of Psychology

BETH A. TRAMMELL, PH.D.

GREGORY DAM, PH.D.

AMANDA KRAHA, PH.D.

INTRODUCTION

Perhaps more than with any other discipline, students come to the task of learning psychology with an abundance of prior knowledge, beliefs, and folk theories. People naturally spend a lot of time theorizing about the minds of others, their intentions, their beliefs, and the causes of their behavior. Consequently, students accumulate a variety of folk theories about human behavior prior to receiving formal instruction on the scientific discipline of psychology. Unfortunately, much of this knowledge consists of misconceptions that often interfere with learning (Lilienfeld, Lynn, Ruscio, & Beyerstein, 2009). This makes teaching psychology difficult because many incorrect student preconceptions regard some of the core ideas and concepts in the field. Traditional teaching methods have been shown to have little effect on reducing student misconceptions (Lamal, 1979; Standing & Huber, 2003; McKeachie, 1960). Here we explore some of the unique affordances of online learning environments that allow instructors to address student misconceptions.

Student misconceptions in psychology are often deeply embedded beliefs, and are strongly supported by personal evidence—making them difficult to change (Hughes, Lyddy & Lambe, 2013). Since it is easier to reject new ideas than to edit one's beliefs, a student's tendency toward confirmation bias may lead them to distort or ignore new information that conflicts with their established beliefs. It is also easier to revise and abandon mistaken intuitions about subatomic particles than to revise knowledge regarding something as personal and immediate as other people. Psychology instructors are therefore confronted with a burden of proof to demonstrate sufficient evidence to reject commonly held beliefs. Evidence for psychological theories is derived from behavior measured under the rigors of scientific methodology, often in laboratory settings. These scientific explanations are often met with skepticism by students and challenged by deeply rooted misconceptions that may be supported by personal experience, misinterpretations of scientific findings in popular press, and the reinforcement of certain myths within the growing sources of information and media (Taylor & Kowalski, 2004).

The overall propensity to acquire and strongly adhere to misconceptions suggests a need for students to develop skills to critically evaluate new information. The goal of instruction is often thought to be for students to demonstrate the acquisition of scientifically supported content knowledge in psychology. However, it is also important to teach students how to critically assess information and distinguish science from pseudoscience. Research on the instruction of critical thinking has demonstrated some promise in effectively reducing student misconceptions and their effect on learning psychology (Bensley, Lilienfeld, & Powell, 2014). It has also been shown that students who score well on critical thinking tests have fewer misconceptions and show a greater reduction of misconceptions as a result of instruction (Kowalski and Taylor, 2004).

Online learning environments provide unique opportunities for instruction that differ from traditional face-to-face (F2F) instruction. For example, online students participate in peer discussions about the content being learned. In F2F settings, it is difficult to initiate discussions that elicit participation by all students. Further, people behave differently online than they would in face-to-face environments in what has been known as the "online disinhibition effect" (Suler, 2004). This effect may reduce some of the social hurdles for students to express their views freely. Online discussions can easily reveal underlying misconceptions. For example, lengthy threaded commentary on the cause and nature of photographic memory or repressed memories, phenomena not supported by scientific evidence, may occur. This provides opportunities for instructors to design interactions that are likely to bring to light student misconceptions. Such interactions can encourage students to make their mistaken preconceptions explicit, which helps focus instruction efforts. We briefly review the literature on student misconceptions in psychology and pedagogical approaches to effectively reducing misconceptions through instruction of critical thinking and principles of deep learning. We then provide a framework for online instruction and some suggested best practices for addressing student misconceptions.

STUDENT MISCONCEPTIONS IN PSYCHOLOGY

Researchers have been interested in folk theories of psychology for decades and recently there has been a renewed interest in studying student misconceptions. Understanding what misconceptions students bring to the task of learning has important implications for instruction. Students who endorse discipline-related misconceptions show decreased levels of learning (Dochy, Segers, & Buehl, 1999), and the number of misconceptions held by students predicts their class grade (Kuhle, Barber & Bristol, 2009). Research efforts have been devoted to cataloguing common student misconceptions and their change with instruction. There have been efforts to increase the efficiency of identifying student misconceptions automatically with computational methods (Sherin, 2013; Dam & Kaufmann, 2008).

Evidence suggests that commonly held misconceptions in psychology (e.g., "we only use 10% of our brain") are widely held by as many as 71% of students entering introductory level courses (Standing & Huber, 2003). Unfortunately, research also has shown that traditional college training has only a small effect on dispelling popular myths and misconceptions. Psychology majors who had completed upper-level coursework in the discipline demonstrated a persistent high 50% acceptance rate of misconceptions (Gaze, 2014). Research also shows that traditional F2F psychology courses are not effective in reducing misconceptions and reduce misconceptions marginally by 6% (Lamal, 1979). In addition, myth rejection increases slowly despite students taking numerous psychology courses (Standing & Huber, 2003; McKeachie, 1960). As a consequence, many students may complete college level training in psychology and still retain many incorrect beliefs.

WHY ARE SOME STUDENT MISCONCEPTIONS SO RESISTANT TO CHANGE?

Roscoe and Chi (2002) proposed that student misconceptions can be classified into distinct categories that depend largely on how interconnected the misconceptions are with other concepts in the student's belief system. Each category of student misconception presents unique challenges with regard to how conceptual change can be affected through instruction. Some misconceptions regard mistaken "factual" claims that are relatively independent of other beliefs the student holds, such as "people only use 10% of their brain." These propositional level misconceptions may be reinforced by popular notions in fiction, media, and false advertising. Propositional level misconceptions can be corrected by introducing the correct and conflicting information: "100% of the brain is active in a healthy person." The consequences of the conceptual edit are minimal to the learner's belief system. The learner need only edit the specific incorrect belief by replacing it with the correct information, which may only entail changes to a few other beliefs. As a result, propositional level misconceptions are perhaps the easiest to address during instruction.

Much more difficult to change are misconceptions that are deeply interconnected and embedded within the student's worldview and belief system. For example, many people believe that explanations in biology are distinct from explanations in psychology and belong to a different conceptual domain (Coley, 1995; Bloom, 2004). For some students, the notion that mental states are identical to material states of the brain runs not only against their common sense intuition, but may also conflict with other strongly held beliefs, such as religious teachings. Students are often reluctant to endorse new information that conflicts with their core beliefs, and the more strongly these beliefs are held, the larger their negative influence on learning (Dole, 2000).

Psychology is a scientific discipline that adheres to standard scientific methodology. One of the broadest and most overarching misconceptions that students have about psychology involves the fundamental nature of the discipline. Many students do not conceive of psychology as a scientific research discipline (Goedeke & Gibson, 2011). Prior to enrolling, students believe that an introductory psychology course may teach personal skills to help improve one's life (Goedeke & Gibson, 2011). This non-scientific view of psychology may lower the standards by which students are willing to accept new information in the domain of psychology. Instructional approaches that focus on teaching psychology as a scientific discipline demonstrate higher rejection rates of commonly held misconceptions (Bensley, Lilienfeld, & Powell, 2014). It is hypothesized that students learn to 'sort out' beliefs that are intuitively appealing and hypotheses that are supported by empirical findings.

The amount of information that students and instructors have access to is increasing at remarkable rates. This increased availability of information creates problems for how knowledge and understanding develop. To effectively increase understanding in a given domain requires critical evaluation of not only the content, but also the source of information. The high levels of student adoption and strong adherence to misconceptions in psychology suggests the need to develop critical thinking skills. It is important that students not only demonstrate knowledge of accepted concepts and theories in psychology, but also develop skills for evaluating new information. Students who demonstrate strong critical thinking skills hold fewer misconceptions than their peers with poorer skills. Critical thinking skills also predict whether existing misconceptions will change as a result of instruction (Kowalski & Taylor, 2004; Bensley, Lilienfeld, & Powell, 2014).

Teaching students to think critically is to teach scientific reasoning. One of the hallmarks of scientific reasoning is to only accept hypotheses and theories that are supported by observable and reproducible empirical evidence. Student success in psychology courses is predicted by students' ability to recognize evidence-based supported claims and practices (Bensley, Lilienfeld, & Powell, 2014). It has been argued that teaching scientific reasoning reduces confirmation biases and serves as a safeguard against reaching conclusions subjectively appealing although incorrect (Lilienfeld, 2002).

Prior to changing any misconceptions, online instructors must first make it easy for the online learner to learn. It goes without saying that students who are unable to navigate the online classroom are unlikely to learn much, much less change their preconceived notions. Therefore, the first step for an online instructor is to minimize confusion in basic online learning at the outset to maximize the chance to change misconceptions. Next, online instructors should examine students' current belief system to inform both the student and the instructor on the current number and degree of misconceptions. Third, students should be taught how to think critically and finally, how to apply examples to their own lives to facilitate learning.

Step 1: Course planning and design. To best assist learning, online instructors must be meticulous in their course planning and organization. Beginners in online course development might hold the idea that you can simply transfer a traditional F2F course to an online environment with the same levels of learning. While there are some parallels, overall this is not the case (Ko & Rossen, 2004). In an online environment instructors must plan not only lessons and assignments, but course structure as well—how the course is designed within a particular learning management system (Ko & Rossen, 2004).

The student's first impression of the course will be from the learning environment, not the instructor themselves (Miller & Doering, 2015). Because of this, students will begin forming opinions of the instructor before they have any interaction with them—bringing to light the importance of a polished, well-designed course environment. Consider the hypothetical student who, upon the start of the semester, logs in to the first day of his/her new course in Introductory Psychology. Once logged in, the student looks for several minutes, finally locating a welcome message after minutes of searching. After reading the welcome, though, the student then must spend additional time searching the course site to get started. This kind of first impression can be a frustrating experience that may reflect poorly upon the instructor and damage the sense of credibility necessary for a successful learning experience.

Creating a sense of instructor presence is considered one essential piece of creating a successful online learning environment (Lehman & Conceição, 2010) that minimizes confusion and will aid in the combating of misconceptions. Instructor presence is defined as "being there" and "being together" with students throughout the online learning experience (Lehman & Conceição, 2010). One method of establishing instructor presence is to convey a sense of enthusiasm about the upcoming course (Ko & Rosen, 2010). This can be done through welcome messages, introductions, or similar introductory activities as the course begins (Lehman & Conceição, 2010). Welcome forums are a common course component to foster presence, and instructors should not only include these in some form, but be sure to participate in them as well (Lewis & Abdul-Hamid, 2006). If class size allows, individually responding to each student's introductory post will further the sense of presence in an online course (Ko & Rosen, 2010). Requiring students to do their own video welcome forum could help students "put a face to a name" that is often a challenge in the online classroom (Suler, 2004). Beyond this, it also allows the instructor to get acquainted with students on a deeper level by understanding the non-verbal cues that are inherently absent in written communication that is the online environment.

Throughout the course, instructors should strive to engage in regular interaction—through course announcements, personal e-mails, or similar methods (Ko & Rosen, 2010). One strategy is to provide a summary of the major objectives of the previous week along with major expectations of the current week. This serves to provide students with a recap of what they should have learned, and what they can expect in the upcoming week. When instructors are engaged and visible in the course, students will be more engaged as well (Conrad, 2004). In addition, by doing this, it could eliminate questions or confusion from students about what is needed for the week. In a F2F classroom, it is common for instructors to give verbal reminders at the beginning or end of class. In the online classroom, this is still an important part of class, but may require an additional email or announcement within the learning management system.

Tone is another important consideration in the online environment. In F2F interactions, students can use both verbal and nonverbal cues to interpret the meaning of feedback. In an online environment, students typically rely on only written forms of communication, thereby limiting the information they use to interpret instructor tone. Because of this, it is essential that instructors carefully craft all messages to convey a positive, reassuring tone in all course interactions and student feedback. One study found the positive effects of syllabi with a positive and friendly tone—students rated the instructor as being warm, approachable, and motivated to teach the course (Harnish & Bridges, 2011).

Instructors should also make it clear in the start of each online course how students can find help when they need it (Pacansky-Brock, 2013). The ability of students to quickly find help when they need it contributes to an overall sense of presence within the course. This includes help for technological difficulties (Will you help? Is there a campus department to help?) but course-related material as well. Some authors (e.g., Ko & Rossen, 2010) suggest the creation of a Frequently Asked Questions (FAQ) page for the course. This gives students a place to look for questions as would be true if a classmate in a F2F class raised his or her hand. Reminding students that such a FAQ page exists is important and might require prompting at the beginning of the course to help students utilize such a resource. Another strategy is to provide additional resources, perhaps curated from various internet sites (Howell Major, 2015). TED Talks and YouTube clips are popular options—however, instructors should carefully evaluate each resource before sharing, particularly broken links and expired web pages.

Step 2: Examine students' current belief system. One relatively simple way to examine current beliefs about psychological concepts is to administer a short questionnaire about common psychological misconceptions. By offering this as a quiz at the outset of the semester, the online instructor does as least two things: 1) He or she gets the students thinking about their own thoughts and the content of the course, but also 2) gets a quick overview of what content is the most misconceived by the students. Several authors have created and critiqued common misconception assessment tools (for overview see McCutcheon, 1991). Although there is no consensus about which assessment tool is the best at capturing all psychological misconceptions, certainly any of these options could serve the aforementioned two goals. Two commonly cited assessment tools are Vaughan's (1977) Test of Common Beliefs and the McCutcheon Test of Misconceptions (1991). More simply, the online instructor could take a list of commonly cited misconceptions and create a short true/false quiz as Kuhle and colleagues (2009) did. In doing this, these researchers found that 83% of students held at least 5 of the 10 most common misbeliefs. Moreover, they found a negative correlation between the number of misconceptions and students' final grade (Kuhle, Barber, & Bristol, 2009). To establish even deeper connection, the online instructor could carefully select from a list of the most common misbeliefs (Gardner & Brown, 2013; Lilienfeld, Lynn, Ruscio, & Beyerstein, 2010) that directly coincide with the course content and quite purposefully select those to assess.

One other means to examine student's current beliefs is to challenge students to consider where their misbeliefs come from. Researchers have suggested misconceptions frequently originate from past personal experiences, previous coursework, and the media (Taylor & Kowalski, 2004), but also our human desire for immediate reconciliation of complicated situations, and selective attention/memory (Lilienfeld, 2010). Here again, the online instructor could create a quick follow-up quiz that would include the common misconceptions as mentioned above and ask which of the aforementioned sources are the culprit. In doing this, it will become easier for the instructor to tailor specific lecture content. For instance, if the majority of students report media as the common source of misconceptions, the instructor could present additional media examples that present accurate information to refute that misconception. More information about refutational strategies in the online classroom will be discussed below. What seems evident here is that there are many methods to measuring students' misconceptions, all of which have advantages, which is an important second step in changing those mistaken beliefs.

Step 3: Teach critical thinking skills and promote deep learning. There are several things that instructors can do to teach critical thinking skills that will empower students to confront and carefully consider their psychological misconceptions. First and foremost, instructors can create an environment with rich discussions and virtual relationships—not only student to instructor, but student to student as well (Lewis & Abdul-Hamid, 2006). These interactions are important for student satisfaction (Su, Bonk, Magjuka, Liu, & Lee, 2005) and student learning (Lewis & Abdul-Hamid, 2006). Online education changes the role of the instructor from expert to facilitator (Ko & Rossen, 2010). Because of this, instructors should take a step back and incorporate activities that allow frequent and meaningful student interaction. Instructors should participate in these discussions, mostly to guide students and keep them on topic (Lewis & Abdul-Hamid, 2006). This sort of interaction fosters constructive learning, and is becoming mandatory in some places (Wilson & Stacey, 2004).

Another interesting strategy to encourage critical thinking and assess misconceptions is illustrated by Chew's (2004) use of ConcepTests. Most courses implement multiple choice formatting for either quizzes or exams. With ConcepTests, the online instructor creates a good multiple choice question that includes a common misconception as one of the choices (Chew 2004). It follows good test construction to have several choices that are logical, but with the ConcepTest approach, the instructor deliberately chooses misconceptions relevant to the course content to get a better understanding of how many students still hold that belief to be true.

The notion of deep learning in higher education is not a new endeavor, but its importance should not be underemphasized. Hacker & Niederhauser (2000) discussed five learning principles that promote deep learning in the classroom. One learning principle requires students to become active participants in learning by giving deeper explanations for what they believe (Hacker and Niederhauser, 2000). It is common for students to respond to forum prompts with their own personal experiences about a matter. For instance, in considering the misconception "Opposites attract," inevitably several students will share their personal experiences about how this is true in their lives, perpetuating the misconception for themselves and promoting it with fellow students. In the online classroom, instructors should require scientific citation for responses in the forum or on assignments. This is not to say that reflection is not a critical part of learning. Rather, this posits that students need to understand how to consume scientific information as it relates to their lives.

Another principle for deep learning includes appropriate use of instructor feedback (Hacker & Niederhauser, 2000). Feedback is an essential component to student learning (Biggs, 1999), particularly in the online classroom. Feedback to students should be both timely and constructive. Everyone will have a different definition of timely—students included. Further, since there is not a start or end time of the online classroom, students may have unrealistic expectations that you will be available at extraordinary times of the day and week (e.g., evenings and weekends). For this reason, it is critical to let students know what they can expect from you with regard to timeliness of feedback on assignments and responses to emails. Feedback should also be constructive—it should provide clear, tangible information about how the student can improve. Employing a competency framework for the course where students can revise their work based on this feedback is also associated with higher levels of learning (Black & Wiliam, 1998).

Step 4: Use refutational teaching and student-oriented examples to facilitate learning. Refutational teaching strategies stem from the literature surrounding conceptual change, whereby students become dissatisfied with their current belief system before change occurs. When aiming to change misconceptions, implementing these principles into teaching has showed the most promising evidence (Kowalski & Taylor, 2009). With refutational teaching, the online instructor would first activate the misconception for the students. For instance, open the learning module with a quotation of "How true is the statement...? We only use 10% of our brains." This introduces students to the topic and gets them to think about what they believe about the statement. Immediately following that activation, refutational teaching posits the true explanation needs to be offered immediately following the activation to argue against, or refute, the misconception. In their study, Kowalski and Taylor (2009) examined the differences in students' misconceptions via various instructional methods (e.g., refutational lectures, refutational text, standard text, standard lecture). Results suggested refutational lectures plus refutational text was superior to any other method and, particularly of interest for the online instructor, refutational text was approximately equal to standard text and lecture together. Since the main method of transmission of information from instructor to student in an online classroom is text-based, this may be a hole in the research where more is needed. In the meantime, it seems to highlight the importance of using video or audio lectures to refute misconceptions, in addition to written or text-based evidence.

While the evidence on refutational teaching is strong and continuing to emerge, some have argued against such approach. Schwarz and colleagues (2007) examined the impact of activating the misconception by using flyers promoting the dispelling of myths surrounding the flu vaccine. They concluded participants continued to hold misconceptions despite seeing the counter-evidence, possibly because of the familiarity bias (we will continue to believe what is familiar to us—our previously held belief) (Schwarz, Sanna,

Skurnik, & Yoon, 2007). This suggests instructors may need to be continually vigilant of implementing formative assessment about the misconceptions of their students throughout the course.

Linking everyday events to course content is another way to aid in the combatting of misconceptions. One popular controversy of late is the blue dress phenomena, where a Tumblr user posted an image of a dress and asked what colors the dress was. A seemingly simple question, the internet erupted into a rage of debate—some saw white and gold while others saw blue and black (Pinker, 2015). The blue dress debate can illustrate several issues of Cognitive Psychology, including perception and bottom-up versus top-down processing, to name a few. Connecting popular media to course topics has the capability to accomplish several instructional goals, such as building credibility with students, staying relevant with course content, and modeling the use of examples, another principle of deep learning (Hacker and Niederhauser, 2000). Indeed, the ability to apply content via a good example shows higher-order understanding according to Bloom's taxonomy. Beyond this, using popular media enhances the student's understanding of psychology and how it applies to everyday life, furthering the instructor's efforts to combat and correct common misconceptions.

CONCLUSION

Addressing student misconceptions in psychology requires careful consideration from the online instructor to teach scientific reasoning and critical thinking. With some purposeful attention, online instructors can gather information about current misconceptions of their students and the appropriate online activities to refute these misconceptions. Although the research on refutational lecturing in an online environment may still be emerging, this type of instruction appears to be the most promising and the most likely to be easily translated into online video or audio lectures to change misconceptions. Continued efforts to expand teaching methodologies into the online classroom are likely to emerge in the coming years as the increase in online education continues to grow.

Bensley, D. A., Lilienfeld, S. O., & Powell, L. A. (2014). A new measure of psychological misconceptions: Relations with academic background, critical thinking, and acceptance of paranormal and pseudoscientific claims. *Learning and Individual Differences, 36,* 9–18.

Biggs, J. (1999). *Teaching for Quality Learning at University.* Buckingham: Open University Press.

Black, P., & Wiliam, D. (1998). Assessment and classroom learning. *Assessment in Education: Principles, Policy & Practice, 5*(1), 7–75.

Bloom, P. (2004). *Descartes' Baby.* New York: Basic Books.

Chew, S. L. (2004). Using ConcepTests for formative assessment. *Psychology Teacher Network, 14*(1), 10–12.

Chi, M. T. H., & Roscoe, R. D. (2002). The processes and challenges of conceptual change. In M. Limon and L. Mason (Eds.), *Reconsidering conceptual change: Issues in theory and practice* (pp. 3–27). Dordrecht, Netherlands: Kluwer Academic Publishers.

Coley, D. C., (1995) Emerging differentiation of folkbiology and folkpsychology: Attributions of biological and psychological properties to living things. *Child Development, 66,* 1856–1874.

Conrad, D. (2004). University instructors' reflections on their first online teaching experiences. *The Journal of Asynchronous Learning Networks, 8,* 31–44.

Dam, G., & Kaufmann, S. (2008). Computer assessment of interview data using latent semantic analysis. *Behavior Research Methods, 40* (1), 8–20.

Dochy, F., Segers, M., & Buehl, M. (1999). The relation between assessment practices and outcomes of studies: The case of research on prior knowledge. *Review of Educational Research, 69*(2), 147–188.

Dole, J. A. (2000). Readers, texts and conceptual change learning. *Reading & Writing Quarterly, 16,* 99–118

Gardner, R. M., & Brown, D. L. (2013). A test of contemporary misconceptions in psychology. *Learning and Individual Differences, 24,* 211–215.

Gaze, C. M., (2014). Popular psychological myths: A comparison of students' beliefs across the psychology major. *Journal of the Scholarship of Teaching and Learning, 14*(2), 46–60.

Goedeke, S., & Gibson, K. (2011). What do new psychology students know about psychology? *Australian Psychologist, 46,* 133–139.

Hacker, D. J., & Niederhauser, D. S. (2000). Promoting deep and durable learning in the online classroom. *New Directions for Teaching and Learning, 2000*(84), 53–63.

Harnish, R. J., & Bridges, K. R. (2011). Effect of syllabus tone: Students' perceptions of instructor and course. *Social Psychology of Education, 14,* 319–330.

Howell Major, C. (2015). *Teaching online: A guide to theory, research, and practice.* Baltimore, MD: Johns Hopkins University Press.

Hughes, S., Lyddy, F., & Lambe, S. (2013). Misconceptions about psychological science: A review. *Psychology Learning and Teaching, 12,* 20–31.

Ko, S., & Rossen, S. (2004). *Teaching online: A practical guide* (3rd ed). New York, New York: Routledge.

Kuhle, B. X., Barber, J. M., & Bristol, A. S. (2009). Predicting students' performance in introductory psychology from their psychology misconceptions. *Journal of Instructional Psychology, 36*(2), 119–125.

Kowalski, P., & Taylor, A. K. (2004). Ability and critical thinking as predictors of change in students' psychological misconceptions. *Journal of Instructional Psychology, 31*(4), 297.

Kowalski, P., & Taylor, A. K. (2009). The effect of refuting misconceptions in the introductory psychology class. *Teaching of Psychology, 36*(3), 153–159.

Lamal, P. (1979). College students' common beliefs about psychology. *Teaching of Psychology, 6*, 155–158.

Lehman, R. M., & Conceição, S. C. O. (2010). *Creating a sense of presence in online teaching: How to "be there" for distance learners.* San Francisco, CA: John Wiley & Sons.

Lewis, C. C., & Abdul-Hamid, H. (2006). Implementing effective online teaching practices: Voices of exemplary faculty. *Innovative Higher Education, 31*, 83–98.

Lilienfeld, S. O. (2010). Can psychology become a science? *Personality and Individual Differences, 49*, 281–288.

Lilienfeld, S. O. (2002). When worlds collide: Social science, politics, and the Rind et al. child sexual abuse meta-analysis. *American Psychologist, 57*, 176–188.

Lilienfeld, S. O., Lynn, S. J., Ruscio, J., & Beyerstein, B. L. (2010). *Great myths of popular psychology: Shattering widespread misconceptions about human behavior.* Chichester, England: Wiley-Blackwell.

McCutcheon, L. E. (1991). A new test of misconceptions about psychology. *Psychological Reports, 68*(2), 647–653.

McKeachie, W. J. (1960). Changes in scores on the Northwestern misconceptions test in six elementary psychology courses. *Journal of Educational Psychology, 57*(4), 240–244.

Miller, C., & Doering, A. (2015). Exploring opportunities for thoughtful technology transformations. In C. Howell Major, *Teaching Online: A Guide to Theory, Research, and Practice* (pp. 126–130). Baltimore, MD: Johns Hopkins University Press.

Pacansky-Brock, M. (2013). *Best practices for teaching with emerging technologies.* New York, New York: Routledge.

Pinker, S. (2015, February 28). Rock star psychologist Steven Pinker explains why #TheDress looked white, not blue. *Forbes.* Retrieved from http://www.forbes.com/sites/matthewherper/2015/02/28/psychologist-and-author-stephen-pinker-explains-thedress/#607a057d611c

Schrodt, P., & Witt, P. L. (2006). Students' attributions of instructor credibility as a function of students' expectations of instructional technology use and nonverbal immediacy. *Communication Education, 55*, 1–20.

Sherin, B. (2013). A computational study of commonsense science: An exploration in the automated analysis of clinical interview data. *Journal of the Learning Sciences, 22*, 600–638.

Standing, L. G., & Huber, H. (2003). Do psychology courses reduce belief in psychological myths? *Social Behavior & Personality, 31*, 585–592.

Su, B., Bonk, C. J., Magjuka, R. J., Liu, X., & Lee, S. (2005). The importance of interaction in web-based education: A program-level case study of online MBA courses. *Journal of Interactive Online Learning, 4*, 1–19.

Suler, J. (2004) The online disinhibition effect. *Cyberpsychology & Behavior* 7(3), 321–326.

Taylor, A. K., & Kowalski, P. (2004). Naïve psychological science: The prevalence, strength, and sources of misconceptions. *The Psychological Record, 54*(1), 15–25.

Wilson, G., & Stacey, E. (2004). Online interaction impacts on learning: Teaching the teachers to teach online. *Australasian Journal of Educational Technology, 20*, 33–48.

7

World Languages (Spanish and French)
Best Practices in Online Second Language Teaching: Theoretical Considerations in Course Design and Implementation

DIANNE BURKE MONEYPENNY, PH.D.

JULIEN SIMON, PH.D.

INTRODUCTION AND OVERVIEW

While completely online (OL) second language (L2) instruction has increased in popularity, resources on how to build and conduct an effective online language class are scarce. The information presented below is based on developing and teaching five years of completely online foreign language courses at Indiana University East (IUE). The online languages project at IUE began with the first year of Spanish courses in 2011. After assessing the first year online program and finding it successful, the online languages experiment was extended. We currently offer all levels of Spanish online, first and second year French online, and first and second year German online based on the original Spanish model, but with some variations.

This chapter combines the best practices of foreign language pedagogy with the best practices of online teaching based on IUE's working model. Where appropriate, the chapter also includes sample activities that can be easily transferred to any online language classroom. Although this chapter will reference second language acquisition research, its main focus (which is also that of the entire volume) will be on best practices in the design and delivery of online language courses. Furthermore, the majority of foreign language teachers are neither linguists nor experts in second language acquisition. Therefore, a discourse on teaching well will take precedence over overly technical language and complex theories.

Outlining theoretical and evidence-based techniques will help ensure quality instruction in the OL classroom. Some of the most fundamental theories of how one learns a language are based on interaction: hearing the language (input), interacting with a speaker of the language (negotiation and sociocultural contexts), and finally, producing the language (output). Table 1 briefly explains the key concepts of Interactionist Theories of Second Language Acquisition.

Table 1. SLA Interactionist Theories

SLA Emphasis	Theorist(s)	Key Points
INPUT	Krashen (1985, 1994)	• One-way comprehensible input is all that is needed. • A second language is acquired unconsciously in manner similar to the acquisition of a first language.
INTERACTION: NEGOTIATION	Pica (1994) Long (1985) Lightbown and Spada (1998) Long and Robinson (as cited in Blake, 2000)	• Conversational • Work with interlocutor toward a goal that requires expressing and clarifying with language • Negotiate for meaning in a significant context • Repetition, clarification, and confirmation checks, may be used to gain understanding
INTERACTION: SOCIOCULTURAL	Vygotsky, 1962	• Interact with more advanced speakers of the language • Scaffolding by more advanced speaker
OUTPUT	Swain (1995)	• Comprehensible output hypothesis

Moneypenny and Aldrich (2016) and many foreign language professionals are in agreement as to how students reach fluency; the students must: 1. Hear a significant amount of speech, 2. Receive input from varied speakers;

3. Create a significant amount of their own speech, 4. Be provided with relevant feedback, and 5. Practice the language in a significant context (Eskenazi 1999; Kenworthy, 1987; Laroy, 1995; Richards & Rodgers, 1986). The American Council for the Teaching of Foreign Languages (ACTFL) also promotes the standards of the 5 Cs (communication, cultures, connections, comparisons, and communities) that are essential to language instruction, regardless of the classroom mode. When learning is occurring in a virtual classroom, other considerations are also appropriate.

It is commonly agreed upon that interaction is key to learning a language, and it is also an indispensable component of distance learning in general (Thurmond, V. & Wambach, K. 2004)[1]. Moore and Kearsley's (1996) Theory of Transactional Distance, a definition of and base model for online interaction, is supported by many scholars (Thurmond 2003)[2]. This theory proposes a three-pronged model of distance learning interaction: learner-content, learner-learner, learner-instructor (Moore & Kearsley 1996), and many also add the interaction of learner-interface (Hillman, Willis, & Gunawardena 1994).

Some scholars have linked the theory of transactional distance to interaction in an OL foreign language context. As Moneypenny and Aldrich cite, Don (2005) found that instructors and students both favor clear instructions, student-instructor contact, audio components, an emphasis on the four language skills, and student-student interaction. To this, Eskenazi (1999) proposes two additions well suited to computer-assisted language learning CALL, 1. Student comfort and 2. Frequent teacher feedback (as cited in Moneypenny & Aldrich 2016). And flipping the dialogue from the classroom to the instructor, according to Hauck (2006) an ideal online L2 teacher must 1. Adapt to and combine different roles, 2. Employ various styles of teaching, and 3. Create new techniques specific to the OL environment (as cited in Moneypenny & Aldrich 2016).

---

1   Thurmond, V., and Wambach, K. cite: Billings, Connors, & Skiba, 2001; Boyle & Wambach, 2001; King & Doerfert, 2000; Meyen & Lian, 1997; Moore & Kearsley, 1996; Muirhead, 2001a, 2001b; Sherry, 1996; Tuovinen, 2000; Wagner, 1994.
2   Thurmond cites Chen, 2002; Crawford, 1999; Ehrlich, 2002; Kirby, 1999; Meyen & Lian, 1997; Navarro & Shoemaker, 2000; Rovai, 2002; Sherry, Fulford, & Zhang, 1998; Smith & Dillon, 1999; Swan, 2001.

Hybrid or blended teaching, wherein students complete a portion of the course online and a portion in a face-to-face setting, can also inform a discussion based on online L2 pedagogies. In "Best Practices for Online Learning: Is it For Everyone" and "Student Learning in Hybrid French and Spanish Courses: An Overview of Languages Online," Blake and Chenoweth et al. (2016) identified special considerations for online language courses: 1) program fluidity (Blake), 2) course organization (Chenoweth, Urshida & Murday 2006), and 3) increased guidance (Chenoweth, Urshida, Murday 2006). Regarding blended learning, Goertler (2009) says a strong course needs analysis of language, development, and computer literacy (including technology assistance and course navigation help), materials designed for realistic goals and per SLA theories, continually evolving course design, consistency of teacher/learner roles, increased input and output options, various opportunities for synchronous and asynchronous interaction, immediate feedback when possible, practice activities, and to use individualized programs/instruction when appropriate. Data collection should also form an integral part of the course via qualitative and quantitative methods and this data should be used to inform teaching (Goertler 2009).

In an effort to condense the information from the many lists above, the chart below organizes the considerations by recommendations for teachers and recommendations for course design.

Table 2. OL L2 Pedagogies

	Teacher	Course
Don (2005)	• Give clear instructions • Make contact with students	• Emphasize four language skills (speaking, listening, writing, and reading) • Facilitate student-student interaction
Eskenazi (1999)	• Make students comfortable • Provide frequent feedback	
Hauck (2006)	• Combine and adapt to different roles • Use different styles of teaching • Develop techniques specific to the OL environment	

	Teacher	Course
Chenoweth, Ushida, Murday (2006)	• Increased guidance	• Organization
Goertler (2009)	• Analyze language, development, and computer literacy • Provide technology assistance • Course navigation help • Consistency or teacher/learner roles • Immediate feedback • Individualized programs/instruction when appropriate • Use data to inform teaching/course revisions	• Designed for realistic goals and per SLA theories • Continually evolving course design • Increased input and output options • Opportunities for synchronous and asynchronous interaction • Practice (or low-stakes) activities • Built-in Quantitative and Qualitative Data collection

As the purpose of this chapter is to illuminate best practices in OL L2 classroom design, we will center on the category of course recommendations above. In summary, an ideal OL L2 course is designed to: 1. Promote input (reading/listening) and output (writing, speaking) language skills, 2. provide four levels of interaction (per SLA theories) between individuals, include synchronous and asynchronous activities (including practice), and 3. harbor built-in data collection that leads to revision.

OPPORTUNITIES TO PRACTICE THE FOUR LANGUAGE SKILLS:

Input

Online teaching is similar to F2F in the area of input, except that communication happens less spontaneously. While it is true that reading and listening skills transfer rather easily into OL teaching, what might be a quick F2F classroom remark, turns into a several minute explanation in the online classroom environment. However there are multiple opportunities to create input online. Reading input can be online or printed textbooks, making use of graphic organizers to explain concepts, and, the authors argue, engaging with cultural images or artworks. For example, several artists can be displayed, and students can react to the productions and describe them or identify their favorite piece and why. Listening can and should occur via videos that introduce units or explain assignments, live or recorded lectures on course content, listening to audio-based exercises, and through a variety of culturally-authentic productions. In short, an input-rich online L2 course should be easy to curate with the wealth of available online resources (YouTube, iTunes University, tourism boards, online art museums, Pinterest, websites).

Output

If input focuses on student reception of various language formats, output focuses on student production of language. Output can be textual, visual, or oral. Textual output is well suited to the online classroom. Students can engage in live scheduled text chats, respond to text questions, write essays or creative works, blog, post and respond to other students, or a myriad of other activities centered on the idea of production of text.

Visual output can often be overlooked in the foreign language classroom, but it can provide students with a creative outlet to demonstrate comprehension of language and culture. For example, instructors could provide students with a series of events or a story using preterit and imperfect tenses. To be more precise, students can then create a comic book strip depicting the story in sequential steps while using art to portray the nuances of the imperfect and preterit tenses. For example, students can be provided with the prompt, *"Juan caminaba y miraba el cielo. El sol brillaba y los pájaros cantaban. De repente, Juan se cayó en un hueco. El hueco era muy oscuro. Juan gritó '¡Ayúdame!' Entonces, unos bomberos vinieron para salvarle a Juan. El les dijo 'Mil gracias.'"* Students would then draw the story scene by scene and demonstrate their understanding of these two past tenses in Spanish. These comic book strips can then spur a comparison and classroom discussion on the various illustration techniques utilized. Therefore, visual output functions as a useful measure of language comprehension and as a catalyst for further output. These activities work well in the online classroom where students can post their images and textually/orally respond to the images of others.

The last type of output to be emphasized is oral output, or students speaking in the target language. Oral output is perhaps one of the most polemic issues for instructors considering online L2 instruction (Kolowich 2011; Parry 2011). While it may seem that the physical classroom is better suited to oral production and exchange, technologies available today can, in essence, equate the two fora. Students can record audio and video responses to questions/ prompts (any AV recording tool, such as VoiceThread, Discussions [LMS: Canvas]); they can create and record online presentations (Adobe Connect); they can record conversations with other students/native speakers (using AV recording tools); they can practice oral production via scheduled group conversation times (Google Hangouts, Conferences [LMS: Canvas]); they can speak one-on-one with instructors via a video conferencing tool (Skype or those listed above); or they can even engage in teletandem video chats with speakers in other countries (Perez-Hernandez, 2014). Of course, there is a distinction between a practiced recorded response and a live and, therefore, spontaneous conversation; this will be discussed further under the asynchronous and synchronous section below.

PROVIDE LEVELS OF INTERACTION

Moore's (1989) theories of Transactional Distance and Interaction address the level of separation between educator and learner in the distance education environment and what strategies should be used to bridge this gap. Communication between educator and learner can be a challenge in the OL course since there are not weekly F2F interactions (as is typical in F2F or hybrid courses). To remedy the distance in the online courses, communication should be required through multiple channels, including email, chat rooms, discussion boards, online conversation hours, and oral exams. To address Moore's Theory of Interaction a number of interactions between learner-learner, learner-content, and learner-instructor should also be incorporated into the course design.

Student to student interaction is vital in any foreign language classroom, but it is especially important to orchestrate online where it may not as naturally occur. Students can be assigned to interact in the learning management software's chatroom. They can collaborate on partnered projects and also respond to one another's comments on a discussion board. Instructors should interact with learners via email on a one to one basis, course announcements to the whole class, videos on course content, as an overseer in discussions, and by providing feedback in assignments. Learners interact with course content (i.e., language and culture) via images, text, videos, music online home-work (such as Pearson's MySpanishLab, MyFrenchLab, or Vista's Supersite), authentic foreign language films (digitized or available via YouTube, Netflix, or Hulu), compositions, and cultural projects.

Learner-interface interactions help to orient students to the online course structure and learning management software. According to Hillman, Willis, & Gunawardena, (1994), learner-interface interaction is essential to students learning the course content and should inform online course design. So, along with the typical introduction to the course goals and expectations, instructors should design an introduction to the LMS layout. For this introductory activity, a Scavenger hunt works well as a first day or first few days exercise. Within the scavenger hunt, the instructor can integrate support center information and training videos along with "get to know you" activities that allow students to experiment with the LMS in a low/no-stakes manner. Below is a sample LMS (Canvas, in this instance) Scavenger hunt utilized in fourth semester Spanish:

"CANVAS SCAVENGER HUNT!:
A. Go to our Chat and in Spanish introduce yourself, where you are from, hobbies, favorite book/movie, etc.
B. Go to your name in the top right corner. This takes you to your Canvas profile. Fill in the information and upload a picture for your profile. This picture will show up whenever you post in the Discussions! It makes us all a little more human!
C. Find your professor's email and send your professor one interesting fact about yourself, in Spanish, of course.
D. Post in Discussions and rank the 4 language skills (speaking, listening, writing, reading) according to difficulty for you and how you will work on the skill this semester. This post can be in English.
This is your classroom. Use it. Click all the links to the left in Canvas and discover the different tools and resources at your disposal. ¡Muy bien! Now you are ready to learn with CANVAS."

Synchronous Activities

Synchronous exercises are those that occur in real time between one or more interlocutors and, as such, involve at least two language skills simultaneously. For example, students in a chat room read and textually respond to each other and thereby use reading comprehension (input) and writing (output) skills. The spontaneous nature of the exercises limits reflection and requires immediate or somewhat immediate responses to prompts. This immediacy is a skill vital to everyday authentic language use; so it is an incredibly important component of any language classroom. However, as the majority of students enroll online courses because of the flexibility of time, and students from many different times zones can enroll in the same class, designing practical real-time activities can present a challenge.

The first step to approximate a realistic synchronous OL class component is to survey students with regard to their schedules. At the onset of the course, students should indicate their general weekly availability for live interaction; whenisgood.net is a useful resource for scheduling with a large group. The instructor can set a time frame for any day of the week. Students then "paint" the times and days that work best for them. Instructors can then log on to the results page and see when the most students are available and when to offer synchronous sessions with foci on writing, speaking, grammar review, etc., so that all students can at least participate in one session per week.

Synchronous text-based activities can occur in the LMS chat room. Students can complete an exercise together, interview each other regarding a topic, practice introductions, and more. While these activities are text centered, the limited response time inherent in a real time "conversation" is an important skill for the language learner to master. In fact, Abrams (2003), found that written chat activities increased posttest F2F discussion and students' oral fluency. Payne and Whitney (2002) found a "direct transfer of skills across modality from writing to speaking does occur" (p. 17) and that students who employed the synchronous text conversation outscored the F2F students who only conversed in the classroom. These studies demonstrate that a significant synchronous textual exchange transfers across language skill domains to positively impact oral proficiency and justify the incorporation of these types of activities in the OL classroom.

In the online courses that form the basis of this chapter, oral and aural practice are a central course requirement. Instructors can offer sessions on grammar (conducted in the target language via Adobe Connect), exam review, and even one-on-one interview exams (via Skype, for example). But, one of the most effective tools used to create an oral/aural exchange is synchronous conversation sessions via computer mediated communication (CMC) (Yanguas 2010; Hampel & Stickler 2012). In spite of being online, these sessions can "make a major contribution to the level of individual practice and the extent of instructor attention, which might even exceed what can be found in traditional classrooms given their burden of 25 to 30 students in a 50-minute period" (Blake, 2008, p. 123).

For the OL courses at IUE, a unique team is assembled to enhance language learning: instructor (M.A./Ph.D.), teacher's assistant (B.A./M.A.), and a supplemental instructor (a student who succeeded in the course in the past). The instructor designs, creates, and curates the class. He/She grades major assignments, holds lessons, gives oral exams, and interacts with students. A teacher's assistant can grade minor assignments, offer online conversation sessions, and interact with students. The supplemental instructor program was created by Dr. Deanna Martin at the University of Missouri-Kansas City. This is essentially a student-led tutoring program that focuses on concept mastery and retention through collaborative learning (Arendale, 1994). This student-tutor in online language classes focuses on grammar learning and test preparation. The team members interact with each other and students in the OL classroom.

The teacher's assistant (who has a minimum B.A. in the target language) offers five-plus sessions per week that all cover the same topic for the assigned period (generally one to two weeks). The sessions are spread to accommodate all students' schedules/time zones and this also ensures smaller session sizes. In the first and second semester Spanish courses, students are required to attend five to seven hours of synchronous small group conversation. In upper level courses, the requirement increases to ten hours. An investigation of the literature reveals that other universities are engaging in similar conversation practice sessions. At IUE the sessions are considered pivotal to language learning and are, thus, mandatory (5–10% of the final course grade) whereas at other institutions, such as Open University in London, twenty hours per semester are offered, but attendance is optional (Heiser & Stickler, 2014).

Regarding assessment of oral production and aural comprehension, although the sessions for the courses in question are mandatory, they are graded based on attendance-only. If a student attends and participates, he/she receives full credit. Although no grade-based feedback is offered, the conversation leader gives "implicit and explicit oral redirection based on pronunciation or grammar throughout the sessions when appropriate," (Moneypenny & Aldrich, 2016, p. 126) acting as the frequent teacher feedback suggested by Eskenazi (1999). In many respects, this model is similar to participation in a face-to-face classroom. A student's every utterance is not graded or corrected, but general immediate feedback is given so that students can experiment with language in a low stakes manner. In fact, online students might even participate more than if they were in the physical classroom (Warschauer, 1996).

Besides instructor/assistant led sessions, recorded live conversations were also considered a useful tactic to ensure oral output. Students can converse with one another per an assigned prompt in lower level courses. In upper level courses (300 level or above), assigning a recorded conversation with a native/heritage speaker of the target language has proved an engaging assignment. With these assignments, often a 20-minute required recording turns into an hour conversation between the student and speaker. The conversations are synchronous, but the assessment is asynchronous.

Asynchronous Activities

More along the lines of the face-to-face classroom homework, asynchronous activities are easier to plan and assign. Students simply complete the activities at their leisure (before the assignment deadline). These activities can take the form of 1) cultural discussions based on target language film, readings, or prompts, 2) compositions, 3) audio recordings, 4) video recordings and postings with student responses, and 5) myriad other asynchronous forms of interaction.

The last essential component to online courses is data collection and subsequent revision based on the findings. While this should occur in all courses, the online environment is uniquely suited to a variety of data collections beyond the typical midterm survey and end of course evaluations. The LMS often collects data related to various course and student factors. For example, the tool "People" allows the instructor to see the roster and also how long students are spending in the course; clicking "Student Interactions Report" shows students' last interaction in the course, their current score, their final score, and their ungraded assignments. Under Quizzes in Canvas, a "Quiz Statistics" button will immediately display the average score, the high and low scores, the standard deviation, the average time to take the test, and a performance analysis via a question-by-question breakdown. These types of automatic data collection tools are available in most, if not all, LMS. Having instant access to this data-rich tool along with student voices should inform course revisions and improvement semester after semester.

The online language courses at Indiana University East have experienced success with the techniques discussed above. At the onset of offering online language, some concern was expressed particularly about oral production. So a specific assessment using the Versant for Spanish exam was built into the online courses at regular intervals. The results, as outlined in the article "Online and Face-to-Face Language Learning: A Comparative Analysis of Oral Proficiency in Introductory Spanish" in the *Journal of Educators Online* by Moneypenny and Aldrich (2016), show that online language students at the end of the first year of courses performed just as well (no significant difference) as the control group, face to face students, in areas of sentence mastery, vocabulary, fluency, and pronunciation. Having these assurances semester after semester catalyzed the development of languages online at IUE.

As discussed, online teaching of languages is a venture worth exploring. The basic principles of good teaching, good teaching online, and best practices in language teaching should meld to inform online language course development. The five years of experimentation in this field at IUE should serve as guide for educators who wish to combine quality instruction with online learning and existent OL L2 theories.

REFERENCES

Abrams, Z. I. (2003). The effect of synchronous and asynchronous CMC on oral performance in German. *Modern Language Journal, 87*(2), 157–167. doi: 10.1111/1540-4781.00184

Arendale, D. R. (1994), Understanding the supplemental instruction model. *New Directions for Teaching and Learning,* 11–21. doi: 10.1002/tl.37219946004

Blake, R. (2000). Computer mediated communication: A window on L2 Spanish interlanguage. *Language Learning and Technology, 4*(1), 120–136.

Blake, R. (2009). The use of technology for second language distance learning. *Modern Language Journal, 93,* 822–825. doi: 10.1111/j.1540-4781.2009.00975

Blake, R. (2012). Best practices in online learning: Is it for everyone? In: F. Rubio, J. J. Thomas, & S. K. Bourns (Eds.), *Hybrid language teaching and learning: Exploring theoretical, pedagogical and curricular issues* (pp. 10–26). Boston, MA: Heinle Cengage Learning.

Chenoweth, N. A., & Murday, K. (2003). Measuring student learning in an online French course. *CALICO Journal, 20*(2), 284–314.

Don, M. (2005). An investigation of the fundamental characteristics in quality online Spanish instruction. *CALICO Journal, 22*(2), 285–306.

Eskenazi, M. (1999). Using a computer in foreign language pronunciation training: What advantages? *CALICO Journal, 16*(3), 447–469.

Goertler, S. (2009), Using Computer-Mediated Communication (CMC) in Language Teaching. *Die Unterrichtspraxis/Teaching German, 42,* 74–84. doi: 10.1111/j.1756-1221.2009.00038.

Hampel, Regine, & Stickler, U. (2012). The use of videoconferencing to support multimodal interaction in an online language classroom. *ReCALL, 24*(2), 116–137.

Hauck, M., & Stickler, U. (2006). What does it take to teach online. *CALICO Journal, 23*(3), 463–475.

Heiser, S., & Stickler, U. (2013). Ready, steady, speak-online: Student training in the use of an online synchronous conferencing tool. *CALICO Journal, 30*(2), 226–251.

Hillman, D. C., Willis, D. J., & Gunawardena, C. N. (1994). Learner-interface interaction in distance education: An extension of contemporary models and strategies for practitioners. *The American Journal of Distance Education, 8*(2), 30–42.

Kenworthy, J. (1987). *Teaching English pronunciation.* Harlow: Longman.

Kolowich, S. (2011). "Expanding language by degree." *Inside Higher Ed.* Retrieved from https://www.insidehighered.com/news/2011/04/25/pennsylvania_public_higher_education_system_will_offer_fully_online_degrees_in_arabic_and_other_languages

Krashen, S.D. (1985). *The Input Hypothesis: Issues and Implications.* Harlow: Longman.

Krashen, S.D. (1994). *The input hypothesis and its rivals, Implicit and Explicit Learning of languages.* Academic Press. London: Ellis, 45–77, doi: 10.1.1.121.728

Laroy, C. (1995). *Pronunciation.* Oxford: Oxford University Press.

Lightbown, P. M., & Spada, N. (1998). *How languages are learned.* Oxford: Oxford University Press.

Long, M., & Robinson, P. (1998). Focus on form: Theory, research and practice. In. C. Doughty & J. Williams (Eds.), *Focus on form in classroom second language acquisition.* (pp. 15–41).

Moneypenny, D., & Aldrich, R. (2016). "Online and face-to-face learning: a comparative analysis of oral proficiency in introductory Spanish." *The Journal of Educators Online, 13*(2), 105–134.

Moore, M. (1989). Three types of interaction. *The American Journal of Distance Education, 3*(2), 1–6.

Moore, M. G., & Kearsley, G. (1996). *Distance education: A systems approach.* Boston, MA: Wadsworth.

Parry, M. (2011). "Foreign-language instruction, digitally speaking." *The Chronicle of Higher Education.* Retrieved from http://www.chronicle.com/article/colleges-map-an-online-future/129604

Payne, J. S., & Whitney, P. J. (2002). Developing L2 oral proficiency through synchronous CMC: Output, working memory, and interlanguage development. *CALICO Journal, 20*(1), 7–32.

Perez-Hernandez, D. (2014/05/05). "Technology provides foreign-language immersion at a distance." *The Chronicle of Higher Education.* Retrieved from http://www.chronicle.com/article/Technology-Provides/146369/

Pica, T. (1994), Research on negotiation: What does it reveal about second-language learning conditions, processes, and outcomes?. *Language Learning, 44*, 493–527. doi: 10.1111/j.1467-1770.1994.tb01115

Richards, J., & Rodgers, T. S. (1986). *Approaches and methods in language teaching: A description and analysis.* Cambridge: Cambridge University Press.

Swain, M. (1995). Three functions of output in second language learning. *Principle and practice in applied linguistics: Studies in honour of H. G. Widdowson,* 125144.

Thurmond, V. A. (2003). *Examination of interaction variables as predictors of students' satisfaction and willingness to enroll in future Web-based courses while controlling for student characteristics.* Universal-Publishers.

Thurmond, V., & Wambach, K. (2004). Understanding interactions in distance education: A review of the literature. *International Journal of Instructional Technology and Distance Learning, 1*(1).

Vygotsky, L. S. (1986). *Thought and language.* (Revised Edition). Cambridge, MA: MIT Press.

8

HISTORY

Teaching History Online:
Old Struggles, New Pathways

JUSTIN CARROLL, PH.D.

CHRISTINE NEMCIK, PH.D.

DARON OLSON, PH.D.

"The past is a foreign country, they do things differently there."
L. P. Hartley

INTRODUCTION

For many who take history courses the sentiments of Hartley, an English nov-
elist, no doubt seem pertinent. History is a peculiar discipline and teaching
it can be difficult. At the core of this difficulty lies the issue of accessibility.
Since history is the study of the past, and often the study of historical actors
long dead, it can only be accessed through its ghosts, namely the artifacts
left behind such as writings, speeches, accounts by others, or in more recent
times video sources. Whereas those who teach other disciplines, including
psychology, sociology, or communications, can have their students refer to
their everyday experiences for context, that is not always possible in history,
especially as one goes further back in time. Moreover, people who lived in
the past more often than not had different moral and societal values than
those that are dominant in contemporary society. A special task facing the

historian, therefore, is to help students *understand the context of past societies*, including their societal values, before they can delve into understanding *why* the events of the past happened. For those who teach history online, this challenge requires the historian to find innovative ways to achieve this goal.

Before considering the innovative ways to teach history online, it is useful to articulate the various challenges of teaching history. In addition to *context*, of particular concern to the historian is the need to teach students about *change over time, causality, contingency,* and *complexity,* or the Five Cs (Andrews and Burke, 2007).

As noted, context poses a special problem to the discipline of history. It is further compounded when one realizes what is called the mirror of context, namely the tendency for students to evaluate the past in terms of moral presentism. This tendency is not limited to students in the United States. Writing on New Zealand students, Martyn Davison observes:

> "Students' knowledge of history is rooted in their own community. They tend to look at history from a social relations point of view so they apply morals to the past. Learners also find it difficult to make sense of the strangeness of the past and that part of New Zealand's history which is about injustice and inequality" (Davison, 2015). Context remains the most difficult of the five concepts to teach (Andrews and Burke, 2007). Yet without context, history becomes insubstantial and as Donna Marie Trimble writes, "For it [is] only when we try to comprehend who the historical leaders were, what they appeared to be in the context of their times, and why the people were ripe for their message and willing to do their bidding, that history matters!" (Trimble, 2010).

Change over time, meanwhile, is the easiest of the concepts to teach to students. They can grasp that new technology changes over time, that laws change, and that different cultural pursuits are enjoyed (Andrew and Burke, 2007). However, students tend to view these changes as elementary and they can at times oversimplify how change over time works as a process. Patrick Manning identifies a common problem among students: "One example of oversimplified global analysis is the listing of a variety of outcomes of different situations, and the assertion that they add up to a pattern." Furthermore, if students offer "no explanation of how the situations were selected or how they relate to each other, this would be a weak statement of global patterns: one needs to identity the process, not just the linked influences and outcomes" (Manning, 2006). For world history in particular, students find it next to impossible to explain changes over time owing to "the added dimensions of changes over longer periods of time and usually across more places as well" (Cohen, 2009).

Explaining causality in history also remains an elusive target and one notices that historians have a much tougher task at hand than do scientists. For instance, Andrews and Burke observe that "scientists can devise experiments to test theories and yield data, but historians cannot alter past conditions to produce new information. Rather they must base their arguments upon the interpretation of partial primary sources that frequently offer multiple explanations for a single event" (Andrew and Burke, 2007, p. 3). For students in history courses, there is a tendency to approach history as being preordained or that it follows an uncomplicated path that is inevitable. Historical events are nearly always multicausal and it is tempting for students to see the one path already traveled by looking backwards than to view the past from the perspective of the historical actors themselves, who are looking forward to a number of possible paths. (Waring, 2010, p. 283). The preference for a teleological view of history among students of history remains a daunting one for the teacher of history to challenge and correct.

Historians also argue that there is contingency in history, or the idea that every historical outcome depends on a number of prior conditions. Moreover, each of these prior conditions depends in turn on still more other conditions, and the pattern continues. Contingency for the historian means that the world is "a magnificently interconnected place." If a single prior condition is changed, any historical outcome could have turned out differently (Andrews and Burke, 2007, p. 3). One can see how contingency can give the impression to the history student of inevitability. At another level, though, contingency has the meaning of accident or luck (Richardson, 2010, pp. 1–2). For historians, human agency also has a place. Historian R. G. Collingwood argued that the natural sciences study regular, law-obeying processes such as the workings of gravity, while historians study the unpredictable actions of conscious, self-aware, and freely acting women and men (Collingwood, 1994, p. 214). David Christian concludes that science has natural laws while history has patterns because humans are the one species capable of sustained innovation and collective learning (Christian, 2009). The capacity of humans for intelligent thought and group action can impact events.

Yet getting students to understand contingency in history remains a daunting problem since many of them cling to the notion that "history is all about facts." Students have a tough time envisioning the past as a series of choices with unforeseen consequences rather than as a predetermined script of human actions. Students need to understand that human actors in the past had choices and that they had to contemplate those choices, assessing how those choices allowed for some and prevented other possibilities. (Bond, 2013, pp. 531–532, 542).

As an approach to the past grounded in multicausal, contextual, changing, and contingent themes, history ascribes to the value of complexity. Andrews and Burke emphasize that "moral, epistemological, and causal complexity distinguish historical thinking from the conception of 'history' held by many non-historians" (Andrews and Burke, 2007, p. 4). One of the best predictors of success among college students is their exposure to complex texts, and history is well suited to offer those opportunities to students. As pointed out by Reisman and Wineburg: "It is in learning to interrogate the reliability and truth claims of a particular source that students begin to engage in the sorts of activities that lie at the heart of historical thinking" (Reisman and Wineburg, 2012, p. 24–25).

Mystery lies at the heart of historical thinking. In his essay on historical thinking Sam Wineburg compares the historian to the detective. Historians see themselves searching for evidence among primary sources to a mystery that can never be completely solved. He adds that historians approach a historical problem with a series of questions and that students should be taught to think in terms of these same questions. They should think about a document's author and its creation, contextualize the document in time and place, closely read the document to understand the language used and what the document says, plus three additional strategies: using background knowledge, reading the silences (what has been left out of the document), and corroborating through other sources. Wineburg states that students need to "think like historians" not because they will become professional historians "but precisely because they won't." He identifies the goals of education as to prepare students to tolerate complexity, to adapt to new situations, and to resist the first answer that comes to mind (Wineburg, 2010, p. 1–3).

NON-TRADITIONAL HISTORY ASSIGNMENTS IN ONLINE COURSES

The act of translating an effective in-class experience or assignment into an effective online course is fraught, complicated, and frustrating. These feelings are especially true as the field of history presents its own special challenges, namely, the need to explain and impart to students the Five Cs: context, change over time, causality, contingency, and complexity. (Andrews and Burke, 2007). Therefore, over the next several pages, this essay will explore how to take an effective and well-conceived series of activities and assignments from a face-to-face upper-level history course on American history and re-imagine and parallel the experience online. In doing so, this essay will show how online assignments fostered intellectually invigorated, asynchronous, and joyous learning environments, and how they also reinforced best practices in online teaching, especially in regard to establishing effective, collaborative discussions and their associated soft skills.

In 2011, as a newly hired faculty member at Indiana University East (IUE), Dr. Justin M. Carroll, an assistant professor of American history, read that the NAEP (2010) tested 7,000 fourth-graders, 11,000 eight-graders, and 12,000 twelfth-graders from across the United States. (p. 1–3) The study (2010) found that 82% of the sampled students have partial or no mastery of their grade-specific historical knowledge. (p. 1–3). With these numbers in mind, he casted about for different ways to develop new face-to-face courses as a way of offering IUE students a strong historical background and introduce them to the Five Cs. Moreover, he also wanted to center their learning experiences on important soft skills that might prepare them for future courses and, much later, the job market—for example: strong communication skills, problem-solving, collaboration, conflict negotiation, and the ability to put new learned information to work. These goals lead him to role-playing games as an effective learning strategy.

Over the past decade, across the United States of America, college history professors have been engaging the Reacting to the Past Pedagogy

(RTTP) developed by Mark Carnes, a professor of Modern American History at Barnard College. RTTP is comprised of role-play games grounded in the past, where students take up roles informed by primary-source and secondary-source readings. Students, playing historical characters, run day-to-day games sessions, in which they argue, debate, negotiate, and scheme their way through pivotal historical moments.

In Dr. Carroll's first course on the American Revolution, he organized it to culminate in a four-week long role-play game entitled: Patriots, Loyalists, and Revolution in New York City, 1775–1776. His students used the historical and historiographical information they learned in the course to invest their characters—loyalists to the British Crown, New York rebels, Hudson valley moderates, African-American slaves, or poor women—with life. Immersed in an eighteenth century British political tradition, Dr. Carroll's students delivered speeches, produced political tracks, worked as factions to promote or stymie colonial rebellion, and, when their moments came, stood up to be leaders. The more they played, the more engaged the students became. For example, one student, who played a New York printer, researched and designed his own unique font based on eighteenth-century typefaces for his weekly newspaper. Likewise, another student wrote the game "gave [the students] a chance to connect with [their] characters, something that is sometimes difficult to do when reading a book." Many of the students grasped that just because events happened one way it did not mean that such events were inevitable. Their version of the American Revolution freed the slaves of New York City, for example.

Reacting to the Past games often capped the end of Dr. Carroll's upper-level history courses; they served as the intellectual testing grounds after weeks of historiographical, theoretical, and historical readings and debates. At the end of the semester, the students worked to put what they learned into action in vibrant and dynamic ways. And when Dr. Carroll was first asked to teach these courses online, he felt worried that he would not be able to recreate a similar intellectual atmosphere and felt, perhaps like many first-time online professors do, that his online classes would be pale imitations.

Then, one spring day, Dr. Carroll walked into his classroom and noticed that most of his students were on their cellphones; some were playing games, others were texting their friends, and in the back corner, two history majors were laughing about a YouTube video they just watched. They saw him enter and rushed to the front of the class, and asked if he had ever seen the popular web series Drunk History or Epic Rap Battles of History. He laughed and said "Yes" and quickly informed them that they would have to talk about the clips later as they were a bit inappropriate. He had an epiphany as they walked back to their seats: the history students enjoy outside of my classroom is not analytical, staid, or rigorous; in fact, it existed in the form of Hollywood films, independently made web series, multiplayer computer games, or iPhone apps. Their history exists in the palm of their hands, and through this, was a new way to approach online courses.

The first upper-level course Dr. Carroll taught online at IUE focused on the history of colonial North America, and, instead of using a role-play game, early in the semester, he asked his students to download a turn-based strategy game called *Sid Meier's Colonization*. Released in 1994 by MicroProse, a now-defunct software publisher and developer, the game focused on European colonization of the Americas, and asked its players to guide French, British, Spanish, or the Dutch colonists in their efforts to found colonies and later start colonial revolutions. The game offered a playable and very standard narrative of colonial North America and the events that lead to the American Revolution, and it served, just like the role-plays had, as the collective and capping experience for every student in the course. Over the semester, they would play the game in conjunction with a series of secondary- and primary-source readings designed to challenge and complicate the narrative of the game and the popular culture that spawned. As the students played the game and did the readings, he created assignments centered on both.

For example, in the seventeenth century, English explorer and the for-mer-governor of Jamestown, John Smith (1884), wrote a document entitled, "Instructions given by way of advice by us whom it hath pleased the King's Majesty to appoint of the Counsel for the intended voyage to Virginia, to be observed by those Captains and company which are sent at this present to plant there." (pp. 33–37) In the narrative, Smith offered detailed advice on how to best establish a planation or colony in North America. Such documents, along with mapmaking and letter writing, written in Spanish, French, English, and Dutch in the sixteenth, seventeenth, and eighteenth centuries, were widely disseminated and read by different agents of colonization across Europe and provided models and techniques of colonization. Smith's work became the grist for an assignment. Dr. Carroll required his students to play

Colonization and follow the advice and examples set forth by John Smith's narrative and see if his words would lead them to success or not. This assignment, grounded in both primary- and secondary-source readings, evolved into a larger online WikiProject where the students collaborated as a class to create their "Guide to Colonization of North America."

However, as the students wrote, edited, and built their "Guide to Colonization of North America," they found their collaboration grow more intense and the guide they created more fraught. After three or four weeks of playing *Colonization* and reading secondary and primary sources, the students began to encounter the silences inherent in the game's narrative colonial North American history. For example, after several online discussions and readings related to the trans-Atlantic slave trade and North American slavery, the students began to notice that the game did not portray African-Americans or African-American slavery at all; it was a conspicuous and problematic absence. It was interesting to see how students negotiated this pointed exclusion; it showed up in their group work and forum conversations. If it is not in the game, some students suggested, it should not be the in game guide either; however, they also admitted that the game ignored one of the central experiences of colonial North America and it needed to be commented on. *Colonization* also failed to portray the histories of women during the period as well through its gameplay. Over the semester, the students, predominately white, effectively rethought and reexamined how popular culture played and continues to play important roles in how the history of minority groups were minimized, excluded, or simply erased.

In terms of best practices, online assignments, particularly, those centered on student discussions or forum interaction, need to and should be designed to help the students demonstrate knowledge, build community, reflect on their learning, build consensus, foster critical thinking, and promote student leadership. In different ways over the length of a semester, the assignments built around the "Guide to Colonization of North America" required and encouraged these best practices; students, to succeed, had to demonstrate their knowledge of colonial North American history. They negotiated different game-play strategies and worked to build agreement within the framework of their guide, and they learned to critically analyze popular culture and communicate its flaws effectively. Instead of a staid series of assignments, for example, with forum posts that required students to answer questions about readings and respond to each other's writing, Dr. Carroll worked to take advantage of the unique digital experience offered by teaching online.

Online assignments, properly conceived and taking advantage of the unique opportunities offered by the medium, can creatively impart to students the Five Cs: *context, change over time, causality, contingency,* and *complexity.* Moreover, as students continue to become more immersed in their digital lives, historical education requires more than the critical analysis of primary sources or the mastery of historiography. It is increasingly clear that students require a language and vocabulary that allows them to critique, deconstruct, and decenter the pervasive and immersive digital worlds they inhabit. In other words, a vibrant online history course can and should help foster the kind of hard and soft skills that can help our students become more effective online citizens as well. Transitioning from face-to-face to online teaching need not be frustrating or destructive to older, popular assignments, but rather, can serve as a creative catalyst to pedagogical development designed to better history students to thrive in an increasingly complex world.

NON-TRADITIONAL HISTORICAL SOURCES IN ONLINE COURSES

When we as educators think about best practices in online teaching, our concerns often naturally focus around how to adapt our face-to-face course content to fit an online setting. As has already been pointed out, however, teaching history presents additional challenges to this adaptation from traditional to online classes. Traditional face-to-face history classes already present a challenge that is not encountered by other disciplines, as historians are working to help students understand different time periods and contexts outside the framework of their own everyday experiences. To do this historians utilize primary-source documents, in addition to textbooks and historical monographs, which allow students to learn from the perspective of those who experienced the historical events as they occurred. Additionally these sources work to enable students to put themselves into the time period and context under study, and therefore to relate to those who lived through the history.

While all historians agree on the significance of using historical monographs and primary-source documents as the foundational texts in our classes, whether they be in traditional class settings or online, it is important to recognize that these text materials do not always reach all learners. How do educators reach those students who proclaim to "hate history," or more significantly those who have difficulties with the language of the past, particularly the further removed the students are time-wise or culturally from the course topic? These are the students who may find themselves closed off to history textbooks, monographs, and primary-source materials. Either they are unwilling or are unable to decipher the writings of present historians or they do not relate to the language of the historical writer in the past. Since a primary recognized practice of undergraduate teaching is to "respect diverse talents and ways of learning" by faculty creating "learning opportunities that appeal to the different ways students will process and attend to information" (Hutchins, 2003), it is then necessary to find other sources to reach and engage these students who are frustrated with the commonly utilized historical texts.

Using fiction, in the form of novels, short stories, poetry, and non-documentary films, is one way to reach out to those students who are struggling with the more traditional historical sources. Fiction is a form of writing with which students have been interacting since elementary school, and many students therefore find it more accessible than a history monograph or than historical documents. In the past, it was not a generally accepted practice to use historical fiction in university-level classes, and most studies on using such sources cover doing so at an elementary or secondary level. Yet, Dr. Christine Nemcik, an assistant professor of history at IUE, found the use of historical fiction and of non-documentary films to be an effective means of generating student interest in the materials, of creating a better understanding of historical events, and of students connecting more easily to the culture of the region and time period under study.

These source materials, however, are not readily used by history faculty in university classroom settings not only because of the necessity of using more conventional source materials, but also at times due to an unease over how to incorporate them into the factual history being covered. As Marcus and Lavine (2006) stipulate, "One challenge teachers face is overcoming skepticism from historians and colleagues, as well as their own doubts, about whether or not film is an appropriate, valuable, and legitimate means for exploring past events, peoples, and ideas." The same skepticism is often encountered with the use of written historical fiction. Nonetheless, Dr. Nemcik has found that these materials, when used alongside monographs and historical documents, prove to engage students not only in the fiction, but with the traditional source materials, and as a result with the historical content as well.

Understandably adapting these sources to an online course setting presents added challenges. In the face-to-face classroom, films can be shown during class, paused to have discussion of historical context, and easily tied through discussion to the traditional historical texts being read. Analyzing with the students the culture of the period, or the historical event being depicted, or of the landscape of the region is done in synchronous interactions. The equivalent is done with written fiction, in the form of novels and short stories, which the students are able to discuss alongside the primary or secondary sources to which they are related, pulling out passages from both as they are interacting in the classroom. The class is able to analyze poetry together in terms of the historical event that is being presented by the professor or covered in the traditional readings. Students are present in the classroom with the professor, which creates fluidity and accountability.

In the online classroom, however, the class does not watch the films together, and they are not always capable of holding synchronous discussions of the fiction. Therefore it becomes necessary to find other ways to make these sources be as effective for the online student as they are face to face. Garrison (2003) states that, "At the core of the properties of asynchronous online learning is the ability to provide collaborative learning experiences at the convenience of the individual. That is, we can have both interaction and independence." And as Mandernach, Gonzales, and Garret (2006) stipulate, "literature has clearly established the importance of ongoing interaction as a vital component contributing to the quality of instruction in asynchronous, online courses." These interactions include not only instructor interaction with the students, as they discuss, but Dr. Nemcik would argue also regular interaction of the students with one another in connection to the course materials.

She has found that incorporating non-traditional history source materials can lead to this type of connection to the content, to the instructor, and to one another. This is additionally where it becomes effective, and perhaps even necessary, to have students become engaged in the collaborative learning process by contributing as both students and "co-instructors" or "co-discussion leaders." As Hutchins (2003) says, "one significant difference between face-face classes and web-based instruction is in the role of the instructor. Knowlton (2000) argued for a student-centered approach to teaching web-based classes by suggesting that faculty use collaborative learning where students guide discussions and work in cohorts on assignments. The instructor, Knowlton explained, must take on the role of facilitator or coach rather than the sole 'giver of knowledge.'"

These collaborative practices are particularly useful when engaging with non-traditional, fictional source materials. This can be done using a variety of methods, depending upon the level of the course and how close or removed students may be from the course content, for example U.S. students in a course on Europe, Latin America, Asia, or the Middle East. In Dr. Nemcik's online history courses, she, therefore, gears the student engagement in the collaborative learning process first to the level of the course and then to the content. In my lower-level U.S. history survey courses, she has had students collaborate by creating Quote, Commentary, Question (QCQ) assignments for the discussion of novels, short stories, and poetry. In these assignments they choose a quote or a stanza from the source, which they decide is clearly related to the historical context of the unit. They then write a commentary of its historical significance, and create an analytical question for class discussion. This requires that they connect the fictive accounts to the historical sources of the unit, and they need to then think of how the students can use the fictional accounts in a historical discussion. After these have been submitted, Dr. Nemick posts the questions in a discussion forum where they interact with one another over what they found to be most significant in the fictional accounts and how these quotes and questions demonstrate what they found to be most compelling about the historical topic itself. In this way students are taking ownership of their learning while discovering the significance of utilizing fiction in the study of history.

In upper-level courses, and courses of less familiar topics than U.S. history, Dr. Nemcik pushes students to engage even further in the collaborative learning process from the very start of the class. For example, in a course on the history of revolutions in Latin America, she has students read essays on the revolutions written by historians, as well as primary source documents from those who participated in or were involved in the revolutions. For each unit of the course they additionally watch a film, and they read either a novel or poetry or short stories written either by people who were involved in the revolution being studied or by those who lived in the society and culture that followed the revolution. In this class, and other similar upper-level classes, students start the semester by creating an agreed-upon discussion that will thread throughout the semester. For example, the very first unit in the revolutions class included reading theories and definitions on revolution, and then collaboration on a class definition of "what is a revolution." Each subsequent unit of the course was then focused on holding up the class-decided definition against the readings and films that the students were examining.

Engaging the students in the collaborative learning process from the start of the semester had the potential for them being significantly engaged in the process throughout the entire course. Nonetheless, the book that Dr. Nemcik had chosen as the primary text for the course, a book of essays by prominent historians of Latin American revolutionary history, was one that contained exceptionally challenging scholarly works on the revolutions. Additionally students read primary-source documents created by revolutionaries, politicians, government agencies, and international organizations. These are the type of sources that have the capability of distancing from the course content the student who is disinterested in history, or those who are unknowledgeable about the culture and history of Latin America.

In this online course, and other similar upper-level online history courses, the use of fictional historical sources—in the form of films, novels, poetry, etc.—is vital to not only helping students to remain engaged in the course content, but also to helping them relate better to the historical primary- and secondary-source materials as well. Having them collaborate in the course materials from the start creates an ownership of the course content and discussions throughout the semester. But that alone is not enough. When engaging with sources of a higher level of academic analysis, many students require a means of breaking down and relating to the material. While that can be done in PowerPoint presentations and lectures (both face to face and online), being "fed" the materials from the instructor is not the most effective learning strategy. Engaging with other related course materials proves to be definitively more effective in allowing them to take on themselves this process of understanding. When this is combined with discussions of the materials, it allows them to have a greater collaborative ownership in the learning of the course content.

As an example, in a unit on the Mexican Revolution in this course, students read essays on the revolution written by present-day historians. They additionally have readings from Porfirio Díaz, Francisco Madero, and Francisco "Pancho" Villa, during which they discuss their thoughts on Mexican history and the revolution. In order to counter all of the historical theory and revolutionary rhetoric in these readings, the students additionally read *The Underdogs: A Novel of the Mexican Revolution*, written by Mariano Azuela, who participated in the Revolution, about a band of "bandits" who fought for Pancho Villa during the Revolution. And they watch the film *Like Water for Chocolate*, which chronicles the life of an elite family in rural Mexico, during the time period of the revolution. These fictional sources allow the students a means to connect with what it meant to be a part of the revolution and what the essence of Mexican culture entailed. This in turn keeps students engaged in the course content and helps them to take ownership in the collaborative process of online learning.

CONCLUSION

For the practitioner of online history teaching, certain challenges must be taken into account. History is complex and nuanced, requiring the student to place the past in context while realizing that change over time, causality, and contingency all play a role in how history is created. Students must also realize that history is an interpretive discipline that is influenced by the society in which the historian resides, by the fact that who writes history changes, that new sources can create new interpretations, and that technology makes previously unavailable sources now available (Talbot, 2009, p. 1–2). James Joll, the British historian, once stated that "The aim of the historian, like that of the artist, is to enlarge our picture of the world, to give us a new way of looking at things." Online teaching is the latest canvas for the historian who wants to enlarge our picture of the world and give us a new way of looking at that world.

REFERENCES

Andrews, T., & Burke, F. (2007). What does it mean to think historically?" *Perspectives on History.* Retrieved from https://www.historians.org/publications-and-directories/perspectives-on-history/january-2007/what-does-it-mean-to-think-historically

Berlin, I. (2000). *Many thousands gone: The first two centuries of slavery in north america.* New York: Belknap Press.

Bond, R. E. (2013). How to create a cult: Make-believe, contingency, and complexity in the history classroom. *The History Teacher, 46*(4), 531–546.

Brown, K. M. (1996). *Good wives, nasty wenches, and anxious patriarchs: gender, race, and power in colonial virginia.* Chapel Hill: University of North Carolina Press.

Carnes, M. C. (2014). *Minds on fire: how role-immersion games transform college.* Cambridge: Harvard University Press.

Christian, D. (2009). Contingency, Pattern, and the S-curve in Human History. *World History Connected, 6*(3). Retrieved from http://worldhistoryconnected.press.illinois.edu/cgi-bin/printpage.cgi

Cohen, S. (2009). The challenging concept of change over time. *World History Connected, 6*(2). Retrieved from http://worldhistoryconnected.press.illinois.edu/6.2/cohen.html

Collingwood, R. G. (1994). *The idea of history,* rev. ed. (p. 214). J. Van der Dussen (Ed.). Oxford and New York: Oxford University Press. Cited in Christian.

Conrad, R. M., & Donaldson, J. A. (2004). *Engaging the online learner: Activities and resources for creative instruction.* Wiley: Jossey-Bass.

Davison, M. (2015). Teaching and learning history. *New Zealand History.* Retrieved from http://www.nzhistory.net.nz/brain-food/teaching-and-learning-history

Garrison, D. R. (2003). Cognitive presence for effective asynchronous online learning: The role of reflective inquiry, self-direction and metacognition. Web. 20 Apr. 2016.

Hutchins, H. M. (2003). Instructional immediacy and the seven principles: Strategies for facilitating online courses. *Online journal of distance learning administration.* Web. 20 Apr. 2016.

Klaus, P., Rohman, J. M., & Hamaker, M. (2007). *The hard truth about soft skills: Workplace lessons smart people wish they'd learned sooner.* New York, NY: HarperCollins.

Mandernach, B. J., Gonzales, R. M., & Garrett, A. L. (2006). An examination of online instructor presence via threaded discussion participation. *MERLOT Journal of Online Learning and Teaching.* Web.

Marcus, A. S. (2007). *Celluloid blackboard: Teaching history with film.* Charlotte, NC: IAP-Information Age Pub.

Martin, P. (2006). Interactions and connections: Locating and managing historical complexity. *The History Teacher, 39*(2), 189. Cited in Cohen.

Meier, S. (1994). Sid Meier's *Colonization* [Computer software]. Hunt Valley, MD: MicroProse.

Offutt, W. M. (2011). *Patriots, loyalists, and revolution in new york city, 1775–1776.* Boston: Longman.

Barnard College (2015). *Reacting to the past.* Retrieved from https://reacting.barnard.edu/

Reisman, A., & Wineburg, S. (2012). "Text complexity" in the history classroom: Teaching to and beyond the common core. *Social Studies Review, 24–29.*

Richardson, H. C. (2010). Contingency. *The Historical Society Blogspot.* Retrieved from http://histsociety.blogspot.com/2010/06/contingency.html

Skukoff, P., & Ahlquist, L. (n.d.). *Epic rap battles of history.* Retrieved April 22, 2016, from http://www.epicrapbattlesofhistory.com/

Smith, J., & Arber, E. (1884). *Works, 1608–1631.* Birmingham: E. Arber.

Talbott, T. (2009). Why does history keep changing? *Random Thoughts on History: My musings on American, African American, Southern, Civil War, Reconstruction, and Public History topics and books.* Retrieved from http://randomthoughtsonhistory.blogspot.com/2009/04/why-does-history-keep-changing.html

Trimble, D. M. (2010). The importance of historical context. *The Importance of Historical Awareness.* Retrieved from https://brilliantstage.wordpress.com/2010/01/17/the-importance-of-historical-context/

Trouillot, M. (1995). *Silencing the past: Power and the production of history.* Boston, MA: Beacon Press.

Waring, Scott M. (2010). Escaping myopia: Teaching students about historical causality. *The History Teacher, 43*(2), 283–288.

Waters, D. (n.d.). Drunk history. Retrieved April 22, 2016, from http://www.cc.com/shows/drunk-history

Wineburg, Sam. (2010). Historical thinking: Memorizing facts and stuff? *TPS Quarterly.* Retrieved from http://www.loc.gov/teachers/tps/quarterly/historical_thinking/article.html

9

FINE ARTS (DRAWING)
Best Practices in Online Teaching for Drawing

CARRIE LONGLEY, M.F.A

KEVIN LONGLEY, M.ED.

INTRODUCTION

Eleven faculty members, two full time and numerous part time, each specializing in a variety of artistic media, deliver both online and face-to-face courses within the fine arts program at Indiana University East. The program offers a B.A. as well as a minor in fine art with courses in drawing, painting, photography, sculpture, ceramics, metalsmithing, and art appreciation. While art appreciation courses have been implemented in the online setting for some time, studio courses have posed unique challenges for virtual delivery. On average, class meeting times for studio courses are twice that of traditional lecture courses, therefore many non-majors have an especially difficult time fitting lengthy class meetings into their busy schedules. The ability to virtually offer this curriculum gives students the flexibility to enroll in these courses and allows the program to reach a much broader student audience.

Recently, Fundamental Studio Drawing and Fundamental Studio 2-D have been introduced as an online option for students. Plans are also in place to introduce Graphic Design and Digital Photography courses into the online setting. The faculty in the program selected these fundamental-level courses due to the exercise-based nature of the course projects and the ease of documenting and virtually assessing two-dimensional student work.

This chapter will explain the strategies that were designed and implemented in the Fundamentals Studio Drawing course. Strategies include: initial problem solving, curriculum planning and design, content creation, and best practices in implementation.

INITIAL PROBLEM SOLVING

The consensus among studio art instructors is that online learning, or e-learning, cannot match face-to-face education because learning technical aspects is difficult and that students must be talked through them instead of shown (Grant, 2002). Other studio instructors believe online instruction can contribute little or nothing to teaching and learning because it is unsuitable for the instructional methods associated with studio disciplines (Souleles, 2015). However, in his article Neil Bennet (2016) states that there is a real opportunity for teaching creativity online, and though difficult, it is the responsibility of art institutions to create a situation to remedy the problem. Nicos Souleles (2015) adds that instructional innovations in e-learning must involve a change of perceptions and practices in teaching and organization. Through research and experimentation, institutions can and should start working towards creating successful online course offerings (Bennett, 2016). Instead of aiming to replace in-studio instructional techniques and strategies, online instruction should contain a wide variety of instructional strategies that can enhance and support a traditional in-studio course (Souleles, 2015).

In order to attain a successful online studio course, the studio itself must be brought to the student in the most authentic way possible. Online course developers must align pedagogies, psychologies, technology, and culture when designing online learning environments, and should allow for flexible approaches to learning (Logan, Allan, Kurien, & Flint, 2007).

In courses that contain a handful of students, to others that contain one hundred, visual and verbal communication has to be the most crucial element to teach in any classroom (Edmundson, 2012). According to Jean Mandernach (2009) there is considerable evidence that well-designed, content-relevant instructor-generated videos (IGV's) can enhance learning outcomes through visual and verbal exchange. The power of video to project aspects of one's self such as physical appearance, tone of voice, and body language, allows for an increased social presence within an online course (Pinsk, Curran, Poirier, & Coulson, 2014). In online courses where instructors provided IGV's students reported a closer connection with the instructor and also conveyed that they received greater individual attention and feedback (Draus, Curran, & Trempus, 2014). With access to more and more innovative online teaching tools, IGV's could be considered a primary tool for creating successful online courses (Draus, Curran, & Trempus, 2014).

CURRICULUM PLANNING AND DESIGN

In designing the curriculum for Fundamental Studio Drawing a curriculum map was created to organize topics and techniques that related to a 100-level drawing course. Since this course is accessible to majors and non-majors, the content needed to focus on basic drawing fundamentals in order to relate to a broad student audience with varying skill levels. The topics included: observational drawing techniques of drawing contours and cross-contours, gesture drawing, sighting and measuring, drawing ellipses, reductive drawing, and value applications. Linear perspective drawing and drawing using the grid system were also included.

These topics were organized into lessons, beginning with the simple and ending with the complex. As the backbone of drawing from life, students were taught how to see and record visual information in the form of contour lines. Exercises included blind contour line drawings, true contour line drawings, and upside-down contour line drawings.

To produce a blind contour line drawing students were asked to draw a reference image without looking at their drawing surface and without lifting their pencil. Instead of looking at their drawing surface, they were asked to scan the contour line of the reference image with their eyes, and try to mimic their eye movement with their pencil. This is the basic process artists use to record visual information.

To build on the concept of seeing and recording visual information, students were asked to complete a true contour line drawing and an upside-down contour line drawing. In order to create a true contour line drawing students were asked to draw the contour line of a reference image by scanning the image with their eyes, then recording the information onto their paper in small increments at a time. Students were also not allowed to lift their pencils to ensure they were scanning and recording slowly. The upside-down drawing consisted of students applying the scanning and recording techniques previously mentioned. The reference image was placed upside-down, and students were asked to scan and record the contour line as accurately as possible. The idea for this exercise comes from Betty Edwards (1986) book, *Drawing on the Artist Within*, where Edwards explains that drawing upside-down helps the brain eliminate preconceptions of what one normally sees, and allows the observer to focus solely on line and shape. As an example, many beginners will render the top of a drinking glass as a perfect circle, when in fact, from the viewers' perspective, this shape should be rendered as a foreshortened circle, or an ellipse. In observational drawing, an ellipse is what we see when we view a circle from its edge, rather than from directly overhead. When drawing an ellipse in perspective, there are two common mistakes often made. One is to draw a football shape where the edges taper to points, the other is to draw two parallel lines connected with curves at each end. In an online setting, an instructor has the advantage of superimposing a brightly colored ellipse over the still life image to reinforce this complex concept. Skills learned from these exercises serve as the foundation for the rest of the course. In other words, the curriculum allows for a scaffolding of skills, building in complexity as the student advances through the course. Terms and skills associated with the overarching theme of observational drawing, as opposed to concept-driven drawing, is what makes this course suitable for online delivery.

The curriculum for Fundamental Studio Drawing advances from seeing and drawing contour lines, to focusing on the technical aspects of drawing in the form of gestural strokes. Students are to combine scanning and recording techniques with gesture drawing to render reference images quickly and loosely. By simple looking at the reference image and drawing what is presented to the eye, students gain solid perceptual skills and hand-eye coordination. At this stage, reference images are kept simple in the form of two-dimensional geometric shapes. The main emphasis of this lesson is rapid drawing, which allows students to begin to scan and record at a faster pace, eliminating the need to be accurate in their depictions of the reference image. At this point, a variety of key drawing vocabulary is introduced in the form of basic perspective techniques (size relationships and overlapping) and open and closed composition.

Expanding on contour line and gesture drawing techniques, students are introduced to basic sighting and measuring techniques to render accuracy while drawing from life. Using the traditional practice of measuring objects with an extended arm, measuring tool, and thumb, students try to draw a simple still life from a reference image composed of a variety of two-dimensional geometric shapes in an overlapping composition. Students are encouraged to find a consistent unit of measure, and relate that unit to all of the objects within the reference image. Horizontal and vertical lines of reference are also introduced to help students maintain the accuracy of visual planes within their drawings. Students are asked to submit their finished work containing the horizontal and vertical lines of reference so the instructor can see their use of this tool.

Picking up on the momentum of observational drawing, a new lesson is presented to students incorporating how sighting and measuring techniques can be applied to drawing three-dimensional form. A reference image of various overlapping three-dimensional forms serves as the still life for this lesson. Along with the application of a consistent unit of measure and lines of reference, students are introduced to a sighting and measuring technique used to record angles. A clock face is introduced to relate the degree of an angle to help students better document the angles present within the reference image. Students are required to complete multiple drawings using solely graphite pencil and solely charcoal (pencil or stick) in order to prepare for the next lesson, adding value (lightness and darkness) to drawings.

Techniques using graphite and charcoal to create value are presented and demonstrated to students. A worksheet containing a blank value scale and blank three-dimensional forms is provided for students to practice shading techniques. Based on a reference image (presented in grayscale), students are to apply values, using graphite and charcoal, to their three-dimensional form drawings.

At this point in the curriculum, students have been introduced to the basic skills required to advance throughout the remainder of the course. A shift occurs from focusing on basic skills in the form of exercises to applying these basic skills to more complex project-based lessons. Several drawing techniques are explored including reductive drawing, linear perspective drawing, drawing using the grid, and drawing ellipses. All of these techniques, with the exception of linear perspective drawing, include the observational drawing techniques previously described.

CONTENT CREATION

With course objectives created, a curriculum outlined, and lessons developed, the task of distributing information to students in an online setting is set. A list of technology needed to create instructor generated videos (IGVs) was compiled and included: Video camera or camera phone, document reader, computer, video editing software, photo editing software, and art materials. With easy accessibility to photo and video editing software on the World Wide Web, it is safe to say that with minimal research and practice, one can make effective high quality IGVs.

The approach used to create the content for this course was sequential in order. A lesson's introduction was written to include clear concise objectives and lesson vocabulary. Using a video camera, or a cellular phone with a video camera, the lesson introduction was recorded. In order to help the quality of the introduction, the written introduction was uploaded into a free teleprompter software application that was downloaded from the Internet. This allows the instructor to maintain eye contact with the camera, and add a smooth flow to the spoken introduction.

Using a document camera connected to a computer with a USB connection, drawing exercises and demonstrations were created and recorded. Focusing the frame of the document camera solely on the drawing surface allows all viewers of the demonstration the same view. This is difficult to replicate in a face-to-face setting, where large groups of students are gathered tightly around an instructor's easel trying to get a clear view of the drawing process (see Figure 1). A conclusion was created in the same manner as the introduction. Within the conclusion the instructor clearly restated the assignment objectives and expectations. Once all introductions, demonstrations, and conclusions are recorded, the video files are uploaded into the video editing software.

Figure 1. Still image showing instructor demonstration (right side) and sighting and measuring 2-dimensional still-life (left side).

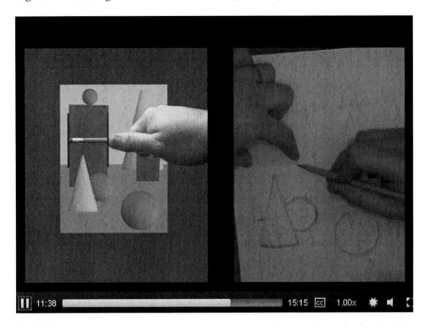

Within the video editing software, video files are placed into a timeline in chronological order. Working from the beginning of the introduction video, still images are created and inserted to enhance key points of the introduction. These still images, in the form of photographs, web images, and edited photographs, are created and enhanced using photo editing software. Still images can be inserted at any point within the video to enhance and illustrate key concepts and points, which is a luxury that is difficult to replicate in a face-to-face classroom (see Figure 2 & Figure 3).

Figure 2. Still image showing proper sighting technique with a red line overlay to convey the extension of the arm.

Figure 3. Still image illustration how to sight and measure angles of objects when drawing from life. The clock overlay is designed to relate the degree of angles to the time frames of a clock.

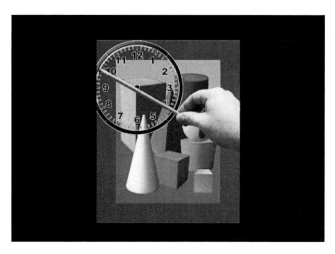

This online capability allows the instructor to reference historical artworks and draw visual connections relevant to the lesson. In a face-to-face setting, technical drawing demonstrations tend to be well over an hour in length and virtually impossible to repeat for absent students with the same rigor and quality. The edited video demonstrations can be distilled to an average of twenty minutes in length and are accessible to students at any time.

Once the content of the video is organized, a voice-over tool, which is usually included in the video software, is used to add dialogue to video introductions, demonstrations, and assignment overviews in a clear concise manner. If the instructor chooses, at this point background music can also be applied to videos, which can be a helpful addition to making longer videos more appealing to view. Videos are finalized and saved in MP4 format which allows them to be uploaded into most learning management systems, YouTube, Vimeo, or other video libraries.

BEST PRACTICES IN IMPLEMENTATION

Importing course content into a learning management system (LMS) can be a time consuming task, yet it is a crucial step in organizing the course structure. Most LMSs contain an area devoted for the course syllabus. Jay Parkes and Mary B. Harris (2002) contend that a course syllabus should drive the course content, serve as a contract between the instructor and students, and should be utilized as a learning tool. It is one thing for a student to just read a syllabus, but quite another for an instructor to talk about course expectations on video simulating the traditional classroom (Brinthaupt, 2011). Thus, it is suggested that instead of being a simple "read only" document, it should be interactive, allowing students to click important links (LMS user manuals and IT support links), watch welcome videos, and utilize course checklists. Including a simple task checklist that contains weekly assignments and obligations allows students the ability to organize and monitor their learning (see Figure 4).

Figure 4. Still image showing the homepage of the LMS where instructor welcome video is embedded.

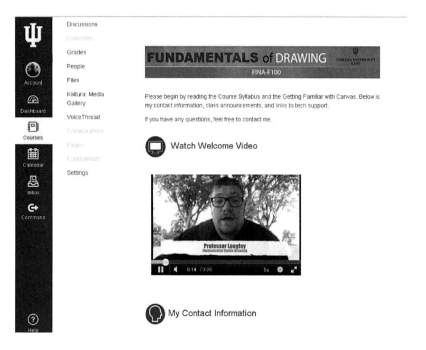

Parkes and Harris (2002) also add that if the syllabus reflects substantial time and effort, the instructor has a right to expect this investment from students as well.

The ability to create pages, or modules, within a course site allows the course designer to organize course content in a chronological order and establish a structure and a routine for the course (see Figure 5).

Figure 5. Still image illustrating the layout of the module page in the LMS.

All modules in the Fundamental Studio Drawing course are arranged into two-week increments. Each two-week increment contains an overview, video tutorial, assignment(s), links to relevant files, and assignment rubrics. To ensure order and ease of use, all modules follow the previously mentioned format.

The overview page is the first item students will view within each module. It is suggested that this page briefly state the goals for the unit, the department learning outcomes that this module addresses, a list of assignments and point values, and assignment due dates. The next page contains a brief description of an instructor-generated video to emphasize the key points of the unit. Below the description, the video is embedded or a link to the video is placed. The video supplies the unit's lecture, demonstrations, and assignment expectations. Below the video, links to the unit's assignments can be found. When these links are clicked, the assignment pages consist of a concise overview of what students are going to complete for assessment. Within this page is a list of required materials (supplies, downloadable files, and reference images), task details, and links to grading rubrics. In some modules, a discussion page has been implemented to allow for peer critiques of artwork. This discussion page uses an embedded Padlet, a free online application that serves as a bulletin board where images and comments can be posted (see Figure 6).

Figure 6. Still image showing the Padlet application imbedded in the LMS.

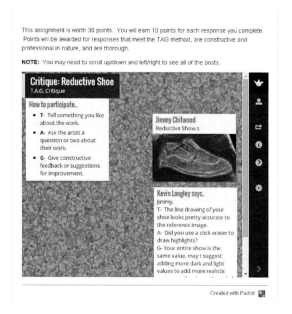

This is also a useful tool for keeping a portfolio of student work. This feature is used for several methods of critique: 1) Students may voluntarily post their work in progress to request feedback from classmates and instructor. This approach encourages peer-to-peer collaboration. 2) Students are required to post in-progress work for a formal mid-point critique where students are evaluated on an assigned number of responses. 3) Students participate in final critique of finished work. In the final critique, students must respond to an assigned number of their peers (i.e., respond to a minimum of three students) using the T.A.G method. T.A.G. is a criticism technique that encourages students to: 1) tell something they like about the work, 2) ask a question about the work, and 3) give the artist a suggestion. In an online setting where students run the risk of working in complete isolation, these discussion pages add a collaborative element to the course and serve as a path to social learning. Also, by utilizing the Padlet, students can become reflective learners, able to scrutinize their own work, which is a skill-set they will need to successfully work with others (Marshall, 2014).

A few other beneficial features of the LMS come in the form of a course calendar tab and course announcements tab. When assignments are created and due dates are set, due dates are automatically pinned to the course calendar. On the LMS home page, due dates appear on a calendar feed to remind students and instructors when assignments are scheduled to be submitted. Another useful tool, the announcement tab, can be used to emphasize assignment due dates, publicize important reminders, and serve as a mass communication source for the entire course. Once an announcement is created, the LMS automatically sends and email to all students and instructors within the course, which eliminates the need for a follow-up email.

STUDENT ASSESSMENT

All modules are designed to be completed in an asynchronous fashion, which gives students the luxury of completing tasks on a schedule that meets their own needs. At the beginning of the course, students are provided with clear guidelines for documenting and submitting their visual works. In addition to these guidelines, students are also provided with visual examples of assignment expectations using a Visual Assessment Rubric (VAR). It is suggested that students compare their work to the VAR prior to submitting for a grade, which, as Hesser (2009) claims, allows students to be involved in all stages of the learning process, from planning to assessment (see Figure 7).

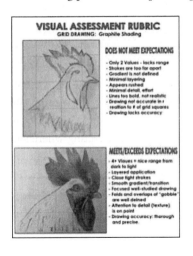

Figure 7. Image of Visual Assessment Rubric to be used by students to compare their work before submission.

Students may document their artwork using various tools, which include scanner, digital camera, camera phone, etc. The resulting image files must be saved as JPEG or PDF format with an image resolution of 300 dpi or higher to ensure clarity. Most instances of poor image submissions occur at the beginning of the course, but are easily remedied when students are instructed to seek assistance from the IT department. Once images are submitted, they are assessed using a rubric connected to course and assignment objectives. One benefit of assessing student work within the LMS is that all submitted files may be downloaded and saved into one folder. This allows the assessor to view all images at once, or one at a time, permitting flexibility in when and how to assess student work.

As is the case with most online courses, academic honesty is a concern. How will the instructor know if the enrolled student is in fact completing the assignment? In an effort to address this issue, an instructor may want to require students to record themselves completing an assignment. In addition, instructors may require students to draw on a much larger scale than a standard 8.5" x 11" piece of paper. This would make it much more challenging for students to simply print and trace.

CONCLUSION

Although online studio art courses are a rarity in higher education, the art department at IU East addressed the need to incorporate online studio courses as a viable option for students. Studio courses most suitable for online delivery include exercise-based, beginning-level courses such as Fundamentals Drawing and Fundamentals Studio 2-D, as well as courses that use digital applications as a tool for visual expression, such as Graphic Design and Digital Photography. With the right equipment, training, and planning, an instructor can successfully virtually deliver studio art curriculum properly aligned with university, department, and course objectives.

REFERENCES

Bennett, N. (2016). Fred deakin is shaking up how art and design is taught at university. *Digital Arts*. Retrieved from http://www.digitalartsonline.co.uk/features/creative-business/why-british-art-design-education-at-university-is-broken-how-we-fix-it/

Brinthaupt, T. M., Fisher, L. S., Gardner, J. G., Raffo, D. M., & Woodard, J. B. (2011). What the best online teachers should do. *MERLOT Journal of Online Learning and Teaching, 7*(4). Retrieved from http://jolt.merlot.org/vol7no4/brinthaupt_1211.htm

Draus, P., Curran, M., & Trempus, M. (2014). The influence of instructor-generated video content on student satisfaction with the engagement in asynchronous online classes. *MERLOT Journal of Online Learning and Teaching, 10*(2). Retrieved from http://jolt.merlot.org/vol10no2/draus_0614.pdf

Edmundson, M. (2012). The trouble with online education. *The New York Times.* Retrieved from http://www.nytimes.com/2012/07/20/opinion/the-trouble-with-online-education.html?_r=2

Edwards, B. (1986). Drawing on the artist within. New York, NY: Simon & Schuster, Inc.

Grant, D. (2002). Distance learning; if you can't draw this... *The New York Times.* Retrieved from http://www.nytimes.com/2002/11/10/education/distance-learning-if-you-can-t-draw-this.html?pagewanted=all

Hesser, J. F. (2009). Personal perspectives on constructivism in a high school art class. *Art Education.* Retrieved from https://www.mica.edu/Documents/Art%20Education/MAAE%20Research/62(4)_ArtEd_July2009_Hesser.pdf

Leong, P., & Ho, C. (n.d.). Constructivist & sociocultural strategies: Theoretical & practical implications for teaching online. Retrieved from http://citeseerx.ist.psu.edu/viewdoc/download?doi=10.1.1.522.3745&rep=rep1&type=pdf

Logan, C., Allen, S., Kurien, A., & Flint, D. (2007). Distributed e-learning in art, design, media: An investigation into current practice. *The Higher Education Academy.* Retrieved from https://www.heacademy.ac.uk/sites/default/files/del1-final-report.pdf

Mandernach, J. (2009). Effect of instructor-personalized multimedia in the online classroom. *The International Review of Research in Open and Distributed Learning.* Retrieved from http://www.irrodl.org/index.php/irrodl/article/view/606/1263

Marshall, M. (2014). Emerging technologies in art education. Retrieved from http://scholarworks.wmich.edu/cgi/viewcontent.cgi?article=1539&context=masters_theses

Parkes, J., & Harris, M. B. (2002). The purposes of a syllabus. *College Teaching, 50*(2). Retrieved from http://jan.ucc.nau.edu/~coesyl-p/syllabus_cline_article_2.pdf

Pinsk, R., Curran, M., Poirier, R., & Coulson, G. (2014). Student perceptions of the use of student-generated video in online discussion as mechanism to establish social presence for non-traditional students: A case study. *Issues in Information Systems, 15*(I), 267–276. Retrieved from http://iacis.org/iis/2014/49_iis_2014_267-276.pdf

Saromines-Ganne, B., & Leong, P. (n.d.). The "art" of online teaching: Teaching visual art virtually. Retrieved from http://www2.hawaii.edu/~peterleo/Electronic_Portfolio/OnlineVisualArt.pdf

Souleles, N. (2015). Elearning in art and design: The elephant in the room. *Research Gate.* Retrieved from https://www.researchgate.net/publication/273458289

10

Sociology, Anthropology, and Geography

Igniting the Passion: Examples for Sociology, Anthropology, and Geography

DENISE BULLOCK, PH.D.

KATHERINE MILLER WOLF, PH.D.

WAZIR MOHAMED, PH.D.

MARC WOLF, M.A.

INTRODUCTION

There are multiple ways in which to stimulate a student's mental activity, which lead to meaningful learning, whether from direct instruction, student driven, or applied. Each of these methods, particularly when combined, serve our institutional requirements—meeting program learning objectives and student learning outcomes. Due diligence through assessment and modification of practices can assure ourselves, as instructors, that our students are learning, affirming our contribution to our students and university. While this is well and good, we suggest that this is not enough. Igniting passion within the student propels their desire for learning outside of the classroom toward meaningful personal, interpersonal, and community/global change. This goal lies at the heart of the disciplines of Sociology, Anthropology, and Geography. Three pedagogical frames—active learning by Chickering and Gamson, experiential learning theory by Kolb, and emancipatory learning by Habermas—will guide this discussion. Strategies and techniques, however, are only tools. Ultimately, instructor/student interaction lights the fire of knowledge.

Active, Experiential, and Emancipatory Learning

Active learning. Active learning has long been recognized as facilitating engaged and motivated learning. Critical thinking and reasoning—common learning objectives for Sociology and Anthropology—is facilitated through active learning, as Hill et al. (2012) state:

> Learning experts maintain that these goals are best achieved through active learning that requires students to expend cognitive energy to reach understanding.... When students reflectively engage by talking about what they know, questioning what they don't, and interacting with instructors and peers, they develop the ability to understand and apply what they have learned. (p. 251)

Traditional educational models of transmitting knowledge to passive recipients has been challenged by pedagogy encouraging active learning, causing an ideological shift in the way we conceive learning and higher education. Briefly, Chickering and Gamson (1987) proposed that active learning is one of the seven good teaching practices in universities and the first of the "six powerful forces in education." From their perspective:

> Learning is not a spectator sport. Students do not learn much just by sitting in classes listening to teachers, memorizing prepackaged assignments, and spitting out answers. They must talk about what they are learning, write about it, relate it to past experiences and apply it to their daily lives. They must make what they learn part of themselves. (Chickering and Gamson, 1987, p. 4)

Facilitating active learning involves thought-provoking and engaging discussions, writing assignments, collaborative exercises, knowledge integrating projects and experiences and internships. Directing student's primary and secondary education almost exclusively toward testing outcomes may make active engagement in the college classroom disconcerting and uncomfortable. Each of the authors have experienced a measure of resistance from students who expect us to simply feed them information needed for the next exam. While teaching to the test will ensure certain knowledge outcomes (at least in the short term), it will not necessarily facilitate the desire for life-long learning or ignite the passion for Sociology, Anthropology, or Geography.

Experiential learning theory. In 1984 David Kolb published his book on Experiential Learning Theory (ELT), which is defined as "the process whereby knowledge is created through the transformation of experience" (Kolb, 1984, p. 41). Experiential Learning Theory is founded on six propositions, two of which we find most compelling in their relationship to potential for profound interpretive oriented learning and integrating course material into one's daily life (Kolb and Kolb, 2005, p. 194). Learning is seen as a progression from acquisition, to specialization, and to integration of knowledge. More specifically, learning shifts from "registrative and performance oriented" (memorization of material) to "interpretive and learning oriented" (practical application of material) to "integrative and development oriented" and finally to deep interpretive oriented (reflective integration of material) (Kolb & Kolb, 2008, p. 50).

Habermas and the sociology of knowledge. Habermas proposed three modes of knowledge acquisition and transmission: technical (or instrumental); practical (or communicative); and, emancipatory (Habermas, 1971; Merriam, 2007; Cranton, 2002; & Tinning, 1992). He suggests that while technical and practical knowledge are important and necessary, we should strive for emancipatory knowledge. Technical knowledge is fact-driven, based on instrumental practicality and objective focus. Drawing upon Marx, Habermas explains that knowledge is based in structures of power and domination. In essence, those in positions of power determine what knowledge serves their interests and therefore, what is disseminated/taught. We do not argue here that all technical knowledge is necessarily directed at maintaining power and control in the hands of the ruling class. Rather, we point out that the potential exists for education and technical knowledge to be directed toward that end. In our discussion, technical knowledge is comprised of the facts, concepts, and theories regarding our material and ideological world, as directed by our disciplines. These facts are derived from research and documentation within our fields of study, and knowledge competencies are measured in our courses through discussion, exams, and writing assignments. Introductory textbooks typically provide the foundation for this technical disciplinary content.

Practical knowledge derives from the communicative and interactive relationship between individuals and their social world. Gaining practical knowledge through dialogue and interaction with others, we are indoctrinated into our culture and social relationships. This reflective process can also be tied to structures of power and dominance (Habermas, 1971). Practical or reflective knowledge rests within the heart of the sociological imagination (Mills, 1959)—the ability to see social forces at work in our everyday lives—and serves as a potential frame for interpretive reflection. Developing a sociological imagination is a key foundational learning outcome for our introductory courses, which provides a foundation for subsequent upper-level coursework. Anthropology also draws upon the same principle, helping students see how their own cultural, physical, and historical context is connected to and contrasted to the unknown *other*.

Finally, emancipatory knowledge engages critical analysis of societal forces at work in our social worlds. Knowledge derives from inquiry into how the status quo is maintained, who benefits and is served from its structural, cultural, and interactional arrangements. Emancipatory knowledge requires critical self-reflection and analysis of the socially constructed and hierarchically ordered nature of our social world. Once acquired, emancipatory knowledge can institute and promote social change. As the course complexity and cognitive learning advances, emphasis on practical and emancipatory knowledge increases, so that in our upper level courses we stimulate higher order cognitive skills and honing sociological imagination through critical analysis.

APPLYING THESE FRAMES OF LEARNING

Clearly, there are overlaps between these three frames. Active learning strategies and scaffolded courses and programs build toward deep learning and emancipatory knowledge, which are central to our goals. At our regional campus, students may come into the educational environment with rigid and fixed notions regarding the social world, with a worldview often framed by media-generated rhetoric or dialogue supporting power and hierarchies of difference. This worldview has often gone unchallenged due to a deficit of critical analysis in their primary and secondary education. For these students (as well as others), the development of critical analysis is a primary objective of our disciplines. One cannot simply begin, however, with critical analysis and emancipatory knowledge. Instead, a foundation of research-supported facts, concepts, and theories (technical knowledge) is established, followed by tasking students with application of this technical knowledge in assignments and discussions, framing their own experiences within this learned context. The result is the development of practical, reflective knowledge. This emancipatory knowledge can be reached in both face-to-face (F2F) and online environments.

The online learning environment provides both opportunities and challenges for students and instructors alike. Debate and conflicting analysis of the effectiveness of online versus traditional, or F2F, for student learning outcomes and satisfaction is ongoing. Recent studies have found that neither student learning nor satisfaction is significantly different for online or F2F when sound pedagogical structure and strategies are used (Driscoll et al., 2012; Bergstrand & Savage, 2013) and when instructor skills are matched with modality (Clark-Ibanez & Scott, 2007). Specifically, matching instructors' dynamic and performative classroom success into the online environment is critical, in the short term. For the long term, changes in technology and ideology regarding higher education, and needs of learning styles require that we must adapt to be successful across learning modalities.

So how is it that we facilitate moving the student from simply the acquisition of content or technical knowledge to the incorporation of a passion that leads to meaningful personal, interpersonal, and community/global change and emancipatory knowledge? How can we ignite that passion in an online course setting? In what follows, we will discuss several factors that we believe allow us to ignite that passion in online (or F2F) class settings: 1) engaging content, 2) passion through personality, 3) personal connection, and 4) an integrated program of study.

ENGAGING CONTENT

Anthropology, Sociology, and Geography are content-heavy disciplines, with courses emphasizing critical, evidence-based analysis, requiring requisite technical knowledge and skills that students are expected to master. Content must also be motivating—if we want to stimulate their sociological imagination and foster emancipatory knowledge. Finding ways to personally connect the student with the course material is key to that motivation. This can be accomplished through a variety of strategies: integration of the instructors own research and/or theories, student research and investigation, and student application of concepts and content (discussed below).

PASSION THROUGH PERSONALITY

As instructors, our presentation of self in the course and our own passion for the material is key to connecting with our students on a personal academic level. As students, we have most likely all had instructors who simply seemed to be going through the motions of teaching. On the other hand, we can all recall those passionate teachers who motivated students toward life-long and deep learning. For Bullock, it was that high school social studies teacher (Paul Cheek) who in 1974 innovatively taught social inequality and social problems through a semester-long, role-playing scenario. Mr. Cheek's passion propelled Bullock toward sociology and activist scholarship.

Displaying our passion for the material through self-presentation is believed much easier in F2F interaction while teaching in an asynchronous and physically detached online environment presents challenges. Most online instructors create presence in online environments. Encouraging contact between students and faculty is one of the "seven principles of good practice" introduced by Chickering & Gamson (1987), allowing students to feel connection to a living person. It does not, however, necessarily move students toward social engagement for positive change. One strategy used is through video and/or audio lectures and vignettes—allowing for instructor's enthusiastic presentation of self. Visual and auditory cues aide in deciphering text/words—confirming or challenging meaning. While there is some debate over the use of PowerPoint slides as an aid in teaching, Hill et al. (2012) found that undergraduates in their study "reported PowerPoint as a useful feature of classroom instruction that improves learning" (p. 246). A principle concern for both students and instructors in this study was the potential loss of active discussion, which is easily handled in F2F settings by facilitating students in active discussion or exercises tied to presented material throughout the class period (Hill et al., 2012). In online environments and its asynchronous structure, conversation is necessarily disconnected from video/audio lectures and embedded PowerPoint slides which become simply another resource for student learning. Video and audio recordings that are not overly produced, allow students to experience their instructors as real people due to occasional quirks and flaws that occur during them, along with instructors' passion for the material.

A second strategy, inquiry-guided learning (IGL) "emphasizes active investigation and knowledge construction rather than passive memorization of content" (Atkinson & Hunt, 2008, p. 1). Inquiry-guided learning requires higher order thinking and application, and is particularly important for upper-level courses and the goal of emancipatory knowledge. Instructors create specific assignments or stimulate IGL through substantive, thought-provoking commenting on submitted work, development of discussion forum questions, or prompting questions that further the students' thinking. IGL promotes deep and emancipatory learning.

PERSONAL CONNECTION

Significant research touts the value of experiential learning. We have high-lighted only a small portion of that research. Our disciplines are ripe with opportunities for applied and active learning at every course level. Our disci-plinary organizations possess course specific resources with content related activity suggestions.[1] For example, Mohamed uses a single commodities approach, such as banana, rice, coffee, sugar, and so forth to stimulate criti-cal discussion on the effects of imbalanced global trade arrangements as well as utilizing the film *Black Gold*, (https://vimeo.com/ondemand/blackgold) to demonstrate how small farmers are marginalized as globalization evolves. Miller Wolf directs students to web-based surveys exploring genealogies and

---

1. See American Sociological Association publications, Teaching Sociology journal and TRAILS (Teaching Resources and Innovation Library for Sociology), both of which provide examples of learn-ing activities. The American Anthropological Association has several resources: Teaching Anthropol-ogy Interest Group (TAIG) Blog for sharing instructional challenges and topic discussion and E-Learn-ing Anthropology Website—a set of resources from the Teaching Anthropology Online Workshop.

individual genetic traits, and Wolf might show a film on current terrorist activities to investigate geographical questions of globalism.

INTEGRATED PROGRAM OF STUDY

An integrated program highlighting human agency and social engagement for positive change reinforces emancipatory learning as students move between courses. Persell et al. (2008), in their survey of scholarly leaders in Sociology—the nine major themes that all sociology students should understand—discovered the importance of trying to improve the world (p. 112, 118–119). Likewise, McKinney et al. (2004) recommended that "Departments should offer community and classroom-based learning experiences that develop students' critical thinking skills and prepare them for lives of civic engagement" (p. 22). Behavioral patterns and personal connections can be established that serve the student long after the individual class or degree is completed. At Indiana University East (IUE), we have a combined Sociology and Anthropology degree that requires a set of core courses (18 credit hours) for both disciplines. Students then choose either an advanced Sociology or Anthropology tract (18 credit hours) to compete degree requirements. Our program focuses on two primary goals: developing an understanding of social justice (tied to structural arrangements and personal and societal/global consequences of inequality), and development and understanding of the importance of human agency. Students graduating with our degree should be able to demonstrate a series of outcomes tied to the five key learning objectives[2].

Assessment planning allows us to target and forecast multiple opportunities to emphasize our programmatic goals. The development of personal motivation and informed human agency is a foundational element because with few instructors or few classes emphasizing the development of human agency and/or civic engagement behavioral patterns, emancipatory knowledge may not be reinforced. It is about being intentional in the way we structure our programs.

---

2. Due to space constraints, we have not listed the individual learning outcomes under each of the five program objectives. We have established five to seven outcomes for each program objective. The authors would be happy to share this information.

In what follows, we will provide four exemplars—two from Sociology, one from Anthropology, and one from Anthropology and Geography—that illustrate how we ignite the passion.

Introduction to Sociology: Denise Bullock

At IUE, the majority of students take Introduction to Sociology, available in both F2F and online formats, to fulfill general education or degree requirements other than Sociology. The introductory course may be our only opportunity to kindle students' sociological imagination. Demographically, our regional students tend to come from economically challenged backgrounds with their pre-college education less focused on critical analysis than their private school and upper-class counterparts. Additionally, many of our students lack exposure to critical analysis and investigation in their home environments. Experiential learning outside of academia has, likewise, been limited for the majority of our regional students. The introductory course is one opportunity to develop sociological imagination through experiential learning. The online environment has the advantage of drawing students from not only our campus region but also across the state and even the world—broadening student exposure to a diversity of ideas and social worlds.

Sociology makes a difference community projects (SMDC). Within the sociology/anthropology program at IUE, we instituted a program in fall 2012 called Sociology Makes a Difference Community Projects (designed originally for F2F classes and adapted for online). One of the primary goals of the SMDC projects was to connect our students with their local communities in specified activities, applying their course content knowledge through active learning and stimulating critical analysis of social issues—thereby linking technical, practical, and emancipatory knowledge. Due to socioeconomic belief systems and life circumstances, many of our regional students lack a sense of their own human agency. They experience social issues and problems in their personal interactions, communities, and the global world, but often feel help-less to create meaningful change. SMDC projects are selected to highlight social issues at a community level through which students can personally participate in collective good for the welfare of others. Students commit to a minimum of 10 hours of community engagement, keep a journal of their experiences, and submit a reflective essay of their project—connecting course content (technical knowledge), personal connection (practical knowledge), and the value of civic engagement (emancipatory knowledge). Our students can and do make a difference in their local communities.

Variance of projects. Some of the projects are group or individually ori-ented, depending upon whether there are collectives of students from the same regional area or more isolated students. Time on a particular project has varied from multiple weeks to a single day of activity. The scale of those affected has also varied from neighborhood to one-on-one engagement. For example, students hosted a neighborhood picnic with food and games, open discussions on landlord/tenant issues, food pantry assistance, and cleanup projects. One student wrote of her experience saying, "This experience helped me realize that by giving time to help others in need, I am not only help-ing them, but also making myself a better person" (personal communication, April 27, 2014). Another student wrote about transforming a small dilapidated area into "pocket park."

> Through this experience, I have learned the true value of teamwork and what it is truly like to clean something ugly up and make it beautiful.... If a community looks nice then it makes the people feel a sense of pride for what they have accomplished, which in turn raises moral[e] and makes the community whole again (personal communication, December 4, 2013).

Because many of our students balance their education with work and family obligations, tailoring projects to individual students is necessary—to reduce burdens on students' time. While many of the instructor-coordinated group projects for the F2F classes are located in Richmond (where IUE is located), projects are easily arranged in the communities in which the students live. Additionally, a supplementary book, *The Engaged Sociologist* (Korgen & White,

2015), provides additional readings and selected projects to give students flexibility in meeting course requirements.

Utilizing the SMDC projects in the online environment. Development of community projects is more challenging for online classes, since there is less opportunity for instructors to draw from established contacts in their own region. I place the onus of finding community engagement projects with the students in order to motivate them to find a project that matches their personal interests and time constraints. Guidelines and examples of appropriate projects are provided to aid students in selection. For example, students are to arrange projects that benefit the community or individuals within the community (in their local area) that are outside of their normal work or volunteer activities. The idea is for the students to step outside of their routine and participate in new experiences. Students are instructed to describe their proposed project and provide contact information for the site and individuals with whom they will be working. I approve the project directly with the host individual, ensuring that the parameters of the activities are appropriate, before students are permitted to participate in the project. Students are then responsible for arranging their schedule with the host site to meet the minimum 10 hours.

Upper-Level Sociology Classes: Wazir Mohamed

Online teaching is challenging for those of us who are more accustomed and experienced with F2F teaching. Because our student population is enlarged by the online environment, the need for adaptation is more pressing. For the upper-level courses, I focus on "inquiry-guided learning," carefully selecting a combination of textbook, monographs, and journal articles to stimulate deep or emancipatory learning. Engaging readings expose students to a variety of ideas and a wide range of examples of the human condition. These challenging and varied readings better prepare students for graduate degrees or deep learning for preparation to work in the global economy that is becoming more diverse, yet less respectful of the diversity of human society.

From this context, my teaching approach in online classes puts less attention on lectures and PowerPoint presentations, and more on reflective discourse between professor and students. In their readings and other resources (films, etc.) students are required to analytically deconstruct the content before they complete reflective discussion posts and essays, in an attempt to avoid the tendency for students to regurgitate trend lines and ideas fed to them in lectures and PowerPoint notes. This enables a process whereby I evaluate how well each student is able to think critically about the subject matter.

Assignments and feedback. In my upper-level classes, coursework entails: assigned readings; discussion board posting, engagement, and debates with their colleagues; completion of weekly essays, and short essay mid-term and final exams. By the end of each semester, students have completed 50–75 pages of reflection on the subject matter. Assignments and exams are geared to ensure that students are learning the material, and to determine whether or not and to what extent the course, as designed and delivered, meets the requirements of the established learning outcomes.

My classes encourage inquiry-guided learning through extensive feedback, which takes different forms. Feedback is used to advise students of their understanding of the subject matter, adjustments to their focus, and different ways they can think about the subject and issues discussed. Firstly, discursive lecture videos (6–8 minutes) engage students and respond to their work—reenforcing what they are doing well, correcting any misconceptions present in their work, and helping them expand their thinking. Secondly, I give them copious written feedback, and encourage them to communicate with me by email, telephone, and online as a means of furthering discourses on subject matter. This gives online students opportunities for real-time connectivity with the subject matter through my presence as an intermediary. Thirdly, through these forms of engagements, students are empowered or are encouraged to give feedback. Comments from students validate these methods. One student from the Global Society course in fall 2015 wrote to say:

> Thanks for all the feedback you give me on my work in your class. I have never had a professor help me so much! Thanks for helping me get focused. I think I understand now that reiterating historical points and general information is not the best use of this class. Exploring the relationships and particulars that enabled this history that formed our modern world is what is important. Only by understanding these relationships and particulars will I begin to understand the why, how, and connections of history that power the world of today. Thanks again for taking the time and effort to help me dig deeper and to get the most

from your class. I am really enjoying it and am hopefully becoming more reflexive (personal communication, October 26, 2015).

This reflection mirrors the following excerpt taken from a note sent by a Social Inequality student in spring 2015. The student wrote:

> I want to thank you for...your time and willingness to share your insight on social inequality with me. I can guarantee you that I will carry your thoughts and words, and the knowledge I have gained throughout this course with me in the future. When I enrolled in your class to satisfy my diversity requirement, I had doubts that I would find enjoyment, satisfaction or reward in any Sociology course, but I was wrong. Your class opened up a place in my mind and my heart that I had let go numb over the years...I am grateful that you structured this course in such a way that I was challenged to be independent—think, research and form strong opinions about the social issues around me (personal communication, spring 2015).

Our task is to structure classes that meet the required technical knowledge while ensuring learning through student feedback. As the student points out above, the structure of the class is very important. I structure my classes to challenge students to develop and think, in order that their inner person can emerge, and that they can see themselves for who they are or can be.

Anthropology: Katherine Miller Wolf

Anthropology is a dynamic field of inquiry that helps us to reflect upon our own culture, identity, and life. In F2F courses, the examples I integrate in my lectures help to ignite students' curiosity and spark a lively debate about the complexities of the human lived experience and the nuances of cultural symbols and meaning. In online teaching, it seems difficult to create an environment in which an organic, passionate discussion can ensue and shift the classroom environment. Yet, the challenge of creating a space in which students enrolled in online courses are afforded the same critical thinking opportunities as in-person learners is one that is happily accepted.

Careful organization and selection of course materials are of paramount importance to the success of online learning. In my view, we must strike a careful balance between the resources we provide to our online learners—streaming media, textbooks, websites, articles, and lectures. The textbook should form a baseline for technical knowledge and serve as a reference for the student as they consider complex articles, powerful documentaries about life in all its iterations and variations, and my lectures draw out key details in anthropology, enhanced by my own fieldwork experiences, which provide unique and engaging examples for students. By sharing my own experiences as an anthropologist, I attempt to create a space in which students feel similarly open to discussing their own views and biases about controversial cultural or global issues. One assignment in particular affords students the opportunity to recognize their own cultural system and to reflect upon their place in the world.

The curious case of body ritual among the Nacirema, presented by Miner (1956), was met with acclaim and chagrin. His ethnography presented a case of ritual violation of the human body by a culture obsessed with beauty, health, and perfection. In excruciating and sometimes uncomfortable detail, he outlines their "barbaric" practices of skin laceration and ritual visits to a holy-mouth man known to cause severe dental pain. This article is the first assignment for students in my Cultural Anthropology classes from which they must consider the practices of this civilization and discuss what conclusions they might draw about the behaviors described therein. Responses vary—"Disgusting!" "Why would you do any of this to your body?" "I could never live among the Nacirema." "I feel nauseous."—but the discussion remains critical and unsympathetic, until the following lecture reveals that Nacirema is simply American spelled backwards and that Miner had written an ethnography that made *Us* appear like a *Them*.

This small exercise creates a personal connection to anthropology through experiential learning when students are confronted by their own ethnocentric bias. After this point, students discover their own passion for understanding culture and develop compassion for those that seem to be different than what they know or understand. Anthropologically, we call this *cultural relativism,* and to help students develop such self-reflexivity is my goal.

Unpacking their own cultural bias can be overwhelming to students in a F2F course during discussions where stronger or louder voices bury others.

In this way, online students have the better opportunity; they can consider controversial or complex topics on their own, carefully collect their thoughts, and only then present them to their classmates. The discussions that ensue are thoughtful, nuanced, and well contextualized in course material because of the unique individual learning environment that online teaching affords.

Throughout the course of the semester, students in any of my online courses (Cultural Anthropology, Human Origins and Prehistory, Cultures of Africa, or Forensic Anthropology) participate in biweekly discussions that require significant writing. These discussions facilitate the learning process more than quizzes or exams, and as such, comprise a significant component of the final grade, since it is through these discussions that students truly grapple with their understanding of the material and reach out to their colleagues to dissect key concepts. Recently, I have implemented a new discussion technique, prompting students to pose a question to their classmates after responding to my discussion prompt. Students have reported that the interaction and resulting discourse from the question/answer process encourages engagement and camaraderie.

One student offered the following on the conclusion of the course:

> I'm actually a better person because of this course. Cultural relativism means much more than I realized. Many topics were painful to deal with, but knowing how the rest of the world actually lives puts things in perspective. In other words, I gained intellectually and ethically (personal communication, 2015).

If students can complete an anthropology or sociology course as a more thoughtful citizen of the world, we have succeeded in passionately providing engaging content that creates a personal connection to the world around us. Such emancipatory learning cannot be accomplished without making the foreign seem familiar and providing the context for critical reflection of one's society and own life. Ultimately, this can bring about positive change in our families, communities, and world.

Anthropology and Geography: Marc Wolf

The goal of any learning exercise is to instill knowledge in the student. Ideally, education objectives—in both online platforms and traditional in-person classes—are the same. Operating under this paradigm, the human aspect of the social sciences should never be overlooked or taken for granted. This creates two challenges not found in F2F classes: the online environment is typically bereft of the F2F interaction between students and teacher and students and other students, and the online setting requires a strong degree of self-motivation by the student. However, examples from prior courses detail how both areas can be successfully addressed.

This discussion will focus on two classes: Indians of North America, and Introduction to Human Geography. Online instruction has often been unfairly maligned, mischaracterized, and downgraded to an inferior form of teaching—it is within these semantics that the academic community strives to uphold ethical and intellectual standards. Online classes are obviously devoid of the personal and more physical aspects of a regular seated class; however, this negativity can be addressed by the power of extreme resource availability in an online setting, where a web search is just a hand motion and new browser tab away. Though this might seem to implicate the instructor of the course in learning quality—specifically in structuring the online content—the exponential access to information that is inherently part of an online design can become a nexus of digital interaction between students and professors. If applied diligently, this can make up for the lack of F2F synergy associated with traditional teaching.

Indians of North America is a 100% online cultural anthropology class. In its first printing, Ozwalt's *This Land Was Theirs* was considered somewhat non-conventional; now in its ninth edition, it has become a widely accepted textbook and the pre-eminent resource for this survey course of later historic era North American Indian cultures. Aside from the usual assessments and weekly web-based activities, exercises engage students beyond a teaching and information rich environment (technical knowledge) to a self-motivational milieu (practical knowledge) where students desire to learn. One exercise requires students to visit/attend a Native American themed event or exhibit. Museums, cultural events, and archaeological sites are possible destinations. Native Americana is ubiquitous in the New World, and the visitation assignment tries to reach the preferences of the student and their local history—no matter the location on the globe. This is another positive for the online environment as opposed to that of the traditional classroom that occupies specific space. The appreciation of Native American resources, diversity, and history takes advantage of the individual student's accessibility to regional state sites, archives, and museums with international appeal, and allows for comments between classmates and sharing within online discussion boards and the posting of communal assignments and projects—deep knowledge—that ignores the spatial restrictions of a single campus.

The online platform should also be fortified with as many *offline* activities as possible. In the case of anthropological courses, instructors are fortunate to take advantage of the plethora of archaeological sites and diverse local history. In almost every state in the United States and around the globe, archaeology is celebrated through dedicatory days, months, exhibits, and other meetings and sponsored events. Not only should students be actively encouraged to participate in further research and visitation of their local resources on their own, but also be afforded the opportunity to experience these with fellow students and instructors through field visitations and other class-associated activities and engagements.

In previous semesters, the Introduction to Human Geography class had been taught F2F. The class met once a week for three-and-a-half hours—somewhat tedious given the timing (5:30 pm, after normal school hours) when students' attention was difficult to maintain even with several participatory activities, games, films, and breaks, in addition to lecture and writing assignments of that week's materials. In its current form, the class is a hybrid—meeting once a week as before, but for a shorter hour-and-fifteen-minute session. Additionally, the class has a robust online component of weekly exercises, readings, web links to follow, and videos to watch. In a hybrid class straddling both virtual and seated classrooms, time is one of most noteworthy aspects of a digital platform. In an atmosphere of deep learning, time translates to exposure. Class in a F2F environment is marked by entrances and seating, by answering general questions about the day's topic or other pressing items, lecturing, discussing, and signing off. Another great attribute of the online format is the flexibility of time, often a concern of the F2F milieu. The hybrid course answers this with dynamic digital content to further stimulate students' movement beyond classroom instruction to multimodality learning where videos about the subject or web searches and additional readings enrich their learning experience.

This attribute of time and access/exposure to resources is exemplified in the hybrid format, and is the power of online instruction. In the case of this geography class, the instructor is tasked with the creation of online materials that are both challenging and informing, but also attractive and inspiring deep learning. Class resources are stimulating, varied, and often changing with the current state of knowledge—creating a foundation for learning. Grading of discussion "postings" provides important IGL opportunities to guide student thinking beyond the level of technical and practical/applied knowledge conveyed through web based submissions. Textbooks and lectures may be a starting point for technical knowledge and another chance for the online teacher and student community to unite. The instructor's choice of reading is crucial in stimulating students to digest the technical information reviewed in class. As mentioned in the initial comments, many academic disciplines are fraught with seemingly mundane facts that together form a more complex and interesting understanding of the relevant topic.

CONCLUSION

In this chapter we argue that, for our disciplines, a focus on registrative or technical knowledge, while necessary and important, is not enough to ignite a passion for lifelong learning and deep or emancipatory knowledge. We have highlighted active learning and experiential strategies to enhance interpretive or practical knowledge. While each of us may utilize differing combinations of strategies—active engagement, instructor presence, and inquiry guided learning—we are each committed to fostering critically reflective and emancipatory knowledge. The online learning environment can be just as effective in the development of emancipatory knowledge as F2F, but adaption is necessary. Those of us who have strong performative skills in the F2F environment must find ways to bring material to life in the online environment. This can include visual and more auditory lectures and feedback. Development of written communication skills may be necessary to simulate inquiry-guided learning through discussion questions and feedback. Whether the student has only one introductory course or completes a degree in our fields, we have to take advantage of those opportunities to stretch their analytical and social imaginations. Students for whom the passion is ignited can create positive change in our social world. We just have to light the match.

REFERENCES

Atkinson, M. P., & Hunt, A. N. (2008). Inquiry-guided learning in sociology. *Teaching Sociology, 36*(1), 1–7. Retrieved from http://www.jstor.org/stable/20058621

Bergstrand, K., & Savage, S. V. (2013). The chalkboard versus the avatar: Comparing the effectiveness of online and inclass courses. *Teaching Sociology, 41*(3), 294–306. Retrieved from http://www.jstor.org/stable/43186514

Chickering, A. W., & Gamson, Z. (1987). Seven principles for good practice in undergraduate education. *AAHE Bulletin, 40*(7), 3–7. Retrieved from http://eric.ed.gov/?id=ED282491

Clark-Ibanez, M., & Scott, L. (2007). Learning to teach online. *Teaching Sociology 36*(1), 34-41. Retrieved from http://www.jstor.org/stable/20058625

Cranton, P. (2002). Teaching for transformation in new directions for adult and continuing education no. 93: pp. 63-71. doi: 10.1002/ace.50

Driscoll, A., Jicha, K., Hunt, A. N., Tichavsky, L., & Thompson, G. (2012). Can online courses deliver in-class results? A comparison of student performance and satisfaction in an online versus a face-to-face introductory sociology course. *Teaching Sociology, 40*(4), 312–331. http://www.jstor.org/stable/41725516

Habermas, J. (1971). *Knowledge & human interest.* Boston: Beacon.

Hill, A., Arford, T., Lubitow, A., & Smollin, L. M. (2012). I'm ambivalent about it: The dilemmas of PowerPoint. *Teaching Sociology, 40*(3), 242–256. Retrieve from http://www.jstor.org/stable/41502756

Kolb, D. A. (1984). *Experiential learning: Experience as the source of learning and development.* Englewood Clift, N.J.: Prentice-Hall.

Kolb, A. Y., & Kolb, D. A. (2005). Learning styles and learning spaces: Enhancing experiential learning in higher education. *Academy of Management Learning & Education, 4*(2), 193–212. Retrieve from http://www.jstor.org/stable/40214287

Korgen, K. O., & White, J. M. (2015). *The engaged sociologist: Connecting the classroom to the community.* (5th ed.). Thousand Oaks, California: Pine Forge Press.

McKinney, K., Howery, C. B., Strand, K. J., Kain, E. L., & White Berheide, C. (2004). *Liberal learning and the sociology major updated: Meeting the challenge of teaching sociology in the twenty-first century. American Sociological Association.* Retrieved from http://www.asanet.org

Merriam, S. B., Caffarella, R. S., & Baumgartner, L. M. (2007). *Learning in adulthood: A comprehensive guide.* (3rd ed.). Retrieved from https://proxy.library.iue.edu/login?url=http://search.ebscohost.com/login.aspx?direct=true&db=nlebk&AN=26069&site=ehost-live&scope=site

Mills, C. W. (1959). *The sociological imagination.* New York: Free Press.

Miner, H. (1956). Body ritual among the nacirema. *American Anthropologist, 58*(3), 503–507. Retrieved from http://www.jstor.org/stable/665280

Persell, C. H., Pfeiffer, K. M., & Syed, S. (2008). How sociological leaders teach: Some key principles. *Teaching Sociology, 36*(2),108-124. http://www.jstor.org/stable/20058636

Tinning, R. (1992). Reading action research: Notes on knowledge and human interests. *Quest, 44*,1–4. Retrieved from https://proxy.library.iue.edu/login?url=http://search.ebscohost.com/login.aspx?direct=true&db=eric&AN=EJ446568&site=ehost-live&scope=site

11

The Proof Is in the Pedagogy: A Philosophical Examination of the Practice of Backward Design

MARY A. COOKSEY, M.A.

INTRODUCTION

Higher education in the twenty-first century is an enterprise driven by innovation and entrepreneurialism. To be bold enough to grow, colleges and universities have had to abandon more traditional modes of course delivery and embrace the newest tools and trends in order to attract and retain the millennial student. Gone are the days that monotone delivery of information to passive college students will pass muster as a highly valued teaching strategy, or one that is even acceptable. Higher education today—whether the institution is big or small, whether course delivery is face to face or on line—is held to a much higher standard—as an activity, as a product, as an enterprise. In its pursuit to "up its game" in the educational marketplace of the twenty-first century, colleges and universities have appealed to a variety of innovative strategies to improve and enhance course creation and delivery. One such strategy is backward design. A course creation protocol gaining worldwide popularity, backward design is exactly what its name implies—designing a thing, in this case a course, by moving backward in thinking and intention. Put another way, backward design invites one to begin at the end, and working outward toward the steps to connect the intention and the output. Backward design moves from finish to start, from the back door to the front, instead of the other way around as a more traditional interpretation of thinking chronology might imply.

In this paper, I will examine backward design as a course creation, or course redesign strategy, and explore its special voracity as an architecture for building high quality on line courses. In particular, the underlying pedagogy of backward design will be exposed and investigated, with the ultimate goal being a measure of its logical soundness, and thus its suitability, to be a key driver in the transformation of philosophy content, specifically ethics, for delivery online.

BACKWARD DESIGN — DEFINITIONS AND DESCRIPTIONS

One of the best characterizations of backward design is that put forth by Ruth Mitchell and Marilyn Willis (1995) in their publication, *Learning in Overdrive: Designing Curriculum, Instruction and Assessment from Standards*. In the introduction to a section of the book entitled "Step Six: Mapping Backward from the Culminating Task to the Learning Sections," the authors invite the reader to imagine Christmas..."in a little shack way out West—the kids snuggled together in the cold, crisp evening, dreaming of a sugarplum morning." They continue by pointing out that stories about these children and these holidays always include an orange or a tangerine being found in Christmas stockings the next day. The authors then pose the question: Can you imagine how complicated it was to move an orange tree all the way to Kansas in 1869? With that inquiry, the heart and soul of backward design is exposed...and the structure of its architecture made accessible to be fully understood.

First appearing in educational literature in the mid-twentieth century as the "mapping backward" strategy referenced in the section title above, backward design as a curricular design model is most generally attributed to the duo of Grant Wiggins and Jay McTighe (1998). In their landmark publication *Understanding by Design*, Wiggins and McTighe define backward design as an approach to curricular design as "purposeful task analysis." They continue by noting that the logic of backward design suggests a planning sequence for curriculum, which has three stages: identification of desired results, the determination of acceptable evidence, and the planning of learning experiences and instruction. Filtered through the lens and language of curriculum design, these steps have come to mean that quality course design begins with the determination of learning outcomes; settling on assessment strategies that will most effectively measure the attainment of those outcomes; and then making decisions about course content, learning activities, and signature assignments that will be most effective in connecting the dots for students (Fink 2003).

This process of beginning course design by "imagining when a course is over...then asking: what is it I hope that students will have learned, that will still be there and have value several years after the course is over?" is a design model that may seem counterintuitive, but which has, in the end, proven to be highly effective in producing the desired results of increased student learning (Fink 2003). In fact, for Fink and many others, backward design is the backbone of creating the most significant learning experiences for students.

Backward design was most readily adopted by those working in public education at the secondary level and below, where standards guided the design process, and easily translated into identifiable and measurable learning outcomes. Multiple resources point to backward design as a quality template to attain desired increases in student learning, and equally as important is the accessibility of the elements of backward design to assessment of that student learning (Fink, 2003; Mitchell & Willis, 1995; Wiggins & McTighe, 1998). Backward design as a general design strategy has become so successfully established that, in 2003, Jay McTighe joined with Robert Thomas in authoring an article entitled "Backward Design for Forward Action," wherein the design strategy is suggested as one which could be applied to successfully solve the problems of an entire school system. They assert that by clearly stating educational goals, teachers and administrators can work backward to create realistic measures for the actual learning situations in which they and their students are engaged, better accounting for the conditions and challenges with which they are confronted. Better fit, better approach, better outcome.

In the past ten years, backward design has come to be embraced as a viable design process for everything from whole program revision to the creation of a better writing experience (Linder, et al., 2014). As its popularity has grown, backward design has become a logical fit for the course revision and redesign made necessary by the migration of multiple courses and whole programs on line. It is the emphasis on learning outcomes of backward design that makes it so appealing. As evidenced in the most recent report from the Lumina Foundation, Learning Outcomes is where we are gaining consensus—among educators, between faculty and students, and for the public and private sector. According to the working paper published by Lumina January 26, 2016, "For more than two decades, employers and policy makers have been asking tough questions about how well our nation's colleges and universities are preparing their graduates to succeed in and to contribute to a changing global workplace and society." The report goes on, "Business leaders consistently express frustration that college graduates are not achieving the broad, cross-cutting learning outcomes they need at high enough levels to fuel a technology-rich, innovation-driven economy" (Hart Research Associates, 2007, 2015; Gallup, 2014). They also complain that current forms of documentation do not provide enough information for anyone outside the Academy to know what the student actually learned. The report continues, stating leaders in higher education, and educators in general, have not ignored these critiques, especially in the face of changing demographics and changing patterns of college attendance. As early as 2002, a panel assembled by Lumina noted in their *Greater Expectations* report that in their progression toward a degree, large numbers of students enroll in multiple institutions, also taking courses online. For them, college can be a revolving door, and newer attendance patterns place greater responsibility on students themselves to create meaningful learning from a supermarket of choices (AAC&U, 2002, p. 2).

More and more, students are "swirling," as the AAC&U report puts it, to collaborate on clarifying expected students' outcomes and clearly demonstrating students' achievements as they progress. These pressures and concerns have driven a steady increase in attention to learning outcomes, according to the Lumina report (2016), how we define and develop them and how well we measure how students are actually achieving them. This is where backward design comes in...both on the level of courses and on the level of whole programs...face to face—but especially online, as it is the latter far more than the former that has come under increased scrutiny in terms of quality output and quality control (Weisenberg & Stacey, 2008).

Using backward design to move course creation more deliberately toward the statement of clearer outcomes and their attainment is changing education in new and fundamental ways (Fink, 2003). Having begun as a strategy to calibrate public school classroom content with pre-set standards mandated by state and local governing bodies, backward design has grown into a pedagogy of its own that is utilized in many ways, to effectively engineer large and small scale projects from their inceptions to the production of desired ends. Beginning from end results and reasoning to the steps and strategies to achieve them has proven to be an extremely effective design process for higher education in course creation, especially the design of courses and curricula on line where the stakes are high and the competition is fierce. Online more than anywhere else, the student must be clear about those learning outcomes for which he or she will be primarily responsible for attaining.

THE TEACHING ONLINE SERIES AND THE P120 EXPERIMENT

The Teaching Online Series is a self-paced professional development module that was created by the Indiana University Information Technology Team along with the Educational Designers. It is aligned with the Quality Matters protocol for high quality on line course delivery, but its idea architecture for course design is based on the principles of backwards design, a very useful model for developing courses for both online and face-to-face settings. As stated in the introduction to the TOS Canvas site: "Biggs (2003) uses the term constructive alignment to describe both the process and underlying theory of backwards design. When teaching a course, content knowledge is not moved in whole from your brain to your student's brain. Students **construct** their personal understanding of the material based on their experience in the course and their prior experiences and understandings of the content and its context."

The TOS introduction continues, "One of the goals of instruction is to support realistic constructions and to dispel misconceptions that can get in the way of their learning. **Alignment** of desired learning outcomes, teaching and learning activities, and assessments provides consistency for the student and supports more accurate constructions of course concepts. Backwards design begins with these desired learning outcomes, clearly stated in measurable terms, and works backwards through assessment activities, teaching and learning activities, and content delivery."

For example, in this course, one of the desired learning outcomes is for you to be able to write clear, measurable learning outcomes for a class that you teach or plan to teach online. To that end, one of the TOS takes faculty through the process for writing clear, measurable learning outcomes, then leads them through the selection process for assessment activities. The TOS provides practice activities both in identifying learning outcomes and in writing learning outcomes in a structured way to help you get the hang of the process. It also provides written narrative about learning outcomes and instructions on how to write them well and how to judge whether outcomes meet the main criteria of being observable and measurable.

In the fall of 2015, the adjunct faculty of the Philosophy Department at Indiana University East began to work through the TOS professional development modules, beginning with a general introduction to online teaching and the virtual classroom, as well as a tour of the online environment and an orientation to the various tools it had to offer. Faculty then moved through modules that captured the various steps of backward design...designating essential learning outcome or ELo's, choosing effective assessment tools to measure for desired outcomes, and from there, developing meaningful learning activities and signature assignments. The experiences of the adjuncts was eye-opening, producing great benefits for them and for their students.

The modules of the TOS move participants through examination of their course content not only for their effectiveness in linking learning activities to outcomes and assessment, but also for the usability and accessibility of their content. Like a Quality Matters review (QM 2016), backward design as applied in Indiana University's TOS compels a full explication of all attributes of an online course, making for a more thorough review of the online class for features that really matter—like usability for a learner who is impaired... or for clear learning outcomes for a student who knows she will transfer and will need to make a case for the content mastered in the class. Such was the experience of the Philosophy faculty. Many had not considered the full accessibility or usability of all features of or content in their courses. Some had not taken the time or invested the effort in connecting every part of every assignment to specific parts or portions of specific learning outcomes. As one associate faculty member put it, "I am really looking at the assignments in my course and making sure that I can explain to students every time why it is that I am asking them to do what I am asking them to do. If I want them to write about a particular ethical situation or problem, what is it that I am trying to accomplish by this? That is what I need to be able to tell them. Until I went through all the parts of the TOS, I don't think I pushed that."

Using the modules of the TOS to guide a review of courses currently being taught, the full-time and part-time faculty of the Philosophy Department appealed to the TOS for guidance in building a new online course shell for Philosophy P120, an introductory class in personal and social ethics. Currently under construction, the P120 Ethics course will have designated learning outcomes that will have been crafted from an assimilation of all of the different learning outcomes that had been previously designated by those full time and associate faculty members who had previously taught the course. Using a tool in the TOS called the Learning Outcomes Generator, each instructor input his or her individual learning outcomes, and the Learning Outcomes Generator will create three outcomes that will be a compilation of all that were input. Building learning outcomes in this way best insures all dimensions of course content are covered, all instructional approaches are considered, and all faculty take ownership of outcomes for having been an integral voice in their stipulation.

Along with shared learning outcomes, the P120 collaborative shell will include shared assessment strategies such that easier comparison and cross section study may occur, facilitating more useful research and more efficient and effective use of assessment data in closing the assessment loop.

Faculty have also collaborated to create signature assignments for the P120 course, including an "ethics autobiography" wherein students map backward to the roots of their moral dispositions and ethical attitudes, using the study to better understand themselves and others in moral decision-making postures in their day-to-day lives. A total of four signature assignments populate the course, each acting as a course milestone in attaining the broader learning outcomes, bringing together the significance of the students' signature work and the attainment of the larger learning goal, helping them see the critical connections between the two.

With the guidance of the TOS and the embedded protocol of backward design, course design for the P120 shell will include all the right stuff to be a high-quality online course. After the designation of shared-learning outcomes, like increased comprehension of essential ethical concepts and constructs, good assessment strategies like a pretest and posttest will be put in place for measuring increased comprehension of essential ethical concepts and constructs. The course will include the integration of meaningful learning activities like viewing media that captures ethical difference in new and innovative ways, broadening an understanding of others, then bringing that experience together with the ethical autobiography that emancipates a broader understanding of self. Together, these experiences enable the student to obtain another shared, essential learning objective of increased understanding of the moral dispositions of self and others.

A PHILOSOPHICAL EXAMINATION OF BACKWARD DESIGN

Backward design is a process of design thinking that has proven to yield tangible and desirable results in improving the quality of course development and redesign in online and face-to-face courses in secondary and in higher education. Staring from the desired end result and reasoning backward through how to bring that result about has been shown to be an effective way to provoke analysis of and reflection upon existing pathways and new connections, for the K–12 teacher, for the Philosophy Professor, for the school board member. In mentally walking through the minutia in between steps to making a desired result happen, best practices and worst ideas emerge, so that what is left in the end is a sleeker, more-effective process. Why does backward design work this way? Why is it a strategy that is so effective? The answers to these questions may be answered in part by the application of the principles of the design as illustrated in the literature, or they may lay in part in the empirical data supplied by the application of backward design through a program like the TOS, but in the end, the best proof of the effectiveness of backward design rests in an analysis of the pedagogy itself.

Backward design proceeds from a logical construct that is deductive in nature. The design process is deductive in that the conclusion is asserted first, and the premises are then derived from the conclusion. Everything that is needed—all the content—to construct the premises is presented in the conclusion. Therefore, the form is deductive, the thread of reasoning moving from the general to the specific. It is this logical basis of backward design that, in the end, makes it so effective.

By starting the course design process with the essential learning outcomes, they are placed prominently in the chronology of importance. Essential learning outcomes are front and center in the selection of assessment tools and strategies, and the marriage of the two drives the selection of learning activities and signature assignments. The learning outcomes will automatically occur if the conditions of the assessment are met, and the conditions of the assessment will be met if the learning activities are completed successfully. And in the end, that is the information desired for educators, stakeholders, and accreditors alike—where is the assurance that students are obtaining the desired learning outcomes? Backward design provides the course creation platform that will be most likely to support student attainment of those essential learning outcomes, and through assessment of signature work, will also provide the evidence of that attainment.

If it can be ascertained that backward design as a pedagogy is sound, then it can be trusted to consistently produce positive results. In other words, if the design process is a good one, no matter the particular course or discipline, high quality course creation will occur. Insofar as backward design is a deductive process which proceeds according to the principles and constructs of logic, its pedagogy is sound; thus, the consequences which result from its application are likewise sound. Backward design works because its structure makes sense. This is as a design process, just as effective when applied to structuring a writing retreat as it is when applied to the restructuring of an entire school system. Because the design process always begins with the desired results, it is of little consequence if that result exists on a large scale (a school system) or a small scale (a single course), the result will be the same. When it comes to the "trustability" of backward design to produce desired results, the proof is in the pedagogy; it will work every time.

THE FUTURE OF PHILOSOPHY ONLINE AND ITS RELATIONSHIP WITH BACKWARD DESIGN

The discipline of Philosophy is in an interesting position with regard to online learning in higher education. Recent studies indicate that online teaching and learning in the field is still new and worthy of further investigation to discover the best methodologies and activities to enhance students' ability in key areas in the discipline, such as philosophical analysis and critical thinking.

Other studies seem to suggest that faculty perceive of face to face and online teaching in the discipline as nearly identical.

In a recent study by Weisenberg and Stacey (2008) comparing the experiences of Australian and Canadian Philosophy professors in teaching face-to-face courses versus teaching online, the predominant finding was that both venues were satiating for both groups, and in fact, the majority of individuals in both groups reported that they found little difference between the two platforms. As the authors of the study describe:

A case-study approach (Stake, 2002) was used, where one university in western Canada and another in the state of Victoria in southern Australia were treated as two separate cases of inquiry, and results were compared between cases. Qualitative data were gathered with a seven-question, open-ended survey that was developed by the researchers; the survey asked participants in the faculties of Education in these two comparable universities to describe their teaching philosophies/approaches within both F2F and online teaching contexts. The survey also gathered demographic data about participants' online and F2F teaching history and experiences, their current teaching workloads, and the size of their classes in both modalities.... Paired t-tests on main TPI scores revealed that participants' teaching preferences were remarkably similar across both modalities and for both universities. There were no significant differences between four of the five teaching preferences (p. 71).

This particular study is one of relatively few on pedagogy and best practices in and attitudes toward teaching Philosophy. The reason for this is because a relatively small number of studies actually exist. The explanation for this relatively small number of pedagogical studies in the field is that in the discipline of Philosophy, the Scholarship of Teaching has yet to be fully recognized as a legitimate field of research. Because of this, full scale, longitudinal projects simply do not get done. Studies that have been done tend to focus on one and done projects or initiatives. This is a misstep by the discipline. All indications are that the scholarship of teaching is very important to discipline success and survival. It is within this field of research that meaningful, longitudinal studies may take place that will further flesh out best practices and high impact teaching techniques that are especially effective in teaching Philosophy online. Likewise, it is in engaging in and interacting with the scholarship of teaching that new teachers begin their journey in professional development, and where they learn how to craft effective learning outcomes and where they become familiar with the full range of assessment tools and techniques available to them for measurement of those outcomes. It is also through deep engagement in the Scholarship of teaching that instructors exchange ideas, network, and compare notes about meaningful learning activities and signature work—both for their students and for themselves.

Legislators, funders, and other stakeholders demand that higher education is delivering on its promise of delivering high-quality teaching, and doing so whether the product is being delivered face to face or online. Turning once again to the most recent Lumina study on learning outcomes, the January 2016 report states that at no time has the interest been higher in the nature and substance of learning outcomes. Drawing from a 2015 study done by NILOA, the National Institute for Learning Outcomes Assessment, 85% of all Chief Academic Officers surveyed reported having a common number of intended learning outcomes for their undergraduate students. 87% reported assessing for these outcomes across the curriculum, and they reported that a majority of this reportage still comes from the departmental level (p. 6). This means, in classes, making the ascertainment of learning outcomes assessment data incredibly important. This point, in turn, punctuates the need for a course design process that puts the outcomes front and center, that employs a process—or pedagogy that is sound—and that uses the soundness of the pedagogy to scaffold meaningful learning activities and signature assignments to create quality course content. And again, this must happen in all face-to-face and online offerings.

Returning to the 2016 Lumina report, the continually increasing call for accountability a decade ago from then Secretary Spellings' Commission on the Future of Higher Education, The American Association of Community Colleges (AACC), the Association of Community College Trustees (ACCT), and the College Board came together in 2009 to create the Voluntary Framework of Accountability (VFA). Among the criteria from the framework was the expectation for learning outcomes. Shortly thereafter, multiple other voluntary accountability plans emerged, most important among them for making this a prominent issue for Philosophy, the Student Achievement Measure, a joint project involving the two major, national organizations AAC&U and AACSU, the American Association of Colleges and Universities and the American Association of State Colleges and Universities respectively (p. 4).

In 2011, the Lumina Foundation released the beta draft of the Degree Qualifications Report, the DQP. The profile describes what degree recipients should know and what they should be able to do (DQP 6). The DQP proposes proficiencies that benchmark the associate's, bachelor's and master's degrees. It "draws on more than a decade of widespread debate and effort across all levels of higher education across the United States and across the world to define learning outcomes that graduates are expected to fulfill in preparation for work, citizenship, global participation and life" (p. 6). The DQP Grid, which lays out learning outcomes, groups them in five categories of learning: specialized knowledge, broad and integrative knowledge, intellectual skills, applied and collaborative learning, and civic and global learning (p. 16). For faculty members, there are five principal values of the DQP, and these values are closely aligned with the components of backward design. According to the DQP descriptive report published by Lumina in October of 2014, the five principal values of the DQP for faculty are:

- It draws faculty into active clarification of how and what they teach in relation to what their students learn.
- It encourages them to examine more fully the content and methods of their field...in relation to priorities that span departmental and school boundaries ('my' course to 'our' course).
- It can help foster purposeful, sustained interaction with colleagues concerning the purposes of colleges and universities.
- The DQP enables faculty to examine assignments they give to students to ensure these assignments foster and properly assess the desired proficiencies.
- Faculty members' collaborative engagement with the DQP reinforces and demonstrates the value of their intentionality for strengthening the quality of both learning and teaching.

Of these five values of the DQP for faculty, several are directly related to the backward design process, the others, indirectly. For Philosophy, and more specifically for Ethics, the implementation of the DQP as a partner in the backward design process for an online course might look like the set of relationships outlined below:

DQP Category: Intellectual Skills (Cross-cutting definitional skill: Ethical reasoning) use of reasoning and resources, communication and diverse perspectives to be brought to bear on situations, both clear and indeterminate, where tensions occur to resolve these conflicts.

At the Bachelor's Level: Analysis of competing claims from recent discovery, scientific contention, or technical practice with respect to benefits and harms to those affected; articulates ethical dilemma inherent in benefits and harms; arrives at a clearly articulated reconciliation of that tension.

P120 Ethics Learning Outcome: Students will analyze a variety of ethical decision making models, and will be able to recognize and articulate the crossroads and common ground between them as applied to current issues in a global society.

P120 Ethics Learning Outcome Assessment Technique: Course essay from Signature Assignment

P120 Signature Assignment: After completing reading and media viewing on the issue of euthanasia[1], outline your stance on voluntary, active euthanasia, referring back to your ethics autobiography for grounding. Then, outline the stance that Dax would take with regard to active, voluntary euthanasia. After that, outline the stance of the American Medical Association. Now, imagine you are a hospital administrator charged with striking a compromise between these three ethical points of view. How might you accomplish this? What are the crossroads and common ground between these three?

Attributes making this a signature assignment: students ground initial analysis in their own history, and students employ their own voices in outlining and analyzing ideas and issues.

CONCLUSION

In the history of education and the development of the skills of the intellect, the pedagogies and practices of Philosophy have always been at the forefront.

---

1   Reading scholarly articles in the text, reviewing the Dax Cowart story, the PBS Frontline programs Facing Death, The Suicide Plan and Living Longer, and reviewing the instructor's original research on end of life issues in the 21st century.

Whether it was the development of the first inklings of scientific thinking of the Milesians in the 5th century B.C., the intellectual challenges of the Classic thinkers a hundred years later, the problem of mind put forth by the French and German idealists 2,000 years later, or the angst and arguments put forth by the existentialists and nihilists of this century or the last, Philosophy is the discipline taking on the hard questions about how we know what we know, why we do what we do, and where we can find the next direction to go to make things better. The discipline promises to take the lead as it continues to embrace innovation in higher education in the 21st century. And as the toolbox of the discipline contains the analytical devices to accurately predict and measure pedagogical through logical analysis, the field itself contains all it needs to continually improve. Starting from the point of continuous improvement to ensure that best practices are put into place to enhance the quality of the classroom is the best application of backward design yet—and again, real evidence that the proof is in the pedagogy indeed.

REFERENCES

Adelman, C., Ewell, P., Gaston, P., & Schneider, C. G. (2014). *The degree qualifications profile.* Indianapolis, Indiana: The Lumina Foundation.

Fink, L. D. (2003). *Creating significant learning experiences: An integrated approach to designing college courses.* San Francisco, CA: Jossey-Bass.

Hart and Associates. (2016). *Recent trends in general education design, learning outcomes and teaching approaches* (pp. 1–15, Rep.). Washington, D.C.: Association of American Colleges and Universities.

Hart Research Associates. (2016). *Trends in learning outcomes: Key findings from a survey among administrators at AAC&U member institutions* (pp. 1–12, Rep.). Washington D.C.: American Association of Colleges and Universities.

Lumina Foundation. (2016). *Learning outcomes: Where we have been; where we need to go* (pp. 1–19 Rep.). Indianapolis, Indiana: The Lumina Foundation.

Mitchell, R., & Willis, M. (1995). *Learning in overdrive: Designing curriculum, instruction, and assessment from standards: A manual for teachers.* Golden, CO: North American Press.

The Teaching On Line Series. (2016). Retreived from https://www.iu.edu.

Van Camp, J. C., Olen, J., & Barry, V. (2015). 11th edition. Stamford Connecticut: Cengage Learning.

Wiggins, G. P., & McTighe, J. (1998). *Understanding by design.* Alexandria, VA: Association for Supervision and Curriculum Development.

PART TWO • NATURAL SCIENCES AND MATHEMATICS

12

BIOLOGICAL SCIENCES
Online Teaching and Learning in Biological Sciences

PARUL KHURANA, PH.D.

NEIL SABINE, PH.D.

INTRODUCTION

Traditional lectures have been the primary mode of instruction for a long time. However, pedagogical research has led to a paradigm shift in pedagogy from instructor-focused lecturing to student-centered active learning. Implementing active learning strategies has been resisted by some instructors because of perceived problems of sufficient coverage of course content. Recent innovations have implemented teaching strategies that take components of both pedagogies to give students a rich learning experience.

Blended or flipped classroom approaches have been developed to promote synchronous and asynchronous learning (Bart, 2014; Bart, 2015). In the blended format students are assigned an online (asynchronous and self-paced) component and a live component (face-to-face and/or online). Blended classrooms give the instructor a wide range of online learning tools and modes of delivering course content. In the flipped classroom, students access course material outside of class (e.g., readings, pre-recorded lectures and research assignments). Class time is then used to help students work through problems they faced mastering concepts individually or in groups. Both blended and flipped classrooms are often problem-based teaching strategies, and collaboration is an important component of classroom activities. Blended and flipped classrooms do not completely remove the synchronous component that online courses routinely do.

Online and active learning strategies have been shown to improve student attitudes, performance and learning in science, engineering and mathematics (Armbruster et al., 2009; Connell et al., 2016; Deslauriers et al., 2011; Freeman et al., 2014; Knight & Wood, 2005; McDaniel et al., 2007; Ryan & Reid, 2016; Stockwell et al., 2015). Significant improvements with asynchronous web-based teaching have been correlated with improvements in technology (Anderson et al., 2008; DeBard & Guidera, 2000; Koehler & Mishra 2005). Online instruction has, in practical terms, become synonymous with distance learning.

Online education presents traditional instructors with opportunities to expand their teaching skills. Instruction in online courses requires that learning modules be designed to engage students in course content and be assessed to gauge student understanding (Downing & Holtz, 2008; Edelson, 2001). Online classes present unique challenges for science and mathematics. These subjects often require students to solve problems, rely on hands-on activities and use demonstrations to visualize concepts and processes (Downing & Holtz, 2008). However, rapid advances in the quality of online resources (e. g., virtual laboratories, free tutorials, and animations) in these disciplines have addressed these challenges. Additionally, learning management systems have become sophisticated enough to embed technological advances and tools seamlessly during course design. The combination of these developments have led to tremendous growth in online science courses and holds much promise for teaching science in the future.

Students now learn in virtual environments as well as they do in physical ones. Several studies have shown that students are as successful in online courses as they are in face-to-face courses, maybe even more so (Alisauskas, 2007; Bernard et al., 2004; Dell et al., 2010; Warren & Holloman, 2005; Weber & Lennon, 2007). New technologies, such as gaming and tablet computers, will continue to offer new opportunities for student learning. Virtual learning environments remove many of the physical limitations of learning science. The future of science education is technology-enhanced learning in which virtual-learning environments will play a pivotal role.

As noted in previous chapters, Indiana University East (IU East) is one of Indiana University's five regional campuses. IU East serves nine counties in Eastern Indiana and has a reciprocity agreement with some counties in southwestern Ohio. Being a primarily commuter campus located in a region without a metropolitan area, IU East faced challenges associated with decreasing enrollment. This led to the adoption of online education and programming that began in 2007. Since then IU East has established itself as a leader in online education within Indiana University, with the enrollment numbers doubling at IU East between 2007 and 2014 (LaForge et al., 2015).

The School of Natural Science and Mathematics (NSM) at IU East offers four Bachelor of Science undergraduate degree programs in Biology, Biochemistry, Human Life Science, and Mathematics; and a Bachelor of Arts in Natural Science and Mathematics degree with four concentrations, four minors, and three certificates. The school also boasts a Master of Arts in Teaching Mathematics degree and a graduate certificate in Mathematics. NSM has seen significant growth in its degree programs over the past several years, and the success of many of these rests on the quality and success of its online courses and programs. In fall 2015, 47% of all the credit hours generated by the school were online (a 9% increase from fall 2014). In the 2015–2016 academic year, 48% of the total credit hours generated were from online classes with an enrollment of 751 students (unduplicated head count). Out of the total online credit hours 36% were from online science classes. This is a large percentage, considering the fact that NSM only offers an online B.S. degree in Mathematics and a B.A. in NSM with a concentration in Mathematics.

Faculty members in NSM practice online teaching in various disciplines, including biology, chemistry, biochemistry, physics, and geology. The instructors were early adopters of online instruction in lab courses as well. Science courses in mental illness and addictions have been offered online since 1996. Beginning in 2000, Zoology was taught using many online components, which helped its transition in to a completely online course in 2005. Online simulations, home kits, case studies, and other online and physical tools helped students successfully apply ideas and concepts taught in both lecture and labs. Since 2005, NSM administrators and faculty have embraced the online teaching environment and have endeavored to develop and teach more classes in this mode. In fall 2015 and spring 2016, a total 33 courses in science were taught completely online, out of which seven were laboratory classes. All the lab classes were lower-level science courses for non-majors. More courses will be offered online in the near future, including upper-level science courses. Furthermore, NSM is creating an exclusively online Masters of Art in Teaching Science graduate degree.

In order to grow and sustain the success of NSM in online education, the faculty and administrators have been proactive in ensuring that they offer a quality learning environment for the students. Professional development opportunities for faculty in online education and the hiring of faculty with online teaching experience have helped in this mission. In 2015, as part of an IU East-wide initiative, NSM full-time faculty were trained and certified in the Level One of Quality Matters (QM), a rubric and program created to evaluate, review and approve online courses. Level One certification ensures that faculty can apply the QM rubric to their online courses. Faculty are consistently seeking training and development opportunities to keep up with the best practices in online teaching and learning in order to deliver online courses that best serve the needs of the students.

ONLINE COURSE DESIGN

An increase in the demand and number of online courses has raised the need for a systematic course design that offers the students social presence, cognitive presence, and teaching presence (Garrison, 2007; Garrison & Vaughn, 2008). The online environment requires innovative ways of sharing and transferring knowledge (Kim & Bonk, 2006). Here we describe some of the best practices and technologies used for online science teaching at IU East.

Canvas is the current learning management system used at IU East. Most courses are organized as modules that are weekly, biweekly, or based on readings or content. Course modules frequently revolve around Instructor-Generated Videos (IGVs) that reinforce concepts and supplement activities or assignments. The IGVs usually provide virtual "mini-lectures," but can also be used to show students a wide variety of online resources that reinforce course content.

One advantage of IGVs is that they are customized by the instructor. In some asynchronous IGVs the instructor talks directly to students while others have video recordings with the instructor talking on the side of the frame that shows the notes being written by the instructor while discussing the concept. Instructors often use Microsoft PowerPoint slides to show images and make important points with narration. Web cameras or document cameras were initially used to make these recordings. Improvements in computer technologies, such as those available on tablet computers, have allowed more sophisticated recordings, and problems or concepts can be handwritten on the computer screen using a digitizer pen. Instructors thus frequently make notes over the PowerPoint slides or on a Microsoft Word or OneNote window. These notes can be saved and provided to the students as a resource along with the slides. The IGVs can thus be used to explain course concepts using video, audio, text, and graphics simultaneously.

There are effective online resources for both synchronous and asynchronous learning and both are typically integrated into online courses. Synchronous learning involves streaming media (e.g., video, images, and text) accompanied by video conferencing and/or chats. Synchronized activities allow students and teachers to ask and answer questions in real time (Hrastinski, 2008).

Asynchronous learning is commonly facilitated by videos, simulations and discussion boards; communication between teacher and student in this mode of instruction is typically written. Asynchronous learning environments provide students with flexibility in accessing course content and completing assignments. Students can decide when is the best time for them to master course content and complete their assessments. Many of our students have a host of commitments outside their academic pursuits. Asynchronous classes allow these students to combine education with work, family and other pressures on their time. Since most of communication in this learning environment is written, students have more time to process the information, reflect on it, and refine their responses than they would in a physical classroom; this leads to more thoughtful comments on class assignments. Synchronous learning therefore tends to emphasize personal participation while asynchronous supports cognitive participation (Hrastinski, 2008). Typically a combination of aspects of both synchronous and asynchronous teaching are most effective at promoting student learning.

Web conferencing tools such as Adobe Connect or Zoom, the active learning platform Echo360, and the video platform Kaltura are some of the tools used by the faculty in NSM to create videos for their courses. All of these tools allow the recording of the computer screen itself, thus giving the instructor the flexibility of using any software to explain or demonstrate course-related applications. Recorded lectures enable the students to master concepts at their own pace since they can slow the videos while taking notes, speed them up if they come across a familiar concept, or even take breaks if needed. Students are often given homework or reading assignments based on the content in videos to enhance their understanding. More recently, some instructors have adopted tools like Zaption to introduce interactive activities within videos. For example, this tool allows the addition of multiple-choice questions within a video so students can assess their understanding during their viewing. Zaption and other tools like Echo360 can uncover real-time data by compiling personal responses to or viewing time of the IGV. Analytical data can give instructors information like how often the video was viewed, which sections were most visited, and which questions were mostly answered incorrectly. This allows faculty to refine instruction that addresses problems with students' learning. Personal student data could be accessed relatively quickly, and this leads to early intervention.

The Internet also provides several opportunities for students to access course-related content in different formats and from different perspectives. Animations, simulations, or videos related to science are freely available on websites and can supplement online courses. Many publishers have animations or videos that are often excellent supplements to explanations in the textbook. For example, microscopic visualization of cellular material has become easier to visualize online over time. It remains difficult to do such experiments in a face-to-face class at small universities because of lack of equipment and/or facilities. Videos of phenomenon caught in real time at the microscopic or organismal level can be especially useful to demonstrate the capabilities of advanced imaging techniques. Practical videos and animations are readily available through websites such as YouTube, and can be embedded on most learning platforms. The education company, Khan Academy, has made several lecture videos freely available on the Internet, and instructors can use them as part of their class or as supplemental information.

Assignments used to assess student understanding in online courses include quizzes, forums/discussion threads, papers, reports, and exams. Papers and reports could be written and submitted as Word documents or text entries that can be graded online. Wikis or Google docs can be used to collaborate and share information on group projects. Software programs like Turnitin are anti-plagiarism tools that are directly integrated into our learning management system. Being aware of the tool, students rarely copy content from other students or from the Internet. Rubrics associated with assignments are often provided to allow students to have a clear understanding of the requirements. Faculty also use the rubrics to grade assignments and provide meaningful and efficient feedback to their students.

Canvas gives faculty the flexibility of creating quizzes and exams online with various types of question formats ranging from multiple choice to essay-type questions. The questions could be picked randomly from a question bank entered into the system. The quizzes may or may not have time limits, have single or multiple attempts, and the answers could be provided to the students' immediately after their attempt or after all the students have completed the task. Canvas also provides analytical data on student responses that helps faculty identify areas of misunderstandings and address them in a timely manner.

Science instructors are now routinely using video projects for assignments in their courses. Very often students are asked to make and post small videos introducing themselves during the first week of the semester. Videos are also very handy when instructors want to incorporate oral presentations into their course. Depending on the discipline, the presentations could be about a lab or experiment, a research topic, or a peer-reviewed scientific article. These could be individual or group assignments. Online students thus get the opportunity to learn and be assessed on their presentation skills along with research, and the instructor gets to know them better.

Student-instructor interaction is more easily seen in face-to-face classes. However, online classes can have substantial interactions between students and between students and the instructor. Most interactions are through email or within the learning management system. In NSM the instructors respond to most student emails within 24 hours but may take as long as 48 hours of receiving them, especially on weekends. A popular tool used in online education to strengthen interaction is the asynchronous threaded discussion board (Chan et al., 2009; Gold, 2001; Hewitt, 2005). The amount of interaction on discussion boards (or forums) varies greatly and depends on course content, the purpose of the discussion, and the length of time a discussion topic remains available. For example, discussion boards can be used to have students solve problems, present perspectives on topics, or answer questions posed by the instructor. The number of students participating in a discussion can vary as well. It can be open to the entire class or may be open to only a small group of students. Collaborative assignments typically use small group discussions. This allows group members to have frank discussions, exchange ideas, and make decisions. It is a good vehicle to solidify social interactions among group members.

Instructors often participate in discussions by posting leading questions and monitoring student conversations. It is important to monitor student threads to ensure that the discussion stays on track and interactions between students remains civil. Instructors can also provide guidance to students about the discussion, to broaden or narrow the topics being discussed, for example. Instructors can also upload media content (e.g., short audio or video recordings) that can easily be posted as part of the thread. Faculty routinely add help sections like "Question and Answer" or "Frequently Asked Questions" to the discussion section of their online courses. Students then have the opportunity to post questions to the instructor whose response is then visible to the entire class.

Another way NSM faculty express a social presence is by holding synchronous virtual office hours. In online classes office hours must take into account that students are often spread across several time zones and have multiple demands on their time. Some office hours are held in the evening to allow flexibility for students with other obligations to attend. However, this is not always the case and faculty meet with some students at their convenience. Virtual office hours often employ Adobe Connect because this allows the instructor and student to share computer screens. The platform can also be used to record the sessions, so they can be made available to students who cannot be present at any of the allotted times. Attending these sessions is usually voluntary; however, some faculty make attending a certain number of office hours mandatory during the semester. This is one way to insure that the student is familiar with the instructor and may be more likely to request help in the future.

One of the biggest challenges for online courses in science is providing students with hands-on laboratory experience (Jeschofnig & Jeschofnig, 2011). A long-standing and viable strategy is the use of home experiment kits. Such kits are best suited for lower-level courses that explore scientific phenomena that do not require expensive instruments (Downing & Holtz, 2008). Several courses like chemistry, anatomy, and physiology routinely use such science kits that students can purchase and use for experiments that can be performed at home. A detailed laboratory guide or instructions for the experiments are usually provided with the kits. Technical advances in computing have been employed in more recent efforts to deliver laboratory or field experience to students via virtual field trips or laboratory simulations (Downing & Holtz, 2008). Simulations and online labs are available on the web for free and they can be purchased through various commercial companies.

SHOWCASE

In the following section, we will highlight a few strategies employed in two different science courses. The goal was to create online courses that were at least as effective as their face-to-face alternative. The courses meet the same objectives as the on-site class, and are designed to take advantage of technology. The examples focus on the use of virtual labs, discussions and rubrics.

Ecology

Ecological Principles (BIOL-L 325) is a 4-credit hour (3 lectures, 1 lab) course that is required for all biology majors. The course is completely online and uses a modular format. Each module gives the readings, lab simulations, and evaluations for the week. An electronic text is used that provides animations, links to research articles, and a variety of questions embedded in the text. Students are evaluated based on their responses to e-text exercises, lab simulations, and a semester-long research project. Adopted simulations replaced field experiences as a part of the virtual learning experience. This shift in lab experience was coincidental with a pedagogical shift as well, from a skills-based approach to lab exercises to a concept-based approach.

For many years the labs were competency-based and conducted outside the classroom. Vegetative analysis, mark and recapture, and determining diversity values were typical labs done in the field. The major problems were the time taken to complete labs in the field and the lack of student expertise in collecting reliable data. It took valuable class time to explain the logistics of the lab. Additional time was needed to assign equipment to students and get to the study site. We had to leave the field in time for students to return their equipment and attend their next class. Students who were absent missed the lab experience. The students who did attend did not have experience with the lab techniques used in the field so it was difficult to get reliable data. We routinely replaced student data with that from studies so students could get a clearer understanding during their analysis. Lastly, bad weather caused lab exercises to be delayed and were then out of synch with concepts discussed in class.

In 1994, some simple computer simulations were used to help support concepts covered in the labs. In 2000, laboratory activities went from skills-based to concept-based and all field exercises were replaced with computer simulations. Field experience was retained, however, it went from a class exercise to an individual exercise. Coincident with the movement to computer simulations for lab activities students began to conduct a semester-long research project in the field.

Laboratory simulations were initially purchased from EcoBeaker (SimBio Software) and were relatively simple (pixels for plants and animals). Advantages of simulations were clearly seen almost immediately. First, simulations could be done asynchronously. Second, a random generator within simulations gave unique values and it was nearly impossible for students to get the same set of values. Third, sample size could easily be manipulated within the simulation or made larger by running the simulation more than once. Repeating the simulation was like repeating the whole experiment again. Over time, the range of experiments for a given concept has increased and the graphics associated with each exercise has substantially improved. However, the greatest advantage of simulations was their ability to compress time and space. This allowed students to investigate ecological concepts in ways that would be impossible to replicate in the field.

Figure 1. Moment in time in one exercise in Isle Royal, an EcoBeaker Simulation.

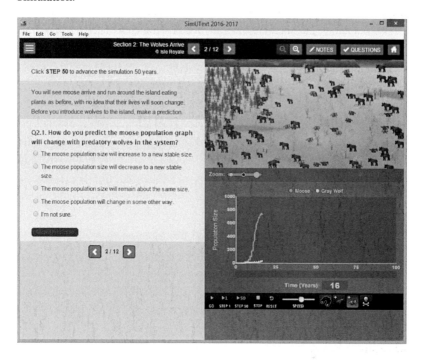

Figure 1 shows an example of an EcoBeaker simulation based on the ecosystem at Isle Royale and the layout is typical of those that students see throughout the semester. There are five exercises with this simulation. This is showing the second section "The Wolves Arrive." In this part of the simulation they can manipulate wolf and moose numbers. Students can run this simulation for as many years as they like and as many organisms as they like either before the simulation begins or as the simulation is running. However, there are minimum values for all simulations to generate reliable data. In this simulation wolves were added in about year 20. The number of moose and wolves are plotted annually and population sizes are graphed over time. Lastly, one can click on each wolf to determine their energy level (ability to hunt moose) and each moose to determine their life stage (baby, juvenile, and adult) and their fat store (indicator of health). Students can test their understanding at the end of each activity. This simulation has a logistic population growth exercise (The Moose Arrive), predator-prey dynamics (The Wolves

Arrive), community dynamics (Changes in the Weather), and statistical testing (Extended Exploration; the t test). Each of these simulations require students to gather, analyze, and interpret data.

Virtual and physical labs can achieve similar objectives such as promoting conceptual understanding, developing inquiry and mathematical skills, and motivating students by using practical examples. Virtual labs have the ability to simplify learning by removing confusing details and compressing time and space (Ford & McCormack, 2000; Trundle & Bell, 2010). These also allow students to see what is unobservable and more easily link that to mathematical equations (van der Meij & de Jong, 2006; Zacharia et al., 2008). Conceptual understanding can also be better supported by virtual labs because students can repeat them until they are comfortable with their understanding (Zacharia et al., 2008). Simulations also tend to have their data clustered around the results of the studies they are based on. Physical labs have more variability in data collected due to inherent errors associated with the expertise of students and/or the equipment they use (Pyatt & Sims, 2012).

Many studies report no difference between physical and virtual labs on student understanding (Triona & Klahr, 2003; Weisner & Lan, 2004; Zacharia & Constantinou, 2008), while some show improved student understanding in virtual labs (Finkelstein et al., 2005; Huppert et al., 2002; Klahr et al., 2007; Olympiou & Zacharia, 2012). Clearly there are advantages to both physical and virtual labs. The field experience for Ecological Principles was best served by having a semester-long research project. Students select a topic of interest and gain experience conducting a complete research study at their own pace and equipment is tailored to their study. An individual approach to field research had the unanticipated advantage of increasing the inventory of field equipment. Buying field equipment for a few students saved money and inventory increased based on student need. It is the combination of field (physical) research and virtual labs that gives students the greatest opportunity to learn (Climent-Bellido et al., 2003; Kollöffel & de Jong, 2013; Olympiou & Zacharia, 2012; Zacharia et al., 2008).

Biochemistry

The CHEM-C 484 Biomolecules and Catabolism lecture course uses a modular format with each module discussing a single chapter and having accompanying activities. Each module also has IGVs in the form of online mini-lectures. There could be two or more mini-videos for each chapter that are less than 20 minutes long. The short videos help avoid streaming issues. Students are expected to read the textbook, write notes, and watch videos to understand course content. Assignments like quizzes are provided online to assess their mastery of the content.

The highlight of the course is the biweekly discussion. It is important to ensure that asynchronous online discussions provide motivation for students to engage in productive conversations with their peers (Rovai, 2007). Effective discussions center on authentic, relatable topics, are task oriented, and encourage communication, thus building a sense of community between the students (Rovai, 2007). These discussion threads can generate the critical dimensions of learning, and students can attain new knowledge through interaction and cognitive engagement (Andresen, 2009, Zhu, 2006). Discussions can thus successfully replace the face-to-face interaction in traditional classrooms.

In the Biomolecules and Catabolism course, topics are selected such that they directly relate to the chapter being studied. These are often topics that have real life applications, like "Diabetes," "Diet or Alcohol Metabolism," and the "Effect of Alcohol on Human Health." Students are asked questions about these topics that generate lively discussion. The expectations for posts are made clear to students and are also available for them to see in the rubric used for grading. Several resources (e.g., YouTube videos, websites, and scientific articles) with background information pertinent to the subject matter are also provided. Students are expected to research the topic and, if tasked, build an opinion about it. They have to post a comment or provide information on some aspect of the question posed. Furthermore, they are required to comment on the posts of other students creating a threaded discussion. Their comments then become a class discussion with each student given sufficient time (two weeks) to compose their contribution. If the discussion topic is such that it generates restricted ideas or if students can only get similar information, the assignments are set up so that the student has to submit his post before other responses are released. This avoids plagiarism and encourages timely submissions.

Figure 2. Screenshot of the CHEM-C 484 Canvas site with Forum Topic 2 introduction.

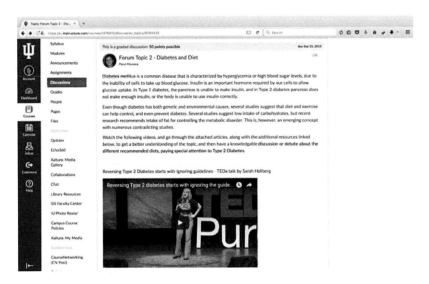

The discussion topic for the second forum of the course, for example, was "Diabetes and Diet" (Figure 2). The students were directed to watch two videos, including a TEDx talk discussing how Type 2 Diabetes starts by ignoring well-known guidelines about carbohydrate intake. Students were also provided scientific literature about dietary fats, carbohydrate restriction, obesity, and diabetes. The literature provided conflicting ideas. Students were asked to summarize what they understood, and express their opinion about effective diets for people with Type 2 Diabetes based on the information provided and their own research. Clear instructions were provided along with an evaluation rubric (Figure 3).

Figure 3. Sample of a rubric used for a discussion thread.

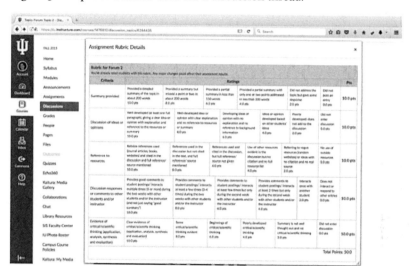

The rubric clearly defines the criteria on how the discussion posting will be evaluated. This includes points for the parts of the topic discussed and the quality of outside resources used (citations required). A detailed summary of the topic, well-developed ideas, and clear evidence of scientific thinking fetches maximum points. Students also receive points for commenting on other student posts. It is mandatory for them to post comments multiple times during the two weeks that the post is open. Bonus points are given to the post that generates the most comments and to the one that is most creative. Students are motivated to look for and post images, videos, or cartoons related to the discussion topic. Students often find images that lay out the scientific information in a clearer and simpler manner. Cartoons related to the topic generate fun comments (example in Figure 4). The discussion thus takes a lively turn. All students appreciate this sort of creativity. The variety of information embedded in posts keep students engaged in the conversation with minimal input from the instructor. Lastly, rubrics streamline the grading process and allow comments from the instructor. Students appreciate this quick feedback and some modify their behavior on subsequent discussions.

Figure 4. A screenshot of a discussion thread showing a cartoon posted by a student as a part of a post.

Such discussions help students gain a wider perspective on the area of study, because they get to look at other's points of view. More importantly, this helps incorporate student-student interaction, which is hard to achieve in any classroom. The timely interactions also create a sense of community among the online students. They go back and forth with comments that generate more ideas and foster critical thinking. Discussions are interactive platforms where information is shared and perspectives are respected.

CONCLUSION

The goal for any instructor is to create a high-quality learning environment for the students, whether the course is taught in a classroom, as a blended or flipped course, or completely online. An asynchronous learning environment provides many opportunities for engagement, and unlike face-to-face classes, can decide when engagement will take place. A good online course hinges upon appropriate course organization and design with useful resources, materials, and assignments that are evaluated in a timely fashion. Having students engaged is the key to all learning. Assignments based on real-world experiences and applications motivate them to learn. Labs and discussions ensure critical thinking and student engagement in online science courses. Clear instructions and expectations, along with creative facilitation and student interactions, foster learning in an online environment.

REFERENCES

Alisauskas, R. (2007). "The Love Triangle" forging links to students using digital technology to deliver content in microbiology courses. *Focus on Microbiology Education, 13*, 13–15.

Anderson, W. L., Mitchell, S. M., & Osgood, M. P. (2008). Gauging the gaps in student problem-solving skills: Assessment of individual and group use of problem-solving strategies using online discussions. *CBE-Life Sciences Education, 7*(2), 254–262.

Andresen, M. A. (2009). Asynchronous discussion forums: Success factors, outcomes, assessments, and limitations. *Educational Technology & Society, 12*(1), 249–257.

Armbruster, P., Patel, M., Johnson, E., & Weiss, M. (2009). Active learning and student-centered pedagogy improve student attitudes and performance in introductory biology. *CBE-Life Sciences Education, 8*(3), 203–213.

Bart, M. (2015). Flipped classroom survey highlights benefits and challenges. *Faculty Focus.* Magna Publications. Retrieved from http://www.facultyfocus.com/articles/blended-flipped-learning/flipped-classroom-survey-highlights-benefits-and-challenges/.

Bart, M. (2014). Blended and flipped: Exploring new models for effective teaching and learning. *Faculty Focus* (Special Report). Madison, WI: Magna Publications.

Bernard, R. M., Abrami, P. C., Lou, Y., Borokhovski, E., Wade, A., Wozney, L., Wallet, P. A., Fiset, M., & Huang, B. (2004). How does distance education compare with classroom instruction? A meta-analysis of the empirical literature. *Review of Educational Research, 74*(3), 379–439.

Chan, J. C. C., Hew, K. F., & Cheung, W. S. (2009). Asynchronous online discussion thread development: examining growth patterns and peer-facilitation techniques. *Journal of Computer Assisted Learning, 25*(5), 438–452.

Climent-Bellido, M. S., Martínez-Jiménez, P., Pontes-Pedrajas, A., & Polo, J. (2003). Learning in chemistry with virtual laboratories. *Journal of Chemical Education, 80*(3), 346.

Connell, G. L., Donovan, D. A., & Chambers, T. G. (2016). Increasing the use of student-centered pedagogies from moderate to high improves student learning and attitudes about biology. *CBE-Life Sciences Education, 15*(1), ar3.

DeBard, R., & Guidera, S. (2000). Adapting asynchronous communication to meet the seven principles of effective teaching. *Journal of Educational Technology Systems, 28*(3), 219–230.

Dell, C. A., Low, C., & Wilker, J. F. (2010). Comparing student achievement in online and face-to-face classes. *Journal of Online Learning and Teaching, 6*(1), 30.

Deslauriers, L., Schelew, E., & Wieman, C. (2011). Improved learning in a large-enrollment physics class. *Science, 332*(6031), 862–864.

Downing, K. F., & Holtz, J. K. (2008). *Online science learning: Best practices and technologies.* Hershey, NY: Information Science Publishing IGI Global.

Edelson, D. C. (2001). Learning-for-use: A framework for the design of technology-supported inquiry activities. *Journal of Research in Science Teaching, 38*(3), 355–385.

Finkelstein, N. D., Adams, W. K., Keller, C. J., Kohl, P. B., Perkins, K. K., Podolefsky, N. S., Reid, S., & LeMaster, R. (2005). When learning about the real world is better done virtually: A study of substituting computer simulations for laboratory equipment. *Physical Review Special Topics-Physics Education Research, 1*(1), 010103.

Ford, D. N., & McCormack, D. E. (2000). Effects of time scale focus on system understanding in decision support systems. *Simulation & Gaming, 31*(3), 309–330.

Freeman, S., Eddy, S. L., McDonough, M., Smith, M. K., Okoroafor, N., Jordt, H., & Wenderoth, M. P. (2014). Active learning increases student performance in science, engineering, and mathematics. *Proceedings of the National Academy of Sciences, 111*(23), 8410–8415.

Garrison, D. R. (2007). Online community of inquiry review: Social, cognitive, and teaching presence issues. *Journal of Asynchronous Learning Networks, 11*(1), 61–72.

Garrison, D. R., & Vaughan, N. D. (2008). *Blended learning in higher education: Framework, principles, and guidelines.* San Francisco, CA: Jossey-Bass John Wiley & Sons, Inc.

Gold, S. (2001). A constructivist approach to online training for online teachers. *Journal of Asynchronous Learning Networks, 5*(1), 35-57.

Hewitt, J. (2005). Toward an understanding of how threads die in asynchronous computer conferences. *The Journal of the Learning Sciences, 14*(4), 567-589.

Hrastinski, S. (2008). Asynchronous and synchronous e-learning. *Educause Quarterly, 31*(4), 51–55.

Huppert, J., Lomask, S. M., & Lazarowitz, R. (2002). Computer simulations in the high school: Students' cognitive stages, science process skills and academic achievement in microbiology. *International Journal of Science Education, 24*(8), 803–821.

Jeschofnig, L., & Jeschofnig, P. (2011). *Teaching lab science courses online: Resources for best practices, tools, and technology.* San Francisco, CA: Jossey-Bass John Wiley & Sons, Inc.

Kim, K., & Bonk, C. J. (2006). The future of online teaching and learning in higher education: The survey says... *Educause Quarterly, 29*(4), 22.

Klahr, D., Triona, L. M., & Williams, C. (2007). Hands on what? The relative effectiveness of physical versus virtual materials in an engineering design project by middle school children. *Journal of Research in Science Teaching, 44*(1), 183–203.

Knight, J. K., & Wood, W. B. (2005). Teaching more by lecturing less. *Cell Biology Education, 4*(4), 298–310.

Koehler, M. J., & Mishra, P. (2005). Teachers learning technology by design. *Journal of computing in teacher education, 21*(3), 94–102.

Kollöffel, B., & de Jong, T. (2013). Conceptual understanding of electrical circuits in secondary vocational engineering education: Combining traditional instruction with inquiry learning in a virtual lab. *Journal of Engineering Education, 102*(3), 375–393.

LaForge, C., You, Y., Alexander, R., & Sabine, N. (2015). Online program development as a growth strategy across diverse academic programs. *International Journal of Instructional Technology and Distance Learning, 12*(8), 25–39.

McDaniel, C. N., Lister, B. C., Hanna, M. H., & Roy, H. (2007). Increased learning observed in redesigned introductory biology course that employed web-enhanced, interactive pedagogy. *CBE-Life Sciences Education, 6*(3), 243–249.

Olympiou, G., & Zacharia, Z. C. (2012). Blending physical and virtual manipulatives: An effort to improve students' conceptual understanding through science laboratory experimentation. *Science Education, 96*(1), 21–47.

Pyatt, K., & Sims, R. (2012). Virtual and physical experimentation in inquiry-based science labs: Attitudes, performance and access. *Journal of Science Education and Technology, 21*(1), 133–147.

Rovai, A. P. (2007). Facilitating online discussions effectively. *The Internet and Higher Education, 10*(1), 77–88.

Ryan, M. D., & Reid, S. A. (2016). Impact of the flipped classroom on student performance and retention: a parallel controlled study in general chemistry. *Journal of Chemical Education, 93*(1), 13–23.

Stockwell, B. R., Stockwell, M. S., Cennamo, M., & Jiang, E. (2015). Blended learning improves science education. *Cell, 162*(5), 933–936.

Triona, L. M., & Klahr, D. (2003). Point and click or grab and heft: Comparing the influence of physical and virtual instructional materials on elementary school students' ability to design experiments. *Cognition and Instruction, 21*(2), 149–173.

Trundle, K. C., & Bell, R. L. (2010). The use of a computer simulation to promote conceptual change: A quasi-experimental study. *Computers & Education, 54*(4), 1078–1088.

van der Meij, J., & de Jong, T. (2006). Supporting students' learning with multiple representations in a dynamic simulation-based learning environment. *Learning and Instruction, 16*(3), 199–212.

Warren, L. L., & Holloman Jr, H. L. (2005). On-line instruction: Are the outcomes the same? *Journal of Instructional Psychology, 32*(2), 148–152.

Weber, J. M., & Lennon, R. (2007). Multi-course comparison of traditional versus web-based course delivery systems. *Journal of Educators Online, 4*(2), 1–19.

Wiesner, T. F., & Lan, W. (2004). Comparison of student learning in physical and simulated unit operations experiments. *Journal of Engineering Education, 93*(3), 195–204.

Zacharia, Z. C., & Constantinou, C. P. (2008). Comparing the influence of physical and virtual manipulatives in the context of the Physics by Inquiry curriculum: The case of undergraduate students' conceptual understanding of heat and temperature. *American Journal of Physics, 76*(4), 425–430.

Zacharia, Z. C., Olympiou, G., & Papaevripidou, M. (2008). Effects of experimenting with physical and virtual manipulatives on students' conceptual understanding in heat and temperature. *Journal of Research in Science Teaching, 45*(9), 1021–1035.

Zhu, E. (2006). Interaction and cognitive engagement: An analysis of four asynchronous online discussions. *Instructional Science, 34*(6), 451–480.

13

MATHEMATICS

Online Teaching and Learning in Mathematics

YOUNG HWAN YOU, PH.D.

JOSH BEAL, PH.D.

INTRODUCTION

With the rapid growth of Internet and computer-based technologies, the methodology of instruction in academia has broadened to include online education. As online education has gained momentum, many researchers have rushed to explore pedagogical approaches to instruction that offer the greatest opportunity for student success. In particular, research has shown that a pedagogy including social, cognitive, and teaching presence, is essential to proper instruction, and facilitates a robust learning experience.

The increase in demand for online mathematics courses at Indiana University East has generated a need for robust and systemized course design based on a proven pedagogical practice. In order to construct such a course design and class facilitation, we have adhered to the online educational framework developed by Garrison and Vaughn (2008). As alluded to above, Garrison and Vaughn suggest that online education should incorporate social presence, cognitive presence, and teaching presence. Social presence motivates a feeling of intimacy and togetherness (Shin, 2002). Cognitive presence is described as the level of critical thinking and inquiry beyond social presence (Bair & Bari, 2014). Teaching presence relates to the process of design, facilitation, and direction through the learning experience in order to realize desired learning outcomes (Garrison, Anderson, Archer, 2000). The goal of this chapter is to further discuss how this pedagogy aligns with so-called "best practices" for teaching mathematics online. We begin with a discussion of efficient course design and continue with a discussion of appropriate instructional tools relevant to upper class mathematics courses. Lastly, we include a discussion on interaction tools and assessment.

COURSE DESIGN

> "Teaching presence begins before the course commences as the teacher, acting as instructional designer, plans and prepares the course of studies, and it continues during the course, as the instructor facilitates the discourse and provides direct instruction when required" (Anderson, Rourk, Garrison, Archer, 2001).

It is worth iterating that teaching presence begins before the course commences. In fact, as an initial step before new course development, the instructor must identify the potential audience of students in order to tailor the design of the course appropriately. At Indiana University East, many students enrolled are non-traditional, part-time, working students, so courses have been designed with this in mind.

A high dropout rate for online classes has been well documented (e.g., Dietz-Uhler, Fisher, & Han, 2008), and the initial designs for upper level online mathematics courses at Indiana University East were not immune to this general problem. However, after careful consideration, the authors realized that a main catalyst for dropouts was due to a gap between the current course material, and an understanding of prerequisite material. Despite having technically acquired the necessary prerequisite credit to begin taking a course, many non-traditional students have not been in a classroom for years, so a more formal review of prerequisite material is essential to their success. Initial course designs did not address this issue, but today, upper level mathematics courses are designed to offer a quick but sufficient review of prerequisite topics. For example, to enroll in Differential Equations, students need to have completed the standard Calculus sequence. However, a sufficient portion of students enrolling in Differential Equations have not taken a Calculus course in years. Feedback from students in our early Differential Equations courses showed that many felt unconfident in their ability to apply past Calculus knowledge to the new material. To remedy this issue, we incorporated a Pre-calculus and Calculus Review during the first week of the course. Of course, the review does not offer a complete summary of Pre-Calculus and Calculus; it only offers a summary of those items, which the authors feel are requisite to begin the study of differential equations. The result of incorporating such review material has been an increase in retention and a decrease in dropout rate.

Along with identifying the potential audience before a course commences, the instructor must become familiar with the underlying learning management system. The learning management system (LMS) serves as a platform on which the course functions. It is here that an instructor will manage instructional and assessment tools. Through the LMS, the instructor should provide a simple, easily accessible learning environment, designed to satisfy requisite learning objectives. For example, Indiana University has adopted Canvas as its learning management system, and the following screen shots give a quick visual of the LMS's appearance for a particular course:

Figure 1

Figure 2

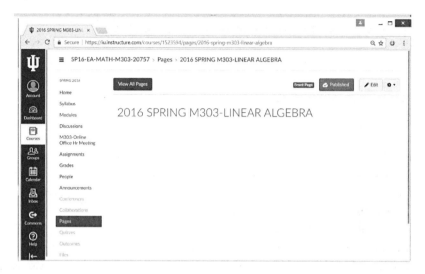

Figure 3

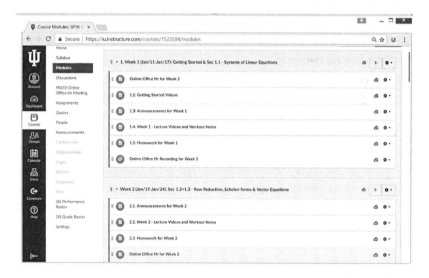

Figure 1 represents an unpublished/undeveloped course, while Figure 2 shows a course that is published and in working order. Notice the changes made in the left tool bar in Figure 2. The updated tool bar includes the minimal amount of tools necessary to the course, and omits several others that are not used. It is important not to inundate students with tools that are not essential to the course. Tools such as Modules, Syllabus, and Discussions are included in an order of importance and frequency of use (the Syllabus tab may not be used as often as Modules for example, but its level of importance dictates that it be positioned above Modules). Figure 3 shows an image of "Modules." One can see how the Module tool can streamline the material and add a level of linearity to the course. It is within "Modules" where the majority of the course functions, serving as the focal point for course notes, and other instructional tools.

MAIN INSTRUCTION TOOLS

Instructor Generated Video (IGV)

Next, in order to promote social, cognitive, and teaching presence in mathematics, a variety of tools should be used. Instructor-Generated Video (IGV), discussion forums, Modules, Wikis, and online office hours are examples of such tools. IGVs, discussion forums, and online office hours, are arguably the most important tools because they promote the greatest level of cognitive presence. This is especially true for upper-level mathematics courses.

Research has indicated that IGVs have a positive influence on student satisfaction and engagement (Draus, Curran, Trempus, 2014; Pan, Sen, Starret, Bonk, Rodgers, Tikoo, Powell, 2012). In particular, Borup, West, and Graham (2012) demonstrated that IGVs enhance social and teaching presence. Students and faculty alike find that IGVs help to diminish the physical gap that is characteristic of an online learning environment, and promote an atmosphere of unity and collaboration. Of course, to promote such an atmosphere of unity, an IGV must be created with careful consideration, not hastily thrown together.

There are generally two ways to create IGVs: 1) the instructor can record a lecture that is similar to a lecture given before a live audience, or 2) the instructor can record a written lecture that is recorded with screen and audio capturing software. We prefer option 2. Experience has shown that this option fosters social, teaching, and cognitive presence, as evidenced by the following evaluation:

> "I like watching his Lecture Videos because you could hear it in his voice how interested he was and it was infectious, and he

explained the material MUCH more clearly than the textbook did."
(Summer 2015, Young You, M313–Elementary Differential Equation
with Applications).

We should emphasize how an instructor's general level of interest in the material, specifically how this interest is conveyed, can increase social presence for the student. Instructors should record their lectures with a level of passion and zeal to increase social and teaching presence so that more students can end a lecture video feeling motivated and eager to learn more.

Before designing a more advanced online mathematics course such as Real Analysis or Differential Equations, the instructor should carefully consider the educational background and mathematical maturity of potential students as well as the level of difficulty of the course. Advanced courses usually include narrated videos created with PowerPoint, Latex (beamer), or other screen-capturing software. Depending on the course, the delivery method of lectures varies. Students enrolled in more rigorous proof-based mathematics courses need sufficient time to contemplate the important propositions and theorems of one section before moving on to the next, and it is clear that certain delivery methods are better suited to this type of learning process than others. It is natural then, to embrace a delivery method that is more traditional. For example, lecture notes from the videos are often written "live" and are available for download as a PDF file. By "live," we mean that the notes become visible as the instructor progresses through the lecture. This method of presentation is often preferred because it mimics the traditional lecture; notes are not simply read by the instructor, they are written and discussed gradually. On the other hand, some instructors prefer to use "completed" lecture notes while recording to minimize the chance of including significant typos and other errors within the video. The following figure shows a screen shot of a portion of a live lecture video.

Figure 4. Screen shot of IGV

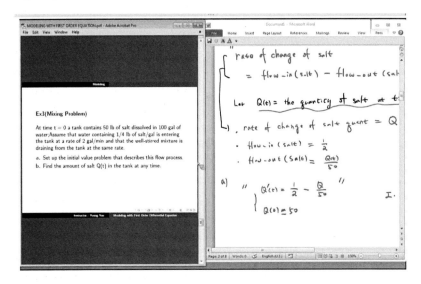

Although there may exist some differences among instructors when it comes to creating IGVs, many still implement similar technologies throughout IGV construction. Typically, these technologies include Adobe Connect, Microsoft Word, OneNote, and a tablet or laptop with a digitizer pen. Adobe Connect is a web conferencing tool that can be used to create lectures and hold virtual office hours. Creating meetings with Adobe Connect is straightforward, and links can be mailed from instructors to students, making it simple for students to meet with the instructor. The creation of video lectures involves a combination of the aforementioned tools. Word and/or OneNote documents are used in lectures to present material and work out example problems. In each case, the instructor will be recorded while giving verbal and written explanations of the respective document. It is essential that IGVs include both a hand-written and verbal explanation because their combination creates a learning atmosphere that is similar to a traditional face-to-face lecture. Handwritten notes created with OneNote are easily partitioned into notebooks, sections, and pages, making it easy for the instructor and student to stay organized. OneNote is also equipped with a feature that makes exporting notebooks, sections, or pages as PDF files very simple. Instructors should also be cognizant of the length of video lectures. Per student evaluations, we have found that lecture videos around 15 minutes maintain student engagement and concentration. Students have reported a level of disengagement for videos exceeding this length.

Like other screen/audio capturing software, Adobe Connect has the ability to record the instructor's voice and screen simultaneously. This is crucial for lectures requiring the demonstration of other software or movement through websites. For example, spreadsheets are used extensively in a Numerical Methods course, so it is necessary for an instructor to record demonstrations involving software like Microsoft Excel. In an upper-level Math Finance course, the instructor may wish to demonstrate workable aspects of an online brokerage, or navigate through financial websites during a recording. Other courses routinely use graphing calculators, requiring an instructor to record demonstrations with a virtual calculator.

On the other hand, Adobe Connect requires an Internet connection, which may lead to obvious problems if the connection is weak. As a way around this potential problem, many instructors choose instead to use screen/audio capturing software that does not require Internet connection (e.g., NCH software). Many of these "Internet-independent" software packages also include tools for editing and combining videos, which clearly help facilitate IGV creation. Any experienced online video creator will agree that it is impossible to control for every type of interruption and interference that may emerge during video creation. For this reason, we recommend video and audio recording software that can be easily paused and edited.

IGVs created in this way give students the opportunity to watch videos according to their own schedules and work at their own pace. This asynchronous aspect of online learning is often what students find most appealing. Throughout an IGV, homework problems are assigned that are similar to other problems demonstrated throughout the lecture. This clearly promotes engagement and understanding.

Faculty and students consistently report a strong impact IGVs have toward a successful completion of the course. In particular, evaluations often include statements about the importance of being able to hear and see the instructor, and how this type of virtual presence, cultivates a feeling of authentic interaction with the instructor. This clearly shows that IGVs raise social presence as well as cognitive presence.

Although students have the freedom to work through IGVs at their own pace and by their own respective clocks, it is still important for the instructor to design a course that will maintain a level of synchrony, and help to keep students on task. This can be achieved by implementing "modules" within the course design. Instructors should consider dividing the course into several sections or modules in order to break down the course into manageable partitions. In our experience, creating a module for each week in the semester/quarter is not only natural, but it partitions the course in the most manageable way as well. Within a (weekly) module, students will find a collection of videos and notes pertaining to that week's material, as well as a homework assignment. Students are free to review the video lectures and notes at their leisure, but homework assignments for that week's module will be submitted by a fixed date. The fixed deadline helps to keep students on task and up to date with current modules. At any fixed date in the semester/quarter, all previously covered course material should be available to students. On the other hand, instructors should be cautious when considering the availability of future modules (course material). In our opinion, instructors should restrict access to modules too far in the future in order to maintain a level of synchrony. We have found that allowing access to modules one week beyond the current week's module does not disrupt the level of synchrony in the class, and provides an opportunity for students to work ahead.

INTERACTION TOOLS

In order to promote social, cognitive, and teaching presence, the instructor must carefully consider methods of interaction (student to student, student to instructor) and the facilitation of these methods. The most apparent difference between online and face-to-face courses is the level of student to student interaction and student to instructor interaction. In a traditional face-to-face course, students have a direct, synchronous way of interaction with the instructor and each other. This is not the case for courses that are taught online, hence interaction must be motivated by other means. The most popular form of interaction in online courses is facilitated by the implementation of asynchronous threaded discussion boards (Hewitt, 2005). Moreover, Al-Shalchi (2009) emphasized that discussions were an essential cognitive component in online education. Many articles highlight the benefits of such asynchronous interaction (Cavana, 2009; Gold, 2001; Morse, 2003), but other methods for promoting interaction are still used, and may vary depending on course material. Upper-level mathematics courses typically implement both synchronous and asynchronous methods of interaction.

It is important in an upper level mathematics course, especially in a so-called "proof-based" mathematics course, for students to collaborate and share ideas. The style of problems that students see in an upper-level mathematics course are much different from those they are familiar with from Calculus, and for students to become more comfortable with proof-based problems, it is advantageous to discuss with their peers the proof techniques that will lead to the solution. In addition, students may be reluctant to seek help from their instructor at first; they may only feel comfortable seeking advice and guidance from their colleagues. It is vital, therefore, that instructors help facilitate instructor to student interaction as well as student-to-student interaction.

In order to simulate student-to-student interaction (e.g., a study group), instructors may partition the class into small groups (5 to 10 students per group). Partitioning the class into groups is particularly advantageous for larger classes because one large discussion forum tends to get convoluted, as each student adds to different threads. A general discussion may still be implemented for all students to communicate with each other. It should also be noted that group settings may be adjusted so that students may view the discussion posts of differing groups, so that collaboration among groups may be possible. However, this feature should be blocked for group assigned discussions.

Allocating students into groups creates a team-spirit mentality, and raises social and cognitive presence. Within their groups, students can feel at ease to discuss a number of topics with their peers, free from any pressure by the instructor.

It is usually beneficial to categorize the discussion boards into general and off-topic discussion, review discussion, and weekly group discussion. The general and off-topic discussion board is available to all students, and offers a platform for introductions, etc. The review discussion board, like the general and off-topic board, is available to all students, but the topics under this board are more relevant to prerequisite material (e.g., Calculus material may be discussed in the review discussion board of a Differential Equations course).

Weekly group discussion boards are assigned to each group. Group members will discuss course content within the group as assigned by the instructor. It is recommended that course content for the weekly discussion boards correspond to weekly modules so that a level of synchrony can be maintained. As mentioned above, features that allow for cross collaboration among groups may be turned on in certain circumstances, but may also be turned off in instances where group members must collaborate strictly within their group. For example, on assigned group projects, group members should not be allowed to collaborate outside their group.

The general and off-topic discussion board serves as an excellent platform for students to introduce themselves and initialize social contact with one another. It is essential to begin an online course by encouraging students to engage with one another, and the discussion board is perfect facilitator of this engagement. As mentioned above, student-to-student interaction contributes immensely to success in an upper-level mathematics course, and the general discussion boards do well at initializing this interaction. It is also worth noting that many non-traditional students offer a level of robustness to the general board through posts detailing their diverse backgrounds and experiences.

Students discuss course content and assignments through both review and weekly group discussion boards. Naturally, the review boards are typically reserved for review material, but may still serve as a platform for discussing current material. Moreover, weekly assignments posted for groups are only accessible to members within the group, promoting an environment for a smaller intensive discussion, while simultaneously improving cognitive presence.

Although discussion forums should serve as a platform for student interaction, it is important that the instructor monitor and participate in them as well. Moreover, the instructor may need to facilitate discussion in order to motivate students to engage with one another. Instructors can encourage this engagement by posting leading questions at the beginning of each week. It has been observed that students tend to respond more to leading questions by the instructor than other postings. For example, in an online Real Analysis class, students may be motivated to contribute their thoughts to leading questions directly relatable to the material such as "*provide an example of a non-convergent sequence that has a convergent subsequence.*" On the other hand, the instructor may pose leading questions that are indirectly related to the material such as "*can you formulate your own conjecture regarding open, closed, and/or compact sets?*" These types of questions, although different in terms of how they relate to the material, are similar in that they promote discussion and collaboration among the students.

On the other hand, within the group discussion forums, the instructor should be less participatory. It is important that the instructor still monitor the group boards, but their presence should be limited. The group forums are designed purely for student-to-student interaction, and the instructor should view these boards as an observer. It is also within group forums and through group projects that students exchange personal contact information (e.g., phone numbers) and develop a deeper academic relationship with one another.

Instructors are advised to consider certain discussion boards as part of overall assessment as well. In particular, instructors should set up grading rubrics for group discussion boards, and determine appropriate assessment strategies for student posts. Our experience has shown that students should contribute at least five substantial posts per week to the group discussion boards. Of course a student's definition of "substantial" may differ from an instructor's definition of substantial, so the notion of "substantial post" should be defined in the syllabus. We also recommend providing examples of substantial posts and "non-substantial" posts within the syllabus to make this notion clearer.

Grading discussion posts can be a bit tedious, especially if the instructor does not wish to close past discussion boards (i.e., discussion boards from previous weeks). In order to manage this tedium, it is advised that instructors restrict accessibility to past group discussion boards. Depending on the learning management system, an instructor may be able to restrict "written" accessibility, but allow "readable" accessibility. In this way, students would still be able to read posts, but unable to write new posts (which is an accessibility feature clearly needed to reduce the tedium of grading posts).

Lastly, the instructor should monitor all discussion boards, and help to guide the students in the correct direction in the event that a post contains misleading or incorrect information. This seems a simple enough task, but it requires a bit of finesse on the part of the instructor. Once an instructor recognizes a post contains an error, it is *not* advised that the instructor make an immediate complete correction. An immediate and complete correction by the instructor eliminates the opportunity for students to identify the error and make corrections. Therefore, it is advised that the instructor simply bring attention to the post, hinting at the possibility of an error. In this way, the instructor is adding a *partial* correction to the error, and providing the students an opportunity to include a complete correction. On the other hand, one bad apple spoils the bunch, and if subtle errors within a discussion forum are allowed to linger too long, they can lead to confusion and hinder a general understanding of the material. For this reason, instructors should also not wait too long to add partial corrections or even complete corrections to errors in posts.

The above-mentioned methods of asynchronous interaction are undoubtedly a useful tool for enhancing online education, but their main purpose is to promote student-to-student interaction. We should iterate that student-to-student interaction is essential for bridging the gap between lower-level mathematics and upper-level mathematics courses. For that reason, instructors are encouraged to implement a variety of asynchronous interaction tools. For example, in an effort to further promote student-to-student interaction, the instructor may encourage students to form virtual study groups, where meetings may take place via Skype. Students consistently provide positive feedback for these study groups, with a common point being that these groups simulate face-to-face study groups, and operate independently of the instructor.

Student to instructor interaction should also be incorporated in order to raise teaching presence and promote a level of academic intimacy between students and instructors. In order to cultivate this interaction, instructors hold synchronous, biweekly virtual office hours via Adobe Connect. Instructors have also had success implementing an office hour schedule that is more fluid and determined by appointments. This type of fluidity works especially well for students with very complicated schedules who are unable to attend regularly scheduled office hours. Needless to say, the instructor must expand their level of availability to accommodate certain students. This level of instructor availability may seem unreasonable for obvious reasons, but experience has shown that it does not lead to an overload of individual appointments.

Platforms like Adobe Connect have made it possible for students and instructors to communicate face-to-face, share screens, swap documents, and record meetings. Chat windows are available for students to communicate with both the instructor and other students, ask questions, add links to relevant sites, etc. Audio options are also available for students, with microphone toggles that students can click on or off. However, large groups of students speaking at once may add confusion to the meeting, so the chat window is typically considered the best option for student interaction. On the other hand, it is difficult for students to input mathematical symbols into the chat box, so instructors encourage students to email questions with large amounts of mathematical text prior to meetings. Of course in almost all meetings, students will want to see problems or explanations worked out in real time. For this reason, instructors are encouraged to use document (Ziggi) cameras or laptop computers that also function as tablets in order to record anything the instructor wishes to write down in real time. The utility of a laptop with tablet option should be emphasized because documents created with a stylus pen can be saved and exported as PDF files.

When scheduling office hours, the instructor should keep in mind the diverse demographics of their students. That is, it is imperative that the instructor remains cognizant of the fact that many online students are non-traditional, and that their schedules may be quite busy during an average business day. For this reason, instructors should consider scheduling office hours during the evening. Some initial empirical evidence has shown that the majority of students are usually available for office hours during the evening (no earlier than 7:00 pm EST). In an online setting, finding appropriate times to schedule office hours can be quite difficult, and it may be necessary to schedule multiple hours in order to accommodate students in different time zones. Instructors are encouraged to facilitate a discussion with their students regarding possible office hour times. Feedback from these discussions helps to identify ideal times to meet.

Office hours sessions are recorded and uploaded to the course website, and links to the recorded video are created for easy access. To encourage participation in office hours, instructors should require students to attend at least four office-hour sessions per semester. Otherwise, student participation in office hours will be low, with the majority of students opting to watch the recorded video, instead of attending the office hour. It should also be noted that many students will not attend non-obligatory office hours because they have simply never attended before, and are unfamiliar with the logistics behind accessing the office hour. An attendance grade for office hours motivates students to overcome this unfamiliarity and engage in a beneficial form of interaction. On the other hand, it may be argued that the notion of required office hours is somewhat inconsistent with the general spirit of online education because it reduces flexibility and forces students in many different time zones to be available for an hour that may be inconvenient. This inconsistency can be removed however, through alternative methods that aim to accommodate students with time-zone issues or conflicting schedules. For example, instructors may conduct phone interviews or assign summaries of the recorded virtual office hour.

For traditional face-to-face classes, set office hours are available to any student from any class the instructor is teaching. That is, office hours for separate courses are not scheduled separately, and students from different courses may meet during a regularly scheduled office hours. This type of scheduling is also appropriate in the online setting, but may require some management by the instructor. Students from several different online courses trying to contribute in one chat room may cause some confusion. In our experience, it can be difficult to manage a chat room of students contributing on topics such as Differential Equations, Abstract Algebra, and Numerical Methods all at once! For this reason, an instructor may wish to schedule separate office hours for separate courses in the online setting.

Experience has also shown that students tend to dislike synchronous components of an online course (e.g., office hours) initially, but towards the end of the course, their attitudes change. For example, many course evaluations illuminate a general contempt for office hours initially, but then show a more favorable view towards the end of the course. Students typically comment that the synchronous style of online office hours helps to clarify general problems with the material and homework, and increases a feeling of togetherness (undoubtedly a perfect example of social presence). Kanuka & Garrison (2004) contend that "If online discourse is to be effective, then instructors must take an active role to assist, or guide, the discussions." But can managing discussion forums and synchronous online office hours become too much of a burden for the instructor? Many educators have asked how facilitating these interaction tools will add to the workload of an instructor.

In general, online instructions requires more time from an instructor than a traditional face-to-face course (Lindsay et al., 2009), but in very large online classes, the increase in workload from monitoring discussion boards and holding synchronous office hours, may become overbearing, and other means of facilitating these interaction tools should be considered. For example, in large classes (60–70 students), the use of a "discussion forums moderator" has proven to be very helpful. Needless to say, moderators should have a good understanding of the course material, and should be vetted to ensure their knowledge is sufficient for making necessary corrections to posts that include errors. Diligent moderators can greatly reduce the workload due to the implementation of interaction tools. Cavanaugh (2006) reported that the time amount of teaching online is nearly double per student time.

ASSESSMENT

Another obvious difference between traditional in class instruction and online instruction is the method behind assessment. In the traditional classroom, exams are administered and proctored by the instructor. Quizzes and other forms of assessment can be directly monitored by the instructor, minimizing the opportunity for academic misconduct. However, in an online class, this type of physical presence is impossible, so other methods must be implemented to maintain the integrity of assessments. For example, online calculus exams can be taken in the presence of a qualified proctor. These proctors are usually affiliated with an academic institution within a reasonable proximity of the student. In particular, the department of mathematics at Indiana University East provided the guideline for a potential proctor and go through an approval process for the proctor. Testing centers are also available at Indiana University East to cater to local students.

For assessments that do not require proctoring, there are sufficient resources available through the learning management system. Through the learning management system, assignments can be created, and restrictions can be imposed via a robust list of assignment options (time limits, availability windows, etc.). When imposing certain restrictions on assignments, instructors should be cognizant of the following: 1) upload and download times of assignment documents, 2) multiple submission options, 3) expected time for completion of assignment, and 4) general computer/Internet issues. Non-proctored assignments should be available for at least twenty-four hours. That is, the availability window should cover a sufficient interval of time so that students can download the assignment, formulate solutions, and re-upload to the learning management system. A twenty-four hour period also ensures that students covering a wide range of time zones, may have the same access to assignments.

Our goal of this chapter has been to describe those functions which raise social, cognitive, and teaching presence, in order to outline best practices in teaching mathematics online. We have attempted to categorize these functions in terms of *course design, instructional tools, interaction,* and *assessment.* In order to effect these best practices, Indiana University East has implemented *Canvas* as a Learning Management System. One learning system, however, should not dictate that all course design be uniform. It is our opinion that course design is dependent on the discipline. In an online mathematics course, the instructor should consider designing an integrated and easy, accessible course layout. Students should feel at ease with the layout after one week. In this way, the process of design, facilitation, and guidance through the course will satisfy the desired learning outcomes, and improve teaching presence.

CONCLUSION

Overall, we feel that significant differences between face-to-face and online instruction are a function of social, cognitive, and teaching presence, and that the best approach to designing an online mathematics course, will raise each type of presence. Social presence motivates a feeling of intimacy and togetherness, and can be raised by including group and general discussion forums within the course design. Cognitive presence, described as the level of inquiry and critical thinking beyond social presence, can be raised through the implementation of Instructor Generated Videos (IGVs). Teaching presence, related to the process of design, facilitation, and direction through the learning experience in order to realize desired learning outcomes, can be raised through the design and implementation of IGVs, virtual office hours, and a good understanding of the learning management system. In our opinion, this type of pedagogical approach should be included within the sphere of best practices for teaching mathematics online, and as evidenced by the following quote from an evaluation, we feel we are working in the right direction:

"The online office hours, combined with the online lectures, pushes this online course to a near on-campus level. The presentation of the material was excellent. I really did not see much difference between the online course and on-site courses that I have taken. Adobe Connect was a good choice because it gives a distance learner the ability to see how the instructor's mind is working. It really inspires confidence."

REFERENCES

Al-Shalchi, O. N. (2009). The effectiveness and development of online discussions. *MERLOT Journal of Online Learning and Teaching, 5*(1), 104–108.

Anderson, T., Rourke, L., Garrison, D. R., & Archer, W. (2001). Assessing teaching presence in a computer conferencing context. *Journal of Asynchronous Learning Networks, 5*(2), 1–17.

Bair, D. E., & Bair, M. A., Ph.D. (2011). Paradoxes of online teaching. *International Journal for the Scholarship of Teaching and Learning, 5*(2), Article 10.

Borup, J., West, R. E., & Graham, C. R. (2012). Improving online social presence through asynchronous video. *The Internet and Higher Education, 15*(3), 195–203. http://dx.doi. org/10.1016/j.iheduc.2011.11.001

Cavana, M. L .P. (2009). Closing the circle: From Dewey to Web 2.0. In C. R. Payne (Ed.), *Information technology and constructivism in higher education: Progressive learning frameworks* (pp. 1–13). Hershey, PA. http://dx.doi.org/10.4018/978-1-60566-654-9.ch001

Cavanaugh, J. (2006). Comparing online time to offline time: The shocking truth. *Distance Education Report, 10*(9), 1–6.

Dietz-Uhler, B., Fisher, A., & Han, A. (2008). Designing online courses to promote student retention. *Journal of Educational Technology Systems, 36*(1), 105–112.

Draus, P. J., Curran, M. J. & Trempus, M.S. (2014). The influence of instructor-generated video content on student satisfaction with and engagement in asynchronous online classes. *MERLOT Journal of Online Learning and Teaching, 10*(2), 240–254. http://jolt.merlot.org/vol10no2/draus_0614.pdf

Garrison, D. R., Anderson, T., & Archer, W. (2000). Critical inquiry in a text-based environment: Computer conferencing in higher education. *The Internet and Higher Education, 2*(2–3), 87–105.

Garrison, D. R., & Vaughn, N. D (2008). *Blended learning in higher education: Framework, principles, and guidelines.* San Francisco, CA: Jossey-Bass Publishers.

Gold, S. (2001). A constructivist approach to online training for online teachers. *Journal of Asynchronous Learning Networks, 5*(1), 35–37.

Hewitt, J. (2005). Toward an understanding of how threads die in asynchronous computer conferences. *The Journal of the Learning Sciences, 14*(4), 567–589. http://dx.doi.org/10.1207/s15327809jls1404_4

Kanuka, H. & Garrison, D. R. (2004). Cognitive presence in online learning. *Journal of Computing in Higher Education, 15*(2), 21–39.

LaForge, C., You, Y., Alexander, R., & Sabine, N. (2015). Online program development as a growth strategy across diverse academic programs. *International Journal of Instructional Technology and Distance Learning, 12*(8), 25–40.

Lindsay, G. M., Jeffrey, J., & Singh, M. (2009). Paradox of a graduate human science curriculum experienced online: A faculty perspective. *Journal of Continuing Education in Nursing, 40*(4), 181–186.

Morse, K. (2003). Does one size fit all? Exploring asynchronous learning in a multicultural environment. *Journal of Asynchronous Learning Networks, 7*(1), 37–55.

Shin, N. (2002). Beyond interaction: The relational construct of transactional presence. *Open Learning, 17*(2), 121–137. http://dx.doi.org/10.1080/0268051022014688 7.

PART THREE • PROFESSIONAL PROGRAMS

14

EDUCATION

Building Online Learning Communities on the Foundation of Teacher Presence

JAMIE BUFFINGTON-ADAMS, PH.D.

DENICE HONAKER, ED.D.

JERRY WILDE, PH.D.

INTRODUCTION

While many have embraced online education as a means for reaching a larger and more diverse student population, for offering platforms through which instruction might be more easily individualized, or for providing both instructors and students with greater convenience, some who have chosen education as a primary pursuit have approached online education with reticence if not outright resistance. From early hopes that children might someday learn in classrooms filled with television screens to futuristic conceptions of artificial intelligence, what educators often fear is not the technology itself but the loss of human connection. Teaching requires a human connection between the teacher and the students, and, to some, the notion that this kind of human connection could be achieved in an online environment is ridiculous and stands in opposition to their most foundational beliefs about learning.

Let us be clear. When we refer to the human connection necessary for learning, we are not talking about mere interaction or collaboration. While those are of course necessary, as educators firmly rooted in sociocultural orientations to our work, our conception of human connection includes the social and emotional facets which elevate interaction and collaboration to develop community.

While a rich history of research exists which illustrates how socioeconomics, race, and other individual or family characteristics are the strongest overall predictors of student success, research has also repeatedly demonstrated that the number one *school-based* influence on a student's development is his or her teacher (Tella, 2008; Ferguson, 1991, 1998; Goldhaber, 2002; Sanders, 1998, 2000). Furthermore, research also indicates that the most effective teachers are not only experts in content but experts in child development, including working with children to build supportive, inclusive, collaborative, and democratic classroom communities (Chaudhry & Arif, 2012; McGarity & Butts, 1984). Therefore, when we think of the classroom as a community, we must also understand that the development of community hinges upon the individual who holds the most power or potential to effect change within the smaller context of the classroom—the teacher. If there is truth to the contention that relationships are an important, or even essential, part of the learning process, then it could be argued that teachers who are effective at building community are providing their students with more productive learning environments. It is our contention that building learning communities and strengthening pedagogical relationships should be a fundamental goal of all educational endeavors whether they take place in elementary face-to-face classrooms or post-secondary online courses.

LITERATURE REVIEW

The concept of a community of inquiry (CoI) was coined as a means of describing interactions that take place within an online class or, in this context, a community of online learners. Rubin and Fernandes (2013) report "online classes are more successful in supporting deep learning when they are characterized by a community of inquiry" (p. 125). According to the CoI view, "Deep and meaningful learning...takes place in a community of inquiry composed of instructors and learners as the key participants in the educational process. The model assumes that in this community, learning occurs through the interaction of three core components: cognitive presence, teaching presence, and social presence" (Rourke et al., 1999, p. 51–52). These three factors attributed to CoI will be examined independently.

Social presence refers to the strength of the relationships and emotional connection among the members of the class. The environment has to be built on trust and provide a safe place for students to take risks. Researchers Garrison and Arbaugh (2007) and Garrison, Anderson and Archer (2010) have identified three elements with regard to social presence: 1) identifying with a learning community, 2) communicating openly in a trusting environment, and 3) developing interpersonal relationships. Of course the genesis of much of the research on social presence dates back to John Dewey who wrote extensively about this topic. One of the cardinal tenets of Dewey's work was that interpersonal relationships are significant in the learning process (Dewey, 1933).

Cognitive presence refers to the ability of students to create meaning through extended communication in the learning community (Garrison, Anderson, & Archer, 2000). It reflects the extent to which students engage in the inquiry process of 1) addressing the problems presented, 2) exploring the concepts and issues that underlie the problems, 3) identify solutions after evaluating pertinent information, and 4) evaluating those solutions and considering further applications (Garrison, Anderson, and Archer, 2001).

Of the three tenets of Community of Inquiry, (social, cognitive, and teaching presence) the most significant for the purposes of this chapter is the latter. Teaching presence in a face-to-face classroom is easily identifiable and presented each time the class meets. Specific teacher behaviors which constitute face-to-face teacher presence have been "identified that show promising relationships to desirable student performance," including using student ideas and contributions, questioning, probing, the interplay of immediate feedback, and the display of teacher affect. (Borich, 2014; Borich, 2008a; Brophy, 2002; Brophy & Good, 1986). However, many of these key behaviors seemingly rely upon the spontaneity of a face-to-face environment, making them challenging to implement in an online learning environment and further making teaching presence in an online context difficult to define but perhaps even more important for the success of the class.

Teaching presence can be thought of as the extent to which the course instructor designs learning experiences, guides and directs student work, and facilitates interaction within the online environment to support learning

(Anderson et al., 2001; Garrison & Arbaugh, 2007; Shea & Bidjerano, 2009; Shea & Bidjerano, 2009b; Rovai, 2007). However, Shea, Swan et al. (2005) investigated the concept of teacher presence and found that 70% of the variance in their factor analysis was accounted for by 1) instructional design and organization and 2) directed facilitation. The authors went on to say, "These results suggest that the indicators identified in the Community of Inquiry Model that are meant to reflect direct instruction do not appear to reliably reveal a latent component of a teaching presence construct" (p. 55).

Shea, Swan et al. (2005) went on to suggest that effective instructional design and the skilled facilitation of discourse have a large positive effect on: 1) student satisfaction, 2) students' sense of being connected to their instructor, and 3) students' perceptions of being supported by their instructor and fellow students. Rovia (2002) reported that an association exists between teacher behaviors and the development of virtual learning communities in online courses. Shea et al. (2003) found significant differences in perceived learning between college students reporting varying levels of interaction with their instructors. Students who reported high levels of interaction with their instructors also reported higher levels of learning from them. Thus, instructional design, discourse facilitation, connectedness, and teacher-student interactions are clearly worthy of additional research related to teacher presence in online courses.

VYGOTSKY'S SOCIAL COGNITIVE LEARNING THEORY, SOCIOCULTURAL THEORY, AND OUR CONCEPTUAL FRAMEWORK

Many theorists have stressed the importance of community in the learning environment. Lev Vygotsky, the famous Russian learning theorist, went so far as to say knowledge is never constructed in isolation. Vygotsky believed that all knowledge is co-constructed because learning always involves more than one person (Vygotsky, 1978). In Vygotsky's theory, learning always happens in the presence or with the assistance of a more knowledgeable other and is always profoundly impacted by one's historical, institutional, and cultural contexts. Of course Vygotsky's work did not include the possibility of online education, but his theory is still relevant when we recognize that virtual learning spaces still rely upon the presence of others and exist in particular historical, institutional, and cultural contexts.

The prevailing theories of Vygotsky's time dichotomized learning and development viewing one as an external and the other as an internal process. Vygotsky (1978) created a much richer framework, which examined their unity and interdependence. He criticized Piaget's theory, in which "maturation is viewed as a precondition of learning but never the result of it" (p. 80). Vygotsky wrote "learning awakens a variety of internal developmental processes that are able to operate only when the child is interacting with people in his environment and in cooperation with his peers. Learning is not development; however, properly organized learning results in mental development and sets in motion a variety of developmental processes that would be impossible apart from learning. Thus learning is a necessary and universal aspect of the process of developing culturally organized, specifically human, psychological functions." (p. 90) Simply stated, Vygotsky believed learning activities profoundly impacted development.

His best known theory is the concept of the zone of proximal development (ZPD), which he defined as "...the distance between the actual developmental level as determined through independent problem solving and the level of potential development as determined through problem solving under adult guidance or in collaboration with more capable peers" (p. 86). Modern day sociocultural theorists have expanded the ZPD to include concepts such as *interactivity* (Chang-Wells & Wells, 1993), *contextualization* (John-Steiner, Panofsky, & Smith, 1994), and the result of the *learners' participation in a community of practice* (Rogoff, 1994).

Vygotsky believed that teachers should create learning environments that maximize students' ability to interact with each other through discussion, collaboration, and feedback.

Sociocultural theory stems largely from the work of Lev Vygotsky. Primarily utilized in the fields of psychology, sociology, and education, sociocultural theory attends to the notion that not only does learning not happen in isolation, but each human's development occurs within specific historical and cultural contexts which have a profound impact on the individual's identity formation and knowledge construction.

To teach from a sociocultural perspective is to acknowledge that each student brings with him or her into the classroom particular bodies of knowledge and ways of being and that none of these is greater or lesser than another. To teach from a sociocultural perspective is to approach students holistically and to recognize that one's social, emotional, physical, and spiritual life and well-being should not, and in truth cannot, be separated from one's intellectual growth and development. To teach from a sociocultural perspective, one must attend to human connections and relationships.

The School of Education at Indiana University East has long operated from a sociocultural perspective articulated in our conceptual framework and what we have lovingly dubbed "the SOE themes." Our conceptual framework holds that an effective teacher is a change agent who keeps the learner at the heart of the classroom by being a global citizen, reflective scholar, and instructional leader.

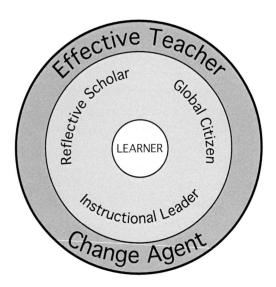

As global citizens, we recognize the value and necessity of multiple perspectives and challenge our students as well as ourselves to purposely interrogate biases, to think critically about global issues, and to seek to change the future. Global citizenry is firmly rooted in a sociocultural perspective which recognizes and values the rich collective of knowledge and perspectives present in any learning environment as well as how the presence of those varied perspectives provides opportunities for learning from one another.

Instructional leadership requires one to be a keen and critical observer who can transform observations into action. Planning and implementing a well-suited curriculum is at the heart of effective instructional leadership. Doing so well always requires knowing one's students. Here again, strands of sociocultural theory run through the School of Education's conceptual framework. To know one's students does not mean to merely know their latest standardized test scores but to know their learning styles and intelligences, their strengths and weaknesses, their backgrounds and communities and to respond to this knowledge by creating a learning environment which capitalizes on what is rich while addressing those areas in which students' demonstrate the greatest need. In short, it means to recognize students as whole and complex learners coming from specific cultural contexts and to use that knowledge to design learning experiences in which that knowledge is not a deficit but an asset.

Lastly, effective educators must be reflective scholars. In order to practice global citizenship and instructional leadership, educators must be capable of examining their roles within the classroom as well as their own practices in order to move themselves forward through a commitment to lifelong learning. So too, working from a sociocultural perspective requires one to conceptualize his/her role as a teacher in broad terms. Reflection should not be limited to one's performance in the classroom but to one's positionality within and work in or for the broader community. Again, our focus is not on isolated knowledge construction but upon reflective practice in light of and in response to one's historical, institutional, and cultural contexts or, in short, to one's community.

BUILDING COMMUNITY THROUGH STRONG INSTRUCTOR PRESENCE

If the ability to develop community in virtual learning spaces hinges upon the strength of an instructor's presence, then ensuring one can construct a clear and consistent presence across the virtual learning space becomes the first concern in designing online learning experiences. In our experiences, the following collection of practices have not only ensured clear and consistent instructor presence but have fostered open communication between instructors and students and hence also fostered the development of community in the virtual classroom.

ORGANIZED COURSES

Actions speak louder than words, or so the old adage goes. In virtual spaces, strong organization of course content communicates volumes to students about the instructor behind the scenes before the instructor him/herself offers official communication. A lack of clear or strong organization can leave students questioning not only what is required of them but whether the instructor knows what he/she is doing or, perhaps worse, whether they care about the course they are teaching. Conversely, a clearly organized course is evidence that an instructor has invested time in presenting course materials, activities, and spaces in logical and accessible fashions.

In our courses, this entails a number of core practices. Though it sounds overly simplistic, we begin by utilizing spaces earmarked for items like the course syllabus or assignment details for housing those integral pieces of course information. While additional electronic copies for downloading may also be stored in areas of courses designated for file storage, each compartment of our online courses contains the information which its title indicates it ought. In addition to ensuring that things are placed appropriately, extraneous tools that students do not need for a particular course are removed or made inactive whenever possible, and tools are rearranged in course menus such that those which will be used most frequently appear at the top. These practices help clarify which areas of the learning management system will be necessary as well as where students might expect to spend the most time or where they might look first for course information.

In terms of organizing course content itself, we rely on modules to group readings, multimedia, assignments, and other supplementary materials into units of study which address specific topics, themes, or essential questions. In one of our courses, each of these modules begins with an introductory page, which provides an overview of the unit via: a list of unit learning objectives; a table detailing weekly readings or viewings as well as assignments with links to each when possible; and a chart indicating which teacher preparation standards, university learning outcomes, and school of education themes the unit meets. In another instructor's courses, each module begins with a "start here" page, which gives a brief overview of the content and overarching questions to be addressed in the module as well as a "check list" for the readings and assignments included in the module. Within this introduction, the instructor includes a podcast or video of him/herself in which he/she attends to common misconceptions, addresses current news/issues associated with the content and topics in the module, and contributes personal experiences to support student understanding. Providing these organized overviews not only clarifies what students are expected to do each unit or each week but also serves as indicators that the instructor has committed time to communicating expectations clearly, to ensuring that student work is designed to meet appropriate standards and learning outcomes, and to supporting students in recognizing current applications of and common misconceptions surrounding unit content.

INTRODUCTORY MATERIALS, INSTRUCTOR PROFILES, AND STUDENT INTRODUCTIONS

In addition to grouping materials into cohesive units of study, we also begin each of our courses with an introductory module which assists students in becoming familiar with the layout of the course, citations for course textbooks accompanied by images of the covers, instructor expectations regarding due dates and communication, campus and course policies, and misconceptions of which students need to be particularly aware as they move forward with course materials. Presented at the beginning of the course, these key pieces of information function as a roadmap which the instructor offers students to assist them in successfully navigating the course and to help ensure that no one gets too lost along the way. In some of our courses, this introductory module is accompanied by a "Getting to Know the Course" assignment in which students are asked simple questions such as, "If the link for an attachment in an Assignment does not work for me, where can I look for the information?" and other items which encourage them to navigate the course to find specific information. Requiring this of students helps the instructor identify who is struggling right away, so he/she can contact them via an electronic message or phone call to address their needs.

Introductory modules in our classes also include a welcome message from the instructor in which he/she shares a bit about him/herself beyond his/her connection to the course content and an asynchronous discussion in which students are asked to introduce themselves and share who they are and where they are in their educational journey. Our introductions as instructors vary widely to fit our personalities. While two of us only use a profile picture and text, another films an introductory message in which he/she is playing the guitar and hosts a short "name that tune" activity to assist students in seeing him/her as a real person with outside interests and a sense of humor.

While the welcome message provides students a glimpse into who their instructor is as a person, the introductory discussion allows students to make connections, to find classmates who share interests or life circumstances, or perhaps to reconnect with someone with whom they have taken classes previously. Conversely, the introductory discussion provides us, as instructors, a window into the unique characteristics of a specific class of students which supports our ability to be responsive to students' needs. For example, it is not unusual for expectant parents to take online classes and to share their upcoming arrival in their introductions. Using this piece of knowledge, we can reach out to students in this situation and work with them to rearrange due dates or design alternatives to group work which might be taking place near due dates. In larger classes, at least one of us has created spreadsheets of student information and updated it throughout the semester as students encountered difficulties with specific assignments which required resubmission or who missed due dates because of illnesses or deaths in the family. The spreadsheet generated from the introductory messages and kept up to date allowed the instructor to respond to student questions or concerns in keeping with their particular situations and contexts.

Also in an effort to remain responsive to students' needs in the online learning environment, one of us specifically asks students to share personal goals for the course as well as fears/challenges they have for the semester in their introductory messages. This information helps the instructor know how to support students as "whole" individuals who may come into the course with additional needs such as help with executive skills or understanding for personal circumstances. Students have responded that having the instructor recognize that there may be additional areas in which they are struggling and to offer assistance means a great deal to them. In addition, the instructor is able to revisit course goals and student needs at the end of the course as a means of modeling how K–12 classroom teachers can support their students in reflecting on their progress as learners and in facing challenges and overcoming adversity.

WEEKLY MESSAGES, ASSIGNMENT FEEDBACK, AND TIMELY COMMUNICATION

Clear course organization, charts detailing weekly expectations, and introductory modules go a long way towards demonstrating instructor presence but not when they are the first and perhaps last time a student hears from the instructor. Consistent and timely communication, which is not only reactive but also proactive ensures that an initially strong instructor presence is maintained throughout the course of the semester. To that end, one practice we have adopted is the weekly message. For example, in courses which adhere to a Monday through Sunday weekly schedule, the instructor begins each week with a "Monday morning message" which not only serves as a reminder of what students should be working on that week but also provides the instructor a chance to encourage the class as a whole, offer redirection, provide helpful tips for completing the week's assignments, or simply communicate how changes in his/her schedule might affect their availability in the coming week.

In addition to weekly messages, each of us has established personal grading policies, which focus not only on students' timeliness in submitting work but on our timeliness in returning feedback. In addition, we understand offering feedback as an extension of teaching, as another opportunity to continue the learning process. Thus, assignment feedback is always ongoing and corrective but also additive in the sense that we strive to not only highlight student errors but to praise great performances, prod thinking with additional questions, offer alternatives to particular choices or perspectives, and engage students in reflecting on their work.

We provide feedback for every assignment, which may seem to be a minimal expectation but conversations with our students inform us that many instructors simply assign a grade to an assignment without any comments whatsoever. Failing to give feedback dismisses perhaps the most teachable moment. Students who perform poorly deserve to know what they need to do to improve. If they don't know precisely what they did wrong, how can they improve?

Conversely, we often hear from students who achieve high scores on assignments and they are just as displeased with the lack of feedback. They also want to know what they did well. Many of our assignments are accompanied by rubrics with measurable criteria that align with the purpose and goals of the assignment, so that feedback can be offered specific to these criteria and students are aware of their strengths in each assignment as well as areas in which they need to spend more time or seek support. This very specific feedback allows the instructor and the student to observe how feedback is used to improve performance on future assignments.

In addition, often we will provide overall feedback to the class before providing individual comments to students. If we see a consistent error or common strength, we want our students to know. This does not take away the responsibility to provide individual responses. It is just another means of supporting student learning. This is also noted in our reflection for that module or assignment so that instructions to that assignment or module can be adjusted for the next semester. This is just one example of how a variety of data is used to inform and adjust instruction.

Since we expect timeliness of our students, we have also learned to expect it of ourselves. Each of us has a communication policy as an instructor that details how quickly students might expect a response to a concern or question. In situations where responding satisfactorily within the allotted time is not possible, we send courtesy messages which inform students that we are aware of their question or concern but need additional time to find answers.

One of us also ensures that at least once each semester he/she schedules a phone, Skype, or FaceTime conversation with each student. These conversations take place mid-semester and allow the instructor to make a more personal connection with the students. This is another practice which students have communicated is meaningful for them as it presents an opportunity to match a name to a face and a voice and makes the instructor seem more approachable. While conversations take less than half an hour, students have an opportunity to ask questions about the course, about the instructor and his/her research, about the program, and about any other concerns they might have. It also allows the instructor to give a brief overview of what will be coming up in the course and to support and encourage students in the work that has already been submitted.

DIFFERENTIATED INSTRUCTION AND ASSESSMENT

When we designed the courses that comprise our School of Education minors in Special Education and Early Childhood Education, which are both entirely online, we did so with education majors in mind. We have found recently that an increasing number of students are non-education majors who take these courses for a variety of reasons. A student might be an expectant mother who is majoring in business management who enrolls in an early childhood course because she wants to learn important information about the development of her unborn child or a criminal justice major in a special education class to prepare him/herself to work in the juvenile justice system after graduation. Approximately 25% of our students are non-education majors. If we are serious about our contention of recognizing students as complex learners who come from specific cultural contexts, then we need to be mindful of our students' differing levels of preparation. We need to make an effort to learn what prior knowledge and experiences our students have and to use that knowledge to design learning experiences in which that knowledge is not a deficit but an asset. In reality, this means we have to differentiate the way we teach and the way we create our assignments.

Thus, in a special education course, the education majors might create an Individualized Education Plan (IEP) whereas the criminal justice major might be charged with an equivalent assignment which is better aligned with his/her future career endeavors. Those enrolled in an early childhood course might develop a set of instructional activities for a class of four year olds, while a parent might develop a set of instructional activities specific to a home environment. Education majors might develop a brochure about developmentally appropriate practice as a tool to support and educate parents, but the same assignment might involve a video developed by a business major as a marketing tool. Differentiation then involves both the purpose of the assignment and the technology in order to make learning relevant to the students in their particular situations and with their unique personal goals.

Thus far, we have focused on practices which strengthen instructor-student relationship, but the notion of community surely encompasses the relationships between students as well. In the traditional face-to-face classroom, students typically develop relationships because of proximity. However, the online classroom lacks this proximity both because it inhabits a virtual space and because students interact asynchronously. Thus, student interaction and the development of student-student relationships is no longer a matter of course but rather something which must be carefully facilitated by the instructor. In our courses, this happens in asynchronous student discussions and through group projects.

Traditionally, classroom discussion has provided students the opportunity to share ideas, ask questions, and be exposed to multiple perspectives while also providing instructors an opportunity to assess students' understanding of topics being discussed. But what do class discussions look like when they are no longer bound by the physical and temporal limits of the face-to-face class session? In the early stages of developing online courses, we attempted to facilitate student interaction by posing prompts or questions to be addressed by students in the online discussion area of our courses. However, without detailed communication regarding the purposes and expectations of online discussion posts and without skilled instructor facilitation, students tended to post their own personal response to the question or prompt and to forego interacting with their classmates in ways which are similar to what happens in face-to-face conversation.

As with any discussion, the instructor's facilitation is key. The expectations we create are crucial to the types of interactions students have. True to the Vygotskian principles discussed previously in this chapter, we believe wholeheartedly that students learn not only from their instructors, but also from their classmates. In fact, students can often be a tremendous learning resource. Most college instructors have experienced a student doing a better job of explaining a confusing concept to fellow students than the professor.

An important component of discussions is when students are responding to classmates' posts. The quality of those interactions is crucial. For example, it is insufficient to simply require students to reply to two posts per assignment. It is isn't about the number or length of the responses that impacts learning. It's about the quality. As instructors, we provide feedback on student responses as a means of differentiating between high quality work that moves the discussion forward through integration of course content and the application of critical thought versus simplistic remarks such as "I agree." This is time intensive but an important part of online teaching. This feedback is the most significant part of instructor presence in discussion forums. We are always pushing students towards the upper end of the Zone of Proximal Development.

Another vehicle through which we facilitate student interaction and the building of student relationships is requiring students to work collaboratively in the online environment. Most learning management systems have tools which allow the instructor to assign students to a group and which also provide student groups with designated spaces to interact as group members. We require students to use these tools and spaces as they collaborate to write behavior intervention plans based on case studies, simulate co-teaching by working with a partner to jointly plan instruction, or participate in jigsaw activities by preparing presentation materials to share with classmates. In requiring students to collaborate online and in structuring those experiences so students can be successful, as instructors, we are not only facilitating the development of student relationships but a skillset which our global community is increasingly demanding.

CONCLUSION

Unsurprisingly, what fosters the interpersonal connections or community, which sociocultural educators believe to a foundation of quality education is the human connection which the teacher him/herself creates and then continues to facilitate via his/her own presence. While we tend to be familiar with what this looks like in a face-to-face classroom, reimagining the building of learning communities in online spaces has challenged educators to rethink how connections are built and maintained and to create and sustain a strong teacher presence. What we find is that the work is not, as some might believe, impossible but strangely remains the same while looking different.

REFERENCES

Chang-Wells, G. L. M., & Wells, G. (1993). Dynamics of discourse: Literacy and the construction of knowledge. In E. A. Forman, N. Minick, & C. A. Stone (Eds.), *Contexts for learning: Sociocultural dynamics in children's development* (pp. 58–90). New York: Oxford University Press.

Chaudhry, N. A. & Arif, M. (2012). Teachers' nonverbal behavior and its impact on student achievement. *International Education Studies, 5*(4), 56–64.

Dewey, J. D. (1933). *How we think.* Boston: D.C. Heath.

Ferguson, R. F. (1991). Paying for public education: New evidence on how and why money matters. *Harvard Journal of Legislation, 28,* 465–498.

Ferguson, R. (1998). Teachers' perceptions and the black-white test score gap. In C. Jencks and M. Phillips (Eds.), *The Black-White Test Score Gap* (pp. 273–317). Washington, DC: Brookings Institution Press.

Garrison, D. R., Anderson, T., & Archer, W. (2000). Critical inquiry in a text-based environment: Computer conferencing in higher education. *The Internet and Higher Education 2*(2–3), 87–105.

Garrison, D. R., Anderson, T., & Archer, W. (2001). Critical thinking, cognitive presence, and computer conferencing in distance education. *American Journal of Distance Education, 15*(1), 7–23.

Garrison, D. R., Anderson, T., & Archer, W. (2010). The first decade of the community of inquiry framework: A retrospective. *The Internet and Higher Education, 13*(1–2), 5–9.

Garrison, D. R., & Arbaugh, J. B. (2007). Researching the community of inquiry framework: Review, issues, and future directions. *The Internet and Higher Education, 10*(3), 157–172.

Goldhaber, D. (2002). The mystery of good teaching: Surveying the evidence on student achievement and teachers' characteristics. *Education Next, 2*(1), 50–55.

John-Steiner, V., Panofsky, C. P., & Smith, L. W. (1994). *Sociocultural approaches to language and literacy: An interactionist perspective.* New York: Cambridge University Press.

McGarity, J., & Butts, D. (1984). The relationship among teacher classroom management behavior, student engagement, and student achievement of middle and high school science students of varying aptitude. *Journal of Research in Science Teaching, 21*(1). 55–61.

Rogoff, B. (1994). Developing understanding of the idea of communities of learners. *Mind, Culture, and Activity, 1,* 209–229.

Rourke, L., Anderson, T., Garrison, D. R., & Archer, W. (1999). Assessing social presence in asynchronous text-based computer conferencing. *Journal of Distance Education, 14*(2), 50–71.

Rovai, A. P. (2002). A preliminary look at structural differences in sense of classroom community between higher education traditional and ALN courses. *Journal of Asynchronous Learning Networks, 6*(1), 41–56.

Rovai, A. P. (2007). Facilitating online discussions effectively. *The Internet and Higher Education, 10*(1), 77–88 (2007).

Rubin, B., & Fernandes, R. (2013). Measuring the community in online classes. *Journal of Asynchronous Learning Networks, 17*(3), 115–136.

Sanders, W. L. (1998). Value added assessment. *School Administrator, 11*(55), 24–27.

Sanders, W. L. (2000). *Value-added assessment from student achievement data.* Cary, NC: Create National Evaluation Institute.

Scott, S., & Palincsar, A. (2013). Sociocultural theory. Retrieved from http://www.education. com/reference/article/sociocultural-theory/

Shea, P., & Bidjerano, T. (2009). Cognitive presence and online learner engagement: A cluster analysis of the community of inquiry framework. *Journal of Computing in Higher Education, 21*(3), 199–217.

Shea, P., & Bidjerano, T. (2009). Community of inquiry as a theoretical framework to foster "epistemic engagement" and "cognitive presence" in online education. *Computers & Education, 52*(3), 543–553.

Shea, P., Fredericksen, E., Pickett, A., & Pelz, W. (2003). A preliminary investigation of teaching presence in the SUNY Learning Network. In J. Bourne and J. C. Moore, (eds.), *Elements of Quality Online Education: Practice and Direction,* pp. 279–312. Needham, MA: Sloan Consortium.

Shea, P., Li, C. S., Swan, K., & Pickett, A. (2005) Developing learning community in online asynchronous college courses: The role of teaching presence. *Journal of Asynchronous Learning Networks, 9*(4), 59–82.

Tella, A. (2008). Teacher variables as predictors of academic achievement of primary school pupils mathematics. *International Electronic Journal of Elementary Education, 1*(1), 16–33.

Vygotsky, L. S. (1978) Mind in society: The development of higher psychological processes. Cambridge, MA: Harvard University Press.

Vygotsky, L. S. (1962). Thought and language. Cambridge, MA: MIT Press. (Original work published in 1934).

15

Economics and Finance
Using Simulation Games to Engage Students in Online Advanced Finance Courses

OI LIN CHEUNG, PH.D.

LITAO ZHONG, PH.D.

STUDENT ENGAGEMENT IN COURSES

Students learn best when they are actively engaged (with appropriate guidance and encouragement for their performance) in the related class activities, in particular the inquiry-based type of learning, as students will have the opportunities to apply and transfer the knowledge they learned in class in personal and/or novel ways (Lévesque, 2006). On the other hand, computer-based simulation games can allow students to gain some hands-on simulated "real world" experiences by applying the textbook theories/concepts they learned in class. In fact, learning occurs when experience is transformed to knowledge (Kolb, 1984). Concrete experience and reflective observation can be used by students to help themselves discover and reflect on social interactions and relationships as well (Godfrey, Illes & Berry, 2005; Kolb, 1984). Active learning is important for students to gain deeper experience and retain lessons (Dewey, 1938), whereas experience affects their cognitive-structure development (Piaget, 1976).

With technology training and computer resources, the type of instructions employed by teachers in general has been very different from what it used to be (Friedman, 2006). And it is found that introducing technology in courses does send out a signal to students that instructors are willing to use emerging technologies to engage the students in the courses (Kroeber, 2005; Pearson, 2010). It may also raise student investment and academic integration (Astin, 1993; Tinto, 1993).

Student engagement (a measure of the quality of learning experience [Robinson & Hullinger, 2008]) has long been deemed to be one of the driving factors for student success in a course. If a person is highly engaged in a learning activity, it is more likely that s/he spends more time on the activity and persists even under unfavorable conditions (Csikszentmihalyi, 2000; Wrzesniewski & Dutton, 2001). It is this persistence that could result in the mastery of the learning (Duckworth, Peterson, Matthews & Kelly, 2007; Ericsson, Krampe & Romer, 1993; Chambliss, 1989).

Student engagement for a course simply refers to the time and effort students put in the course as well as the effort and involvement the instructor(s) made to effectively teach the course (Jacobi, Astin & Ayala, 1987; Kuh, 2003; Karaksha, Grant, Anoopkumar-Dukie, Nirthanan & Davey, 2013). As early as 1969, it was found that the time a student spent on a learning task varies directly with his/her understanding of the task (Kuh, 2009). In other words, no student will be able to succeed in a course without putting into it enough time and effort. How much time and effort will be enough for a particular course depends on the level and the nature of the course as well as the background of the individual student. Thus, one of the major roles of the instructor(s) is to motivate the students to put the required time and effort into the course. This can be facilitated by implementing a purposeful course design that promotes student-student and student-instructor interactions and communication as well as student participation in the course (Johnson, 2003; Weiss, Knowlton, & Speck, 2000). Building into the course appropriate class activities will not only help convey the essential knowledge but also help motivate students to work hard to succeed in the course.

There are several ways instructors have been using to engage students in their courses, be they face-to-face or online. Some examples include discussion forums, socializing groups, collaboration projects, and simulation games. With the advance of technology, these student-engaging practices can be conducted (more effectively and efficiently) online. Thus, there should be not much difficulty in incorporating them in completely online courses. In other words, these practices which are effective in the classroom setting can be easily extrapolated to the online setting.

Recently the use of games in teaching has become more popular. Video games are familiar to college students. They enable students to experiment and learn in the virtual environment. With video games, students can be encouraged to take risks that they would not take in the real world. This feature will let students see and learn from the possible consequences of their actions (that might be deviated from the students' comfort zone or situated outside social boundaries such as those related to law or morality) in an engaging and "safe" environment (Gee's 2003; McDaniel & Telep, 2009). For video games to achieve an educational goal, their design must include these three primary elements: challenge, fantasy, and curiosity (Malone, 1981). Video games can also be made to represent processes natively; in particular, ongoing human interactions are represented by computer processes and observed through game programs (Bogost, 2007). Game characteristics such as competition, goals, rules, challenge, choice, and fantasy can actually be incorporated to the interests and benefits of students in different teaching methods (Charsky & Mims, 2008). However, when using video games in online courses, instructors need to be narrow and focus on activities or examples that can engage and arouse students' interests (McDaniel & Telep, 2009).

Online simulation games, on the other hand, by providing various simulated scenarios, enable students to practice their acquired knowledge, which would otherwise be impossible or infeasible. Building on the concept of student engagement that the more students practice what they learn, the better understanding they have from their learning (Kuh, 2009), online simulation games are recently widely used in the design of business courses (international finance [Seiver, 2013], investment [Pavlik & Nienhaus, 2004; King & Jennings, 2004; Ascioglu & Kugele, 2005; Norton & Singleton, 2005], marketing [Gillentine & Schulz, 2001], operational management [Pasin & Giroux, 2011], personal finance [Huang & Hsu, 2011], and strategic management [Shannon, Krumwiede & Street, 2010]). The move away from an instructional teaching approach towards a student-centered learning approach resulted in the design of curricula around student learning outcomes instead of course contents (Ramsden, 2003). This has also led to the proliferated application of online simulation games in courses, particularly those offered in business programs. In addition to producing equivalent learning outcomes as (and/or better learning performance than) the traditional learning methods, computer game-based learning adds to the enjoyment of student learning. In most cases, these games offer an interactive way for students to practice their acquired knowledge repeatedly without feeling that they are actually reinforcing their memory of the materials (Ebner & Holzinger, 2007; Huang & Hsu, 2011). As a result, a substantial number of instructors have extensively employed stock market trading and portfolio management simulations (for instance, StockTrak) in teaching finance courses (McClatchey & Kuhlemeyer, 2000).

Such extensive use has also inspired lots of research with respect to various aspects—results show that the experiential nature of the games contributes to students' learning and enjoyment (Alonzi, Lange & Simkins, 2000; King & Jennings, 2004; Ascioglu & Kugele, 2005); the computer-based simulation might be used to effectively assess certain investment skills (Lekvin, 2005); and the stock market simulation is an effective tool in engaging and motivating students to learn, thus increasing their knowledge of investments and financial markets with no lectures or reading assignments (Moffit, Stull & McKinnery, 2010). Thanks to the advances in computer technology and Internet speed, students of international finance classes can now be engaged in currency trading that is real time, real world, and 'round the clock using a platform such as OANDA. Students' feedback confirmed its value and that their OANDA experience enhances their learning—students who traded more intensively are found to have better exam scores (Seiver, 2013). However, as computer-games are not as efficient in delivering extensive and complicated knowledge compared with lectures, it is recommended that they be used as course supplements only (Ebner & Holzinger, 2007).

TEACHING INVESTMENT WITH STOCKTRAK AND INTERNATIONAL FINANCE WITH OANDA

In this article, we focus on the discussion of engaging students by using online simulation games. The two examples that have been used in our online advanced finance courses will be examined—investment project incorporated in BUS-F 303 Intermediate Investments (taught by Oi Lin Cheung, Ph.D.) and currency trading game adopted in BUS-F 494 International Finance (taught by Litao Zhong, Ph.D.). Both examples will let students apply the knowledge learned from the courses to simulated "real world" situations—a practical way of preparing students for a professional career. Requiring a final report from the students at the end of the project/game completes the development of their mental capacities to think at different levels: memorization, analysis, synthesis, making judgments, and application. Students have been found to be most engaged in analytical coursework, followed by coursework that requires application of theories and concepts to solve problems. Memorization, synthesis, and making judgments received equal emphasis from students (Robinson & Hullinger, 2008). "Hands-on" experience in online courses will certainly help students in the learning process in various ways: keeping students engaged in the course contents, allowing them to learn more, and enabling them to enjoy learning (Moreillon, 2015). Students who were brought up with substantial exposure to advances in technologies are, in general, good at, and comfortable in, performing in simulation-based virtual settings. They expect more than the traditional teaching approaches for them to be engaged in their learning process (Prensky, 2009). The proliferation of various types of e-tools has occurred as a result. However, successful e-tools should have contents that align with course objectives (Grigg & Stephens 1998; Nieder, Borges & Pearson, 2011; Charsky & Ressler, 2011; Karaksha, Grant, Anoopkumar-Dukie, Nirthanan & Davey, 2013). The e-tools particularly help students with a visual learning style. It is easier for them to learn from diagrams and pictures than written text—which is a unique characteristic of the Generation Y students (Hunt, Eagle & Kitchen, 2004; Lindquist & Long, 2011; Karaksha, Grant, Anoopkumar-Dukie, Nirthanan & Davey, 2013). Although students have positive attitudes towards the application of technology in their learning process by incorporating animations or the like to texts, they do not seem to be in favor of replacing traditional lectures with those tools. Thus, technology-based teaching methods are recommended to serve as supplements to traditional lectures. Even so, for the e-tools to be effective supplements for engaging students, instructors need to make students understand the importance and relevance of those tools relative to the assessment of learning outcomes. The role of instructors should be more towards providing encouragement to students in their self-directed learning and their construction of knowledge and ideas. If students see the value of their class activities—how they will work towards their ultimate goal of passing the course—they will be more likely to be involved in those activities. Instructors can convey this value to their students by sending emails and/or posting announcements frequently (Biggs & Tang, 2007; Karaksha, Grant, Anoopkumar-Dukie, Nirthanan & Davey, 2013).

We will discuss our two examples based on the three general factors of student success in a course activity: 1) the nature of the task, 2) the supporting structure of the learning tool, and 3) the connection to students' interest and development (Lévesque, 2006). In addition, we will also discuss whether students are learning what we intend for them to learn by comparing the investment project and currency trading game to the specific outcomes/objectives of the courses (Robinson & Hullinger, 2008). Furthermore, we also cover the ways we employ promoting students' participation and engagement in the activities.

Table 1. Teaching Investment with StockTrak and International Finance with OANDA

Discussion Item	BUS-F 303 Intermediate Investments	BUS-F 494 International Finance
Nature of Task	Investment Project: $500,000 virtual money (in U.S. dollars) to invest in equities, bonds, mutual funds, options and futures listed on the U.S. exchanges and NASDAQ.	Currency Trading Game: $100,000 virtual money (in U.S. dollars) to trade various currencies.
Supporting Structure	StockTrak Global Portfolio Simulations (http://www.stocktrak.com/)	OANDA (http://www.oanda.com/)

Discussion Item	BUS-F 303 Intermediate Investments	BUS-F 494 International Finance
Assessment Criteria	• Ability to formulate investment strategies (both short-term and long-term) • Ability to comply with the short-term investment strategy • Participation in the project • Ability to distinguish the long-term investment strategy from the short-term one • Ability to identify the way(s) to achieve the long-term strategy • Overall organization and coherence of the final report	• A thorough list of all currency trades • Ability to calculate profit or loss of each trade and the profit or loss ratio of the portfolio • Ability to explain the trend of currencies and identify the factors related to the currency changes • Ability to apply the course knowledge and theories to the project • Ability to address after-game reflection and experience • Overall organization and coherence of the immediate and final reports
Connection to Students' Interests and Development	Since the two courses are among the core courses for the Finance Concentration in our Bachelor of Science in Business Administration (B.S.B.A.) degree program, the investment project and the currency trading game should provide some close to real-world simulated trading experience for the finance majors (or any interested students) to prepare them for their future careers in investment and currency trading respectively.	

Discussion Item	BUS-F 303 Intermediate Investments	BUS-F 494 International Finance
Course Specific Outcomes/Objectives	On completion of this course, students should be able to • show how an optimal investment portfolio can be formed (LO-P1) • compare and contrast the aspects of active and passive investment strategies (LO-P2) • demonstrate how bonds, stock, options, and futures are priced (LO-P3) • analyze the form of informational efficiency of a security market (LO-P4) • evaluate the performance of portfolios (LO-P5) • discuss the risk and returns of investing domestically versus internationally (LO-P6)	After completing this course, students should be able to • understand how international capital markets work (LO-G1) • explain the differences between foreign exchange spot and forward markets (LO-G2) • explain the concepts of international parity relations, such as interest rate parity, purchasing power parity, and the international fisher equation (LO-G3) • employ models to forecast foreign exchange rates (LO-G4) • understand exchange rate exposure for a multinational corporation (LO-G5) • use currency derivatives to hedge currency risk (LO-G6) • make international investment and capital budgeting decisions (LO-G7).
Additional Incentive for Student Participation and Engagement	Students share trading experiences for bonus points by posting both their most successful and least successful trades on the discussion forums within the course site.	Extra credit for students' outstanding performance as measured by their trading profit ratios.

Notes: *The assessment criteria are extracted from the investment project/currency trading game descriptions and requirements. The course specific outcomes/objectives are extracted from the corresponding course syllabi.*

For the investment project implemented in BUS-F 303 Intermediate Investments, students have $500,000 to invest. They can make use of this amount to trade in security types including equities, bonds, mutual funds, options, and futures. They are allowed to trade in these types of securities which are listed on the U.S. exchanges (including Amex, NYSE, NYSEARCA, and OTCBB) and NASDAQ only. In order not to overwhelm the students, all foreign markets are excluded from this project. Students can buy, sell, trade on margin, and sell short stocks. They can also buy, sell, and write actively traded stock options. They can buy and sell bonds, mutual funds, and futures as well. However, they cannot long (buy) and short (sell) any of the same securities at the same time.

Students must subscribe to StockTrak, register with StockTrak for the course, and make payment to StockTrak for their subscribed accounts. The maximum number of transactions they can make for this investment project is 300. Each buy is counted as one transaction, and each sell is also counted as one transaction. They are allowed to trade for twelve weeks. On the StockTrak Global Portfolio Simulations website, students see links for Open Positions, Transaction History, Order History, Summary, Rankings, and Graph My Portfolio under Quick Nav > PORTFOLIO, and Stocks, Options, Mutual Funds, Futures, Bonds, and Spots under Quick Nav > TRADING, where they can learn how the system works after they are done with their registration. They are provided with "Helpful Information" within each link. There are many other resources provided by StockTrak in their accounts. After they have logged into their accounts, students see My Portfolio (where they can review their transactions, account summary, class ranking, etc.), Trading (where they can place their orders for stock, mutual fund, bond, options, and futures for this investment project), Quotes (where they can look up ticker symbols, option chains, economic calendar, etc.), and Research (where they can find links to stock and financial market news and research). In case students have any question about their accounts and the security trading using the simulations system, they can reach the StockTrak customer service for help during their office hours by phone. Students can also email them at any time.

Students are required to derive both a short-term and a long-term investment strategy with respect to their investment objectives (return requirement and risk tolerance) and their investment constraints (related to liquidity, time horizon, regulatory and legal aspects, as well as tax considerations). They need to justify their two formulated strategies as well. Then they make their trades according to their short-term strategy throughout the twelve-week trading period.

At the end of the twelve-week trading period, after closing out all their outstanding positions, students have to note what total amount of cash they have and compare it with the initial amount that they are endowed to trade with in order to determine their profit/loss percentage. They will earn points on their simulated realized returns pro-rata to the return requirements they identified in their short-term investment strategy mentioned above.

Students are expected to be an active investor in this investment project. They are required to trade at least once each week during the twelve-week trading period. They will earn points for each week of trading. The objective of this investment project is to enable students to become more familiar with the selected types of securities (from students' simulated trading in the securities). They are expected to trade at least a couple of times in each security type. They will earn points for each type of the securities they traded. They don't have to include all the security types each week. However, throughout the twelve-week trading period, they must have all the security types in their portfolios.

Each time when students trade in any security, they have to make sure their trading complies with the overall short-term investment strategy they formulated. They need to discuss in their final report how their shortterm investment strategy has been achieved by their trading. They are also expected to discuss how they will trade differently if they are not facing the time constraints in their investment horizon and if they are completely free to choose any security types to trade.

When formulating their own strategies, students will have to study traditional strategies and research about emerging strategies, including the active and passive ones, that they might be able to adopt/adjust and then use in the project (contribute to the accomplishment of LO-P2). Or, they can create new strategies if they do not find existing ones work for them. In addition, students are expected to create their best investment portfolios to achieve their formulated short-term strategies (contribute to the accomplishment of LO-P1). For students to include the type and quantity of securities in their portfolios, they need to have some idea on how the security types are priced (contribute to the accomplishment of LO-P3), the return and risk structures of those securities investing in the domestic markets (partially contribute to the accomplishment of LO-P6) and how their prices might be affected (contribute to the accomplishment of LO-P4). After the trading period has ended, students need to write a final report commenting on, including but not limited to, how they have complied with their short-term investment strategies with respect to their return requirements. To do this, they need to be able to evaluate the performance of their portfolios (contribute to the accomplishment of LO-P5). Thus, this investment project can well serve as a great supplement to the course lectures.

Students tend to forget about the preparation required for major course assignments if they are not constantly reminded of the assignment particulars and due dates since those big assignments usually require/allow for a relatively long period of time for students' preparation before their final reports are due. One way to keep students informed and engaged in the preparation of those assignments is to include some small and related assignments during the assigned preparation period of those major assignments. Over the twelve-week trading period of the investment project, students are able to earn bonus points if they share their trading experiences by posting their most successful and least successful trades on the discussion forums within the course site. In their posting for each of these trades, they are required to include in which security (ticker symbol and name of the security must be quoted); at what price and quantity; by what kind of trade (buy/sell/short sell); and when the trade was made, their reason(s) for making such a trade and why they consider it as their most/least successful trade up till the point of posting with reference to their short-term strategies. They can do this twice—one time in the first half of the trading period and the other time in the second half of the trading period. In addition, they are encouraged to leave their constructive comments to the trades posted by their fellow classmates. This is a very fair means of giving bonus point assignments, as everybody in the class should have their most successful and least successful trades to share and have an equal chance of earning the bonus points.

For the currency trading game adopted in BUS-F 494 International Finance, students need to subscribe a practice account on OANDA. The practice account endows them with $100,000 of virtual money to invest in a wide range of currencies streaming with live market data. Students can either buy or sell a currency against another based on their investment strategy. Unlike other financial markets, the FOREX market runs 24 hours a day (except weekends). This feature grants our online students, particularly those who reside in other countries, more freedom to trade the various currencies at their own pace on OANDA.

The OANDA trading platform is easy-to-navigate and interactive. On the homepage, students can see their open trades, account summary (displaying as Net Asset Value, Unrealized Profit & Loss, and Realized Profit & Loss), and live quotes of selected currencies. In addition to the basic functions, OANDA offers more advanced functions to assist students in their trades; for example, Technical Analysis (where students can access market experts' in-depth market analysis and trading advice), Market Pulse (which is a comprehensive site for analysis and news on FOREX, commodities, and global indices), and Trading Forums (where students can exchange information and experience if they want). Taking into consideration that most investors do not have much knowledge on foreign exchange rates and/or background in online currency trading, OANDA provides a six-lesson tutorial series as basic training for beginners. The series covers all aspects of FOREX including theories and trading terminologies. This resource is highly beneficial to students working on the currency trading game.

Students need to fulfill some assigned requirements to complete the game. First, they are expected to be active traders throughout the semester. Participation points are awarded to students according to their activeness on trading. During the semester, they must trade actively for at least ten weeks. Points are awarded to students for each week of their trading. Second, at the end of each month, students are required to summarize their monthly trading activities in a report. They are expected to include in their reports information on the currencies they have traded during the month such as the price and quantity at which they have traded for each currency; their account aggregate net worth and profit/loss; the value trends of their traded currencies in the month; the reason(s) that caused the value changes in their traded currencies; and the expectations on their traded currencies for the next month. Third, students are required to write a final report to summarize their experience. The final report covers a full analysis on their currency trades, including the value trend of each of their traded currencies for the game, introducing and explaining any factors related to the value changes in their traded currencies during the time period, calculating their profit or loss ratio, and elaborating their post-game experience—what they learned from this game, what knowledge from this course they have applied in this game, etc.

The FOREX market is very volatile and hard to predict. A savvy investor needs to continuously absorb the latest market news to facilitate making the right investment decisions. Reading *The Wall Street Journal* (WSJ) does not only help students understand concepts and knowledge learned from the course, but also keeps them alert to any potential financial market changes. In order to make students frequently browse the FOREX-related news, a separate but related piece of coursework is assigned to them. They are required to read the WSJ regularly and write reflections on four articles, which are related to international finance during the semester. They can subscribe to the WSJ at a student promotional rate that is lower than the regular rate. In their reflection of each article, students are required to write a brief summary of the article, explain how the article is related to the course materials and the currency trading game, and discuss how they can apply the information in the article to their currency trades.

The currency trading game on OANDA offers substantial hands-on experience to students. In addition, it (together with the WSJ article reflections) provides students with opportunities to better grasp the abstract concepts, terminologies, and theories in their readings and apply those concepts/terminologies/theories accordingly in their currency trading. Moreover, it contributes to the accomplishment of most of the course learning objectives. The trading in various currencies enables students to know how the global currency market operates (contribute to the accomplishment of LO-G1). Placing the trade orders on OANDA reinforces students on the currency quotations in the spot and forward markets (contribute to the accomplishment of LO-G2). In order to make better investments, students need to apply the fundamental and/or technical analysis technique(s) mentioned in the textbook to forecast the currency trends (contribute to the accomplishment of LO-G4). The reading of WSJ offers students clues on how the different international capital markets are connected (contribute to the accomplishment of LO-G1), how the macroeconomic factors, such as interest rates and price levels, affect currency values (contribute to the accomplishment of LO-G3), and how currency values impact the operations, budgeting, and cash flows of multinational companies (contribute to the accomplishment of LO-G5, G6, and G7). Again, this currency trading game has worked well as a great tool, supplemental to the course lectures.

In order to promote students' enthusiasm in participating in the currency trading game, extra credit is offered to them based on their performance as measured by their end-of-period profit ratios. They are rewarded with one extra point for each percent of the profit they have made. Those extra points will be added to the students' final course grades. The higher their profit ratios, the more extra credit they will be able to earn. On the other hand, the students will not be penalized for their resulting losses. They will still receive the grades for the required assignments.

EFFECTIVENESS OF THE TWO CLASS ACTIVITIES

From our observations, these kinds of class activities are well received by students. For the investment project, since most of the students do not have any experience in doing anything like this before, they find it interesting and like being able to practice investments. They enjoy seeing how their stocks and how other stocks are doing. The project gives them an insight on how to go about buying and selling various types of securities. It also offers them the freedom to play around and apply what they have learned from the course without worrying about losing any real money. In addition, the project is a great way to expose them to security trading and gain some valuable learning experience. Students can learn how to make investment decisions and track their progress as well. The supporting system (StockTrak) is very interactive and associated with real stocks. Students in general do not have difficulty in using such a system. For the currency trading game, most students are intrigued by it since none of them have had prior experience with currency trading. Some of them didn't even know currencies can be traded like stocks.

The game broadens their vision on how to buy and sell currencies, how different countries' currencies are linked to each other, and how the currency values are affected by macroeconomic conditions. Some students' investment potential was exploited in this game that inspired them to explore currencies in great depth and even invest with real funds.

CONCLUSION

No course can be successful without substantive student engagement. If instructors can build into courses some types of activities that can arouse the interests of students and promote their engagement accordingly, it adds to students' enjoyment of the course in addition to learning the necessary theories and concepts from the courses, particularly those that are geared towards their career paths such as the advanced finance courses offered as part of the core course curriculum in the finance concentration within a business bachelor degree program. The investment project and currency trading game provided two examples that can be included in the advanced finance courses as great tools, supplemental to the course lectures. Certainly, more such activities embedded in the courses within a business program will be very beneficial to students in terms of helping them acquire the necessary skills and/or exposures to work in the various business fields.

REFERENCES

Alonzi, P., Lange, D., & Simkins, B. (2000). An innovative approach in teaching futures: A participatory futures trading simulation. *Financial Practice and Education, 20*(1), 228–238.
Ascioglu, A., & Kugele, L. (2005). Using trading simulations to teach market microstructure concepts. *Journal of Financial Education*, 69-81.
Astin, A. (1993). *What matters in college: Four critical years revisited.* San Francisco, CA: Jossey Bass.
Biggs, J., & Tang, C. (2007). Teaching according to how students learn. In *Teaching for quality learning at university*, 4th edition (pp. 15–30). Berkshire, England: Open University Press (McGraw-Hill Education).
Bogost, I. (2007). *Persuasive games: The expressive power of videogames.* Cambridge: The MIT Press.

Chambliss, D. (1989). The mundanity of excellence: An ethnographic report on stratification and Olympic swimmers. *Sociology Theory, 7,* 8–17.

Charsky, D., & Mims, C. (2008). Integrating commercial off-the-shelf video games into school curriculums. *TechTrends, 52*(5), 38–44.

Charsky, D., & Ressler W. (2011). Games are made for fun: Lessons on the effects of concept maps in the classroom use of computer games. *Computer & Education, 56*(3), 604–615.

Csikszentmihalyi, M. (2000). *Beyond boredom and anxiety: Experiencing flow in work and play* (25th anniversary edition). Jossey-Bass: San Francisco.

Dewey, J. (1938). *Experience and education.* The MacMillan Company: New York.

Duckworth, A., Peterson, C., Matthews, M., & Kelly, D. (2007). Grit: Perseverance and passion for long-time goals. *Journal of Personality and Social Psychology, 92*(6), 1087–1101.

Ebner, M., & Holzinger, A. (2007). Successful implementation of user-centered game based learning in higher education: An example from civil engineering. *Computers & Education, 49,* 837–890.

Ericsson, K., Krampe R., & Romer, C. (1993). The role of deliberate practice in the acquisition of expert performance. *Psychological Review, 100*(3), 363–406.

Friedman, A. (2006). World history teachers' use of digital primary sources: The effect of training. *Theory and Research in Social Education, 34*(1), 124–141.

Gee, J. (2003). *What video games have to teach us about learning and literacy?* New York: Palgrave Macmillan.

Gillentine, A., & Schulz, J. (2001). Marketing and fantasy football league: Utilization of simulation to enhance sport marketing concepts. *Journal of Marketing Education, 23*(3), 178–186.

Godfrey, P., Illes, L., & Berry, G. (2005). Creating breadth in business education through service-learning. *Academy of Management Learning & Education, 4*(3), 309–323.

Grigg P., & Stephen, C. (1998). Computer-assisted learning in dentistry a view from the UK. *Journal of Dentistry, 26*(5–6), 387–395.

Huang C., & Hsu, C. (2011). Using online games to teach personal finance concepts. *American Journal of Business Education, 4*(12), 33–38.

Hunt, L., Eagle, L., & Kitchen, P. (2004). Balancing marketing education and information technology: Matching needs or needing a better match? *Journal of Marketing Education, 26*(1), 75–88.

Jacobi, M., Astin, A., & Ayala, F., Jr. (1987). *College student outcomes assessment.* Washington, DC: Clearinghouse on Higher Education.

Johnson, J. (2003). *Distance education: The complete guide to design, delivery, and improvement.* New York: Columbia University Press.

Karaksha, A., Grant, G., Anoopkumar-Dukie, S., Nirthanan, N., & Davey, A. (2013). Student engagement in pharmacology courses using online learning tools. *American Journal of Pharmaceutical Education, 77*(6), Article 125, 1–10.

King, D., & Jennings, W. (2004). The impact of augmenting traditional instruction with technology-based experiential exercise. *Journal of Financial Education, 30,* 9–25.

Kolb, D. (1984). *Experiential learning: Experience as the source of learning and development.* Prentice-Hall: Englewood Cliffs, NJ.

Kroeber, C. (2005). Introducing multimedia presentations and a course website to an introductory sociology course: How technology affects student perceptions of teaching effectiveness. *Teaching Sociology, 33*(3), 285–300.

Kuh, G. (2003). What we're learning about student engagement from NSSE. *Change, 35,* 24–31.

Kuh, G. (2009). The national survey of student engagement: Conceptual and empirical foundations. *New Directions for Institutional Research,* Spring 2009, (141), 5–20.

Levkin, B. (2005). Some evidence regarding computer-based financial instrument trading simulations and their use as an assessment tool. *Journal of Financial Education, 31,* 23–33.

Lévesque, S. (2006). Learning by playing: Engaging students in digital history. *Canadian Issues,* 68–71.

Lindquist, T., & Long, H. (2011). How can educational technology facilitate student engagement with online primary sources? A user needs assessment. *Library Hi Tech, 29*(2), 224–241.

Malone, T. (1981). Toward a theory of intrinsically motivating instruction. *Cognitive Science, 4,* 333–369.

Moreillon, J. (2015). Increasing interactivity in the online learning environment: Using digital tools to support students in socially constructed meaning-making. *TechTrends, 59*(3), 41–47.

McClatchey, C., & Kuhlemeyer, G. (2000). Incorporating stock market games into classroom: A survey of faculty teaching investments. *Financial Practice and Education, 10*(2), 201–221.

McDaniel, R., & Telep, P. (2009). Best practices for integrating game-based learning into online teaching. *Journal of Online Learning and Teaching, 5*(2), 424–438.

Moffit, T., Stull, C., & McKinnery, H. (2010). Learning through equity trading simulation. *American Journal of Business Education, 3*(2), 65–73.

Nieder, G., Borges, J., & Pearson J. (2011). Medical student use of online lectures: Exam performance, learning styles, achievement motivation and gender. *The Journal of the International Association of Medical Science Educators, 21*(3), 222–228.

Norton, E., & Singleton, J. (2005). Using professional investment analysis software in the classroom. *Advance in Financial Education,* 135–157.

Pasin, F., & Giroux, H. (2011). The impact of a simulation game on operations management education. *Computers & Education, 57,* 1240–1254.

Pavlik. R., & Nienhaus, B. (2004). Learning from a simple options trading game. *Journal of Economics and Finance Education, 3,* 21–29.

Pearson, A. (2010). Real problems, virtual solutions: Engaging students online. *Teaching Sociology, 38*(3), 207–214.

Piaget, J. (1976). *The grasp of consciousness: Action and concept in the young child.* Harvard University Press: Cambridge.

Prensky, M. (2009). Sapiens digital: From digital immigrants and digital natives to digital wisdom. *Innovate, 5*(3): 1–9.

Ramsden, P. (2003). *Learning to teach in higher education: Approaches to learning* (2nd ed.). New Fetter Lane, London: Routledge Falmer.

Robinson, C., & Hullinger, H. (2008). New benchmarks in higher education: Student engagement in online learning. *Journal of Education for Business*, 101–108.

Seiver, D. (2013). Incorporating a real-time FX trading platform in an international business finance class. *Journal of Financial Education*, 53–65.

Shannon, P., Krumwiede, K., & Street, J. (2010). Using simulation to explore lean manufacturing implementation strategies. *Journal of Management Education, 34*, 280–302.

Tinto, V. (1993). *Leaving college: Rethinking the causes and cures of student attrition* (2nd ed.). Chicago, IL: University of Chicago Press.

Weiss, R., Knowlton, D., & Speck, B. (2000). *Principles of effective teaching in the online classroom.* San Francisco: Jossey-Bass.

Wrzesniewski, A., & Dutton, J. (2001). Crafting a job: Revisioning employees as active crafters of their work. *Academy of Management Review, 6*(2), 179–201.

Nursing

Meeting QSEN Competencies in the Online Environment

PAULA KERLER BAUMANN, PH.D., RN

TONYA BREYMIER, PH.D., RN, CNE, COI

KAREN CLARK, ED.D., RN

INTRODUCTION

Nurses make up the largest portion of the health care team. There are over three million nurses in the United States with over 80% actively practicing within nursing (AACN, 2016). Despite the large number of nurses currently practicing, it is expected that the rising need for nursing care will outpace the numbers entering the profession. A growing nursing shortage is anticipated.

Currently there are three typical pathways to become a Registered Nurse (RN). These include three-year, hospital-based diploma programs, associate degree programs, and baccalaureate programs. All three routes of education currently take the same licensure exam to become a RN. Despite using the same licensure process, research has consistently supported that nurses who hold a bachelor of science (B.S.N.) in nursing are best able to meet the complex needs of patients and our rapidly changing health care system (Aiken, 2014; Kutney-Lee et al., 2015; Yakusheva, Lindrooth, & Weiss, 2014). Ensuring that RNs achieve a minimum of a B.S.N. has become a priority nationally.

The Institute of Medicine (IOM) report "The Future of Nursing" set a goal to increase the proportion of the nursing workforce with a B.S.N. from 50 to 80 percent by 2020 (2010). One strategy to meet this goal is to have diploma and associate degree nurses return to school to obtain a bachelor's degree. This is accomplished through post-licensure RN to B.S.N. programs where a student, already a RN, returns to school to obtain their baccalaureate degree. Most of the coursework associate or diploma-prepared nurses need to move on to a B.S.N. can be provided online. Online education creates flexibility, particularly for busy, working nurses, and provides an additional skill set to students who will use technology throughout their nursing career (IOM, 2010). In a study by Davidson, Metzger, and Finley (2014), graduation rates of both a hybrid and an online RN to B.S.N. program exceeded the national graduation rate of 80%. The hybrid program had a 92% graduation rate while the online program was 88%, providing support that online courses and programs can assist more RNs in obtaining their B.S.N. degree.

The IOM report (2010) states "nurses should achieve higher levels of education and training through an improved education system that promotes seamless academic progression" (p. 163). In order to provide more access to quality education for post-licensure students and practicing nurses, online coursework and programs need to be offered as an option for students. Best practices for online education must be incorporated in these nursing programs. A review of the literature on best practices in online education is provided.

ONLINE BEST PRACTICES

Based on Chickering and Gamson's and Chickering and Ehrmann's work as cited in Hammerling (2012) the following best practices for online learning were noted: communication between students and faculty, learning opportunities between and among students, active listening, prompt feedback, effective time management, high expectations, and respect for diverse ways of learning. Scherling (2011) identified these best practices in online collaborative learning: sufficient time to complete team activities, encouraging the team to set their norms in advance, and ensuring the assignment is authentic and applicable to real word issues. Faculty monitoring of team progress, presence, opportunity for peer evaluation, and evaluation of the experience are also best practices.

In addition, research related to online learning has supported the importance of peer interaction not only related to learning but also in feeling a sense of community (Mayne & Wu, 2011). Students reported that peer-to-peer interaction helps to create a sense of community, which has been cited as important for student persistence and retention (Sitzman, 2010). Assignments, which promote a sense of social presence have been found to promote learning and should be considered as a best practice in online courses (Cobb, 2011). In regard to course design, research has identified clarity of assignments, assignments being meaningful, engaging learning activities, and manageable class size impact course outcomes (Burress et al., 2008). The use of videos and podcasts helps to increase a sense of community in the class, and students perceived they aided in learning (Kardong-Edgren & Emerson, 2010). Researchers have also studied the role of the instructor in online classes, finding that some of the best practices for online learning include instructor presence and communication, oftentimes included as instructor caring behaviors (Cobb, 2011). Students also want instructors to provide clear expectations, and timely and worthwhile feedback (Bonnel & Boehm, 2011; Gallagher-Lepak, Reilly, & Killion, 2009).

The remainder of this chapter will discuss implementation of best practices in online teaching within nursing education. As a framework for the discussion, an examination of how Quality and Safety Education for Nurses (QSEN) competencies can be met in an online learning environment will be presented.

QSEN

Since the landmark Institute of Medicine (IOM) Report *To Err Is Human* (1999), there has been a heightened awareness by the public about quality and safety issues within health care. Safer patient care and the development of the cues and standards to promote safety and quality were needed. Six competencies were identified by the IOM as crucial to creating a culture of safety and quality within health care. In 2007, The Robert Wood Johnson Foundation funded a project to assemble experts to further define the six competencies and identify the knowledge, skills, and attitudes (KSA) required to meet the core competencies (Cronenwett et al., 2007). From this project, the Quality Safety and Education for Nurses competencies were developed. The six competencies include: patient-centered care, teamwork and collaboration, evidence-based practice, quality improvement, safety, and informatics. The QSEN website has a complete listing of the KSAs for each competency and should be threaded through all nursing programs at the undergraduate and graduate level.

The QSEN website is a valuable resource when planning learning activities and assignments. The website has a collection of submitted assignments that can be used, including those suitable for online learning. There are a variety of case studies and client scenarios. In addition, the American Association of Colleges of Nurses (AACN), in collaboration with the Robert Wood Johnson Foundation, developed web-based learning modules and a link for additional QSEN resources for the six QSEN competencies. This chapter will discuss how QSEN competencies can be met by nursing students through online programming using best practices in online education, as required in undergraduate and graduate curriculums.

PATIENT-CENTERED CARE

KSAs of Patient-Centered Care: The QSEN competency of Patient-Centered Care recognizes "the patient or designee as the source of control and full partner in providing compassionate and coordinated care based on respect for patient's preferences, values, and needs" (Cronenwett et al., 2007, pp. 123–124). Patient-centered care is demonstrated through respecting the client and family, including their values and culture, clearly communicating with them, and using best practices in delivering care. It is about working with the client and family, not completing the care within a vacuum of evidence and protocol (Sherwood & Zomorodi, 2014).

The KSAs associated with this competency should be inherent in student learning outcomes and integrated into the type of learning experience used in the online environment. Undergraduate students focus on KSAs that are fundamental to beginning practice. Graduate student KSAs build on those foundational KSAs and expand to a more advanced level consistent with their advanced roles and expectations. Core KSAs include use of effective interpersonal communication skills, understanding boundaries of therapeutic relationships, application of individualized care, client advocacy, conflict management/resolution, use of shared decision-making, and care coordination (Sherwood & Zomorodi, 2014).

ONLINE LEARNING ACTIVITIES

Learning modules must address the KSAs and assignments must be tailored to evaluate the understanding of the concepts. Integration of multimedia provides a context for students to apply patient-centered care competencies and reflect on the activities portrayed in relationship to improve quality and safety. Assignments that focus on the use of reflective practice such as unfolding case studies and virtual simulations promote critical problem solving, which ultimately improve future nursing actions as well as enhance reflective practice (Sherwood & Zomorodi, 2014).

Relationship building, collaboration and interaction are essential parts of nursing. Students need to observe role modeling related to relationship building as well as opportunities for practice (Cornelius & Smith Glasgow, 2007). One way to facilitate such skill acquisition is to create a welcoming environment within the online classroom. Students need to feel connected to peers in an online classroom. The use of introductory forum postings that require pictures, video, and safe self-disclosure create connections for students based on similarities and differences. Completing an art therapy assignment by drawing something that represents who they are along with a brief introduction is an example of how this might be accomplished. This self-disclosure promotes a sense of camaraderie.

CONSIDERATIONS IN THE ONLINE ENVIRONMENT

Active engagement in learning is imperative if students are to grow in KSAs. Projects that require students to research topics and apply them to contextual situations, present case studies, respond to video clips, or write in a journal stimulate active engagement and learning (Chenot & Daniel, 2010). Coursework that requires students to view situations from the client or family members' perspective via web-based modules are essential throughout the educational program. Analysis of patient interview data and peer discussions regarding the data supplied facilitates understanding of the patient experience (Hayes, 2013). The National League for Nursing Advancing Care Excellence for Seniors (ACES) curriculum promotes the integration of QSEN competencies while providing access to unfolding case studies over time in a variety of contexts that promotes individualized care and communication. These case studies include audio files, web-based text documents, and other pertinent information (Fonneris et al., 2012). Resources such as these are available for use and frequently at no cost.

Communication is an essential aspect of patient-centered care. Forum discussions, analysis of communication excerpts between health care professionals or between nurses and clients/family, and scenario-based situations afford students the chance to evaluate effective communication and interpersonal skills. Use of the communication technique "Situation, Background, Assessment, Recommendation" (SBAR) in scenarios offers the student the occasion to practice effective interaction. Presenting SBAR reports, similar to shift handoffs, to a peer for required feedback will foster greater comfort and experience with what is considered one of the lesser achieved competencies of new nurses (Stallkamp, 2015; Chenot & Daniel, 2010). SBAR reports could be presented via audio, video, or in written form to others within the online environment.

Designing space in the course for student interaction about content, assignments, or discussing other issues generates dialogue. Assignments such as discussion forums, promote interaction, foster increased connectedness, and support social presence. Active involvement by the faculty member through timely feedback provides appropriate relationship modeling and teaching presence while communicating a sense of respect and connectivity.

TEAMWORK AND COLLABORATION

KSAs of Teamwork and Collaboration: QSEN defines teamwork and collaboration as being able to: "Function effectively within nursing and interprofessional teams, fostering open communication, mutual respect, and shared decision-making to achieve quality patient care" (Cronenwett et al.,

2007, p. 125). KSAs for teamwork and collaboration include: recognition of personal strengths and weaknesses as a team member, recognizing the impact of communication style differences, and respect for the diversity of each team member and the different roles (Cronenwett et al., 2007). Learners will create their own improvement plans for effective team membership, seek input from other members, address conflict, and foster attitudes of respect for differing perspectives and ideals.

There are challenges within the online learning environment for teamwork and collaboration. An imbalanced level of commitment, unshared goals, and difficulties in communication make group work challenging. In addition, lack of negotiation skills, lack of instructor support, and inconsistent levels of quality and effort are common problems (Muuro, Wagacha, Oboko, & Kihorg, 2014; MacNeill, Telner, Sparaaggis-Agaliotis, & Hanna, 2014).

Benefits of Online Learning Activities: When applying best practices for online teamwork and collaboration the environment should support positive interdependence among learners and provide them with experience and skills to apply to future experiences. Successful collaboration supports more positive learning experiences, better goal/outcome attainment, improved individual accountability, enhanced trust, effective communication skills, and a feeling of working within a cohesive and caring learning community (Chang & Hannafin, 2015). When designing assignments that include teamwork and collaboration, the level of the learner, the experiences the learner brings to the classroom, and the authentic nature of the assignment should be considered (Scherling, 2011; Williams, Morgan, & Cameron, 2011).

Considerations in the Online Environment: When students come with limited knowledge or experience in teamwork and collaboration, the online activity may need to be leveled (Chang & Hannafin, 2015). Activities early in the semester may need to teach the students how to work as a team member, identify and recognize the various roles of a team, and introduce the conflict resolution process. The University of California–Berkeley has free team-building and conflict resolution tutorials on their website that can easily be integrated into online assignments. After learners complete tutorials, they can develop team expectations and conflict resolution practices as a group.

Learners with limited experience in teamwork and collaboration may benefit from smaller team membership as they learn how the team functions, how roles are attained, how goals are established and how conflict resolution works. According to Chang and Hannafin (2015), the larger the group the larger the incidence of "social loafing." Learners may engage more readily if the team is smaller in number. When individual learners exhibit a lack of participation, through simple procrastination or deeper, trust-related issues masquerading as procrastination, the team has an increased tendency to fall off track and conflict can ensue (Peterson, 2012; Smith, 2011). Conflict resolution skills are imperative, and faculty presence can thwart negative outcomes by intervening and providing guidance.

Faculty presence is an important factor not only for successful online learning but also successful teamwork and collaboration. Faculty presence and involvement can enhance the team performance and elevate the learning experience (Peterson, 2012). The online environment can pose challenges for the learners to communicate effectively. Creation of online "work rooms" or discussion forums for the teams to converse and exchange ideas can facilitate team communication. Digital communication and organizational tools may enhance the teamwork and collaboration environment; however, adding more tools without sufficient support and faculty comfort level with the tools can cause frustration on the part of both the educator and the students (Wong & Abbruzzese, 2011).

Teamwork and collaboration assignment examples include: presentations, debates, case studies, cultural comparisons, and current events. Following best practices for effective online teamwork and collaboration are the first step toward effective design. Clear directions and rubrics for the assignment are imperative. According to Scherling (2011), offering opportunity for learner self-reflection and peer evaluation can enhance the teamwork and collaboration experience. After a successful teamwork experience(s), the learner will carry strategies from the experience forward to apply to future situations.

EVIDENCE-BASED PRACTICE

KSAs of Evidence-based Practice: The use of sound evidence forms a foundation for best practice. Yet, trial and error, tradition, current practice, or expert opinion often govern practice leading to quality and safety issues. For this reason, one of the six QSEN competencies is related to evidence-based practice (EBP). This competency drives nursing to "integrate best current evidence with clinical expertise and patient/family preferences and values for delivery of optimal health care" (Cronenwett et al., 2007, p. 126), which positively impacts health care outcomes related to patient care, safety, satisfaction, and cost management (Chan, 2013; Miller, Ward, & Young, 2010).

KSAs for evidence-based practice include creating a desire to question, understanding research processes and ethical guidelines, the ability to locate and evaluate the best evidence, use current evidence in care interventions, and determine how to integrate client preference and beliefs with known evidence (Sherwood & Zomorodi, 2014; Melnyk, Fineout-Overholt, Stillwell & Williamson, 2010). Pre-licensure education should focus on helping students locate, read, evaluate, and apply the evidence. Education for students at more advanced levels should promote development of competencies associated with translating evidence to clinical practice or discovering new evidence (Chan, 2013).

Benefits of Online Learning Activities: Learning research processes can be like learning a foreign language. Courses in research or evidence-based practice need to begin by defining terms and research paradigms that guide research. Teaching of ethical guidelines should be addressed in ways that students understand the harm that may result when they are not followed.

Students must be taught how to effectively question. Asking questions that include the population of interest, the intervention or area of interest, comparison or control group, outcome and time frame are known as PICOT questions. PICOT questioning makes searching the existing evidence easier (Winters & Echeverri, 2012; Melnyk et al., 2010). Locating the evidence is often a barrier for students. Good library instruction on databases such as CINAHL and Cochrane Database of Systematic Review (CDSR) assists students in more efficient evidence searching. Use of the terms outlined in the PICOT question singularly and in combinations should provide hearty but streamlined results. Using systematic review databases such as CDSR can provide students with an assurance that the evidence has been reviewed for rigor and is considered quality (Rolloff, 2010).

Evaluating the evidence is essential and must become a habit for the practicing nurse. Article critiques allow the student to demonstrate personal knowledge of good research and how an article meets those standards. Assisting the student to learn to quickly appraise the evidence for validity, usefulness, and importance is essential for its use in the clinical arena (Melnyk et al., 2010).

Considerations in the Online Environment: Students need to have a sound understanding of basic research concepts. Use of varying approaches to facilitate this understanding may include multimedia, interactive content assignments, podcasts, synchronous chats, or asynchronous discussions into research articles where application of the process can be broken into smaller blocks of learning.

To address the ethics of research and EBP, viewing YouTube videos or other multimedia expose the horrors of research gone wrong. Requiring students to analyze the issues associated with ethical violations illustrates the reality of such breaches. For example, stories of the Tuskegee airmen bring life to the necessity for ethical guidelines in research.

To assist students in meeting the KSAs for EBP, the faculty should focus on the use and evaluation of evidence. Development and sharing of PICOT questions in discussion forums provides for insight into the initial steps associated with evidence generation. PICOT questions should be used as a beginning point for location and evaluation of existing evidence. Exercises that require searching in the database and reporting of evidence will assist students in developing the critical skill of evidence location (Winters & Echeverri, 2012; Melnyk et al., 2010). Assignments that require students to determine the credibility, validity, and reliability of the information can be done in discussion forums, through chats, or written rapid critical appraisals (Christie, Hamill, & Power, 2012; Winters & Echeverri, 2012; Stillwell, Fineout-Overholt, Melnyk, & Williamson, 2010). Suppling articles for students decreases frustration in securing appropriate evidence and makes better use of student time when evidence location is not part of the assignment.

Incorporation of unfolding case studies via podcast, serialized video, or virtual simulation situated in the clinical environment provides the students the chance to examine the use of evidence within that context. Asking students to apply the most current evidence to the scenario, keeping in mind client and family preference, creates the opportunity for student dialogue about best practice and patient-centered care via online discussions.

KSAs of Quality Improvement: The QSEN competency for quality improvement is defined as to "use data to monitor the outcomes of care processes and use improvement methods to design and test changes to continuously improve the quality and safety of health care systems" (Cronenwett et al., 2007, p. 127). Some of the skills that undergraduate students should obtain related to quality improvement are use of quality measures to understand performance, identification of gaps between local and best practices, and use of measures to evaluate the effect of change (Cronenwett et al., 2007).

Benefits of Online Learning Activities : Designing online assignments for quality improvement should focus on active learning and peer-to-peer interaction (Cobb, 2011). Having students actively evaluating data and creating plans for change engages the learners and allows for innovative ideas and solutions. There are numerous online resources that relate to quality improvement. Use of these online websites, case studies, and video clips can help students meet the KSAs for quality.

The Institute for Healthcare Improvement (IHI) has resources for virtual training and audio and video programs related to quality. These can be used to either provide more information to the student or as a supplement for assignments. Providing different formats for learning allows students with different learning preferences to have a variety of options for understanding the concepts.

The Agency for Healthcare Research and Quality (AHRQ) website has a Training Catalog section that provides classroom and online activities related to quality and safety. Having students complete a reflective paper or participate in a discussion forum after a learning activity will allow students to reflect on how quality can be compromised and nursing's role related to quality of care (Bonnel & Boehm, 2011).

Considerations in the Online Environment: One assignment that can be used in the online environment with post-licensure students is for students to do their own individual assessment of their healthcare environment and identify one area where the current practice does not reflect what is known to be best practice. Then, within the group, they select one of the examples they want to work on and come up with a plan for change to improve quality on this unit. Group work, although sometimes complicated in an online environment, is a best practice (Cobb, 2011). By designing group sites with chat rooms, discussion forums, video conferencing options, and peer feedback, the projects can aid in student learning (Cobb, 2011).

Students can use reflective journaling to write about examples of quality initiatives and where process variations have occurred in clinical. Students can then post in discussion forums and debate what changes should be made and how to best implement the changes. If students are not in a clinical site, an online case study can be posed to students and, through use of process improvement tools, identify needed changes, or students can go to the National Quality Forum website and download the nursing-sensitive care report and discuss some of the standards.

Students should also be encouraged to develop plans for change. Creating a new way of doing based on the evidence to improve quality of care is the highest level of cognitive process (Krathwohl, 2002). Particularly students at the graduate level can engage in "Plan, Do, Study, Act" (PDSA) in regard to improving quality in their own practice. Having students use evidence and benchmarks to identify areas of concern and then plan for change allows for students to gain necessary quality improvement skills.

SAFETY

KSAs of Safety: The safety competency is defined as to "minimize risk of harm to patients and providers through both system effectiveness and individual performance" (Cronenwett et al., 2007, p. 128). Some of the skills related to safety include effective use of technology and standardized practices that support quality and safety, use of appropriate strategies to reduce reliance on memory, use of national patient safety resources for professional development, and focusing attention on safety in care settings (Cronenwett et al., 2007).

Helping students to understand that safety is not only their responsibility, but the entire system's responsibility is essential. Students need to practice forward thinking to identify both current potential risks to safety and how to prevent future errors. Quality and safety, although different, work closely together. Some of the same online sites for quality can be used as resources for the safety standard.

Benefits of Online Learning Activities: Safety is a major concern not only for health care workers, but for patients, families, and society as a whole. The biggest contributing factor to errors in health care is poor communication (Starmer et al., 2014). Some of the most cited characteristics of a quality online course reported by students are specific to clear and effective communication, including interaction among peers, clarity of assignments and expectations, faculty communications of respect and encouragement, and frequent, timely feedback (Bonnel & Boehm, 2011; Cobb, 2011; Mann, 2014). By modeling effective communication using best practices students can become used to communicating at an appropriate level.

Assignment rubrics are essential for communicating clear expectations of student work (Bonnel & Boehm, 2011). Rubrics help to take the guesswork out of what is required from the assignment and decrease student errors when completing the assignment. They also improve the efficiency and speed of grading and providing feedback to students on their work. Rubrics can explicitly address communication clarity and be related to the safety standards.

An online environment allows for discussion among peers and faculty who can provide an additional perspective. Assignments related to the safety standard could include having students reflect on choices they have made providing care and considering what they might do differently in the future. Post-licensure students can have a discussion about errors that have occurred within their own facility or during their practice. Discussion and reflection about how the error could have been prevented or what could have been done differently contributes to the learning experience. Varied perspectives and a team approach is valuable in an online course and can provide innovative ideas for improving patient safety.

Technology plays a significant role in patient safety initiatives to help reduce errors and harm to patients (Cronenwett et al., 2007). Similar to removing memorization and using aids to improve safety within health care, using the technology in an online course is a logical approach to reinforce those habits. Students can not only learn about safety in an online course or assignment but can practice some of the skills that improve safety. Regular use of online course technology helps to increase general technology skills as well as use digital tools to quickly access data and reinforce the concept of finding the correct information rather than relying on memory. Clear communication, use of online resources, teamwork and peer assistance, and technological aids such as reminders and alerts are important skills that students will need in their future practice.

Considerations in the Online Environment: Some online assignments utilize the National Patient Safety Goals for the year. Students can select one goal and prepare a brief presentation about what they are seeing within healthcare and how the facilities where they work are matching up to these safety goals. The presentations can form the basis for further discussion of the issues. Becoming comfortable presenting information and analysis to a group is another important skill for practice and can be done through video recordings or narrated presentations. Alternatively, students can select a goal and then identify a few strategies that they can implement in their own practice to provide safer care as part of a reflective journal or paper.

A scenario about a patient situation or an unfolding case study can be provided for students and then, through discussion forums or small group work, they can identify areas where either safety breakdowns occurred or where potential near misses are present and then identify plans to improve safety. The QSEN website has video clips of patient and family experiences that are true stories. The Office of Disease Prevention and Health promotion website has a computer-based unfolding video simulation called "Partnering to Heal" that demonstrates how a culture of safety can alter patient outcomes. This can be motivating to students who find these true stories to be quite powerful learning tools.

Another resource to use for quality is the AHRQ website. The section discussing the program TeamSTEPPS has several video clips that can be used to discuss strategies to reduce reliance on memory to improve safety. The videos demonstrate effective communication aids geared toward patient safety. The site also has the video clip chronicling Sue Sheridan's story related to breakdowns in patient safety that directly impacted her family. The story provides an excellent chance for students to work in groups to identify safety improvements to rewrite the Sheridan story. The video is closed captioned, which is important in online learning to meet the needs of all online students.

KSAs of Informatics: The informatics QSEN competency is defined as being able to, "use information and technology to communicate, manage knowledge, mitigate error, and support decision-making" (Cronenwett et al., 2007, p. 129). The KSAs for informatics includes: understanding the importance of information and technology to enhance quality and safety of patient care; utilizing information technology for decision-making, monitoring, and documentation to communicate patient care and patient outcomes; valuing the importance of lifelong learning relative to technology; embracing clinical decision-support through information and technology; and valuing the role of the nurse in all stages of technology implementation to enhance patient care. Nursing informatics competencies need to be integrated across the curriculum and include teaching and learning pedagogies that not only enhance and embrace the competencies but also include professional communication, health policy, HIPAA, ethics, and professional writing (McGonigle, Hunter, Sipes, & Hebda, 2014).

    Benefits of Online Learning Activities: Computer literacy, information literacy, and professional development and leadership are three domains of nursing informatics containing specific competencies for undergraduate and graduate nursing education. Button, Harrington, and Belan (2014) evaluated multiple studies between 2001 and 2012 focusing on issues students and educators had with e-learning. Results revealed that students and educators alike had low-level computer literacy skills for e-learning and information communication technology (ICT). Providing effective technology support and training for students and faculty alike can improve computer literacy related to both e-learning and practice.

    The Technology Informatics Guiding Educational Reform (TIGER) initiative is a web-based environment that provides multiple types and levels of faculty development for nurse educators, in addition to informatics information and education for clinicians, administrators, and healthcare professionals. The aim is to provide development of inter-professional teams to elevate and enhance their informatics KSAs for safe, quality healthcare (Skiba, 2013).

    Considerations in the Online Environment: Multiple formats and teaching strategies can be utilized to support students in achieving the informatics competencies (Spencer, 2012). Informatics knowledge can be integrated into discussion forums pertaining to: general health informatics topics, electronic health record documentation principles, virtual simulations relative to safe medication administration, and the benefits and limitations of mobile communication technologies (Spencer, 2012).

Using various telehealth modalities through the online environment, students can find and retrieve data and information for use in problem-solving and monitoring outcomes (Spencer, 2012). Nurses will not only need to find data, but must also learn how to extract, organize, and analyze data to inform safe, quality care (Francisco, 2011, p. 101). Assigning WebQuests connected to blogging exercises will provide students with opportunities to retrieve, evaluate, and apply information. This can facilitate higher orders of thinking and promote writing through professional communication (Roland, Johnson, & Swain, 2011). Various tools for WebQuests and blogging are WordPress, Questgarden.com, and Webquest.org.

Attitudes toward nursing informatics are enhanced by lifelong learning, use of technology with an ethical and professional demeanor, and continuous seeking of best practices and evidence-based practices for safe, quality care (Spencer, 2012). Health policy, HIPAA, and ethics assignments can utilize social media sites such as Facebook, LinkedIn, and Twitter. Students create accounts, follow professional organizations who set nursing informatics policies, report on informatics hot topics, and blog with inter-professional practitioners across the globe. Such assignments will provide students with information evaluation practice and elicit professional networking while enhancing professional writing skills (Schmitt, Sims-Giddens, & Booth, 2012).

Students require positive role modeling to acquire the KSAs toward electronic health records education and other facets of technology integration and adoption are no different. Nurse educators can utilize a variety of faculty development and informatics toolkits from various professional organizations including: TIGER VLE, ANA social media toolkit, National League for Nursing informatics toolkit, Registered Nurses Association of Ontario e-health toolkit, and the QSEN website. Students are more likely to embrace technology and the KSAs toward nursing informatics when nurse educators embrace them and engage in lifelong learning with technology and nursing informatics.

SUMMARY

QSEN competencies should be integrated into undergraduate and graduate nursing education programs for safe, quality nursing care. Acquisition of the KSAs in the online learning environment is possible when best practices are followed. With an increasing enrollment in online learning, nursing education is not exempt from acknowledging the value of online learning and nursing faculty should design assignments/activities to fully integrate each QSEN competency in the online learning environment.

REFERENCES

Aiken, L. (2014). Baccalaureate nurses and hospital outcomes: More evidence. *Medical Care, 52*(10), 861–863.

American Association of Colleges of Nurses. (2016). Nursing fact sheet. Retrieved from http://www.aacn.nche.edu/media-relations/fact-sheets/nursing-fact-sheet

Bonnel, W., & Boehm, H. (2011). Improving feedback to students online: Teaching tips from experienced faculty. *The Journal of Continuing Education in Nursing, 42*(11), 503–509.

Burress, N. M., Billings, D., Brownrigg, V., Skiba, D., & Connors, H. (2009). Class size as it related to use of technology, educational practices, and outcomes, in web-based nursing courses. *Journal of Professional Nursing, 25*, 33–41.

Button, D., Harrington, A., & Belan, I. (2014). E-learning & information communication technology (ICT) in nursing education: A review of the literature. *Nurse Education Today, 34*, 1311–1323.

Chan, S. (2013). Taking evidence-based nursing practice to the next level. *International Journal of Nursing Practice, 19*(Suppl. 3), 1–2.

Chang, Y., & Hannafin, M. J. (2015). The uses (and misuses) of collaborative distance education technologies: Implications for the debate on transience in technology. *The Quarterly Review of Distance Education, 16*(2), 77–92.

Chenot, T. M., & Daniel, L. G. (2010). Frameworks for patient safety in the nursing curriculum. *Journal of Nursing Education, 49*(10), 559–568.

Cobb, S. C. (2011). Social presence, satisfaction, and perceived learning of RN to BSN students in web-based nursing courses. *Nursing Education Perspectives, 32*(2), 115–119.

Cornelius, F., & Smith Glasglow, M. E. (2007). The development and infrastructure needs required for success—one college's model: Online nursing education at Drexel University. *TechTrends, 51*(6), 32–35.

Cronenwett L., Sherwood, G., Barnsteiner, J., Disch, J., Johnson, J., Mitchell, P.,...Warren, J. (2007). Quality and safety education for nurses, *Nursing Outlook, 55*(3), 122–131.

Davidson, S., Metzger, R., & Finley, S. (2014). Comparison of hybrid and completely online RN-to-BSN curricula: Aspects of program structure that lead to success. *The Journal of Continuing Education in Nursing, 45*(5), 219–224.

Dodge, B. (2015). *WebQuest.Org*. Retrieved from http://webquest.org/

Fornneris, S. G., Crownover, J. G., Dorsey, L., Leahy, N., Maas, N. A., Wong, L.,...Zavertnik, J. E. (2012). Integrating QSEN and ACES: An NLN simulation leader project. *Nursing Education Perspectives, 33*(3), 184–187.

Franscisco, P. (2011). The quest for quality: Turning data into information. *Nursing Economics, 29*(2), 101–103.

Gallagher-Lepak, S., Reilly, J., & Killion, C. (2009). Nursing student perceptions of community in online learning. *Contemporary Nurse, 32*(1–2), 133–146.

Hammerling, J. A. (2012). Best practices in undergraduate clinical laboratory science online education and effective use of educational technology tools. *Lab Medicine, 43*(6), 313–319.

Hayes, C. A. (2013). Use of institute for healthcare improvement (IHI) open school course in a prelicensure nursing program. QSEN Institute. Retrieved from http://qsen.org/use-of-institute-for-healthcare-improvement-ihi-open-school-courses-in-a-prelicensure-nursing-program

Institute of Medicine (IOM). (2010). *The future of nursing: Leading change, advancing health.* Retrieved from http://books.nap.edu/openbook.php?record_id=12956&page=R1

Kardong-Edgren, S., & Emerson, R. (2010). Student adoption and perception of lecture podcasts in undergraduate BSN nursing courses. *Journal of Nursing Education, 49*, 398–401.

Kohn, L. T., Corrigan, J., & Donaldson, M. S. (2000). *To err is human: Building a safer health system.* Washington, D.C.: National Academy Press.

Krathwohl, D. R. (2002). A revision of Bloom's taxonomy: An overview. *Theory into Practice, 41*(4), 212–218.

Kutney-Lee, A., Witkoski, A. W., Sloane, D. M., Cimiotti, J.P., Quinn, L. W., & Aiken, L. H. (2015). Changes in patient and nurse outcomes associated with Magnet hospital recognition. *Medical Care, 53*(6), 864-869.

MacNeill, H., Telner, D., Sparaaggis-Agaliotis, A., & Hanna, E. (2014). All for one and one for all: Understanding health professionals' experience in individual versus collaborative online learning. *Journal of Continuing Education in the Health Professions, 34*(2), 102–111.

Mann, J. C. (2014). A pilot study of RN-BSN completion students' preferred instructor online classroom caring behaviors. *The ABNF Journal, 25*(2), 33–39.

Mayne, L., & Wu, Q. (2011). Creating and measuring social presence in online graduate nursing courses. *Nursing Education Perspectives, 32*(2), 110–114.

McGonigle, D., Hunter, K., Sipes, C., & Hebda, T. (2014). Why nurses need to understand nursing informatics. *AORN Journal, 100*(3), 324–327.

Melynk, B. M., Fineout-Overholt, E., Stillwell, S. B., & Williamson, K. M. (2010). The seven steps of evidence-based practice. *American Journal of Nursing, 110*(1), 51–53.

Miller, L. L., Ward, D., & Young, H. M. (2010). Evidence-based practices in nursing. *Journal of the American Society on Aging, 34*(1), 72–77.

Muuro, M. E., Wagacha, W. P., Oboko, R., & Kihorg, J. (2014). Students perceived challenges in online collaborative learning: A case of higher learning institutions in Nairobi, Kenya. *The International Review of Research in Open and Distance Learning, 15*(2), 132–161.

Peterson, C. H. (2012). Building the emotional intelligence and effective functioning of student work groups: Evaluation of an instructional program. *College Teaching, 60,* 112–121.

Questgarden (2015). *Questgarden: Where great webquests grow.* Retrieved from: http://questgarden.com/

Roland, E. J., Johnson, C., & Swain, D. (2011). "Blogging" as an educational enhancement tool for improved student performance: A pilot study in undergraduate nursing education. *New Review of Information Networking, 16,* 151–166.

Rolloff, M. (2010). A constructivist model for teaching evidence-based practice. *Nursing Education Perspectives, 31*(5), 290–293.

Scherling, S. E. (2011). Designing and fostering effective online group projects. *Adult Learning, 22*(2), 13–18.

Schmitt, T. L., Sims-Giddens, S. S., & Booth, R. G. (2012). Social media use in nursing education. *Online Journal of Issues in Nursing, 17*(3), 1.

Sherwood, G. & Zomorodi, M. (2014). A new mindset for quality and safety: The QSEN competencies redefine nurses' roles in practice. *Nephrology Nursing Journal, 41*(1), 15–22.

Sitzman, K. (2010). Student-preferred caring behaviors in online nursing education. *Nursing Education Perspectives, 31*(3), 171–178.

Skiba, D. (2013). Back to School: TIGER and the VLE. Why faculty need to access this site. *Nursing Education Perspectives, 34*(5), 356–359.

Smith, R. O. (2011). Trust in online collaborative groups: A constructivist psychodynamic view. *Adult Learning, 22*(2), 19–23.

Spencer, J. A. (2012). Integrating informatics in undergraduate nursing curricula: Using the QSEN framework as a guide. *Journal of Nursing Education, 51*(12), 697–701.

Stahlkamp, M. S. (2015). I-SBAR reporting for the nursing student. QSEN Institute. Retrieved from http://qsen.org/sbar-reporting-for-the-novice-nursing-student/

Starmer, A., Spector, N., Srivastava, R., West, D., Rosenbluth, G., Allen,.A.,...Landrigan, C. (2014). Changes in medical errors after implementation of a handoff program. *New England Journal of Medicine, 371,* 1803–1812.

Stillwell, S. B., Fineout-Overholt, E., Melnyk, B. M., & Williamson, K. M. (2010). Searching for the evidence. *American Journal of Nursing, 110*(5), 41–47.

Williams, K. C., Morgan, K., & Cameron, B. A. (2011). How do students define their roles and responsibilities in online learning group projects? *Distance Education, 32*(1), 49–62.

Winters, C. A., & Echeverri, R. (2012). Teaching strategies to support evidence-based practice. *Critical Care Nurse, 32*(3), 49–54.

Wong, C. K., & Abbruzzese, L. D. (2011). Collaborative learning strategies using online communities. *Journal of Physical Therapy Education, 25*(3), 81–87.

WordPress.com. (n.d.). WordPress. Retrieved from: https://wordpress.com/

Yakusheva, O., Lindrooth, R., & Weiss, M. (2014). Economic evaluation of the 80% baccalaureate nurse workforce recommendation. *Medical Care, 55*(10), 864–869.

INTRODUCTION

Dr. Ross Alexander serves as Vice President for Academic Affairs and Provost at the University of North Alabama. He formerly served as Dean of the School of Humanities and Social Sciences and Professor of Political Science at Indiana University East. Dr. Alexander earned a Ph.D. in Political Science from Northern Illinois University and an M.P.A. from Arizona State University. He has been teaching graduate and undergraduate courses at the university level for 19 years, including 14 years online, primarily in public administration and policy, American politics, and political theory. Dr. Alexander has taught over 50 online courses and developed and designed over 20, while also earning Quality Matters Level One certification and a certificate in Online Teaching from the University System of Georgia. Dr. Alexander has authored or co-authored over 20 peer-reviewed journal articles and book chapters in the areas of American national government, state and local government, public budgeting and finance, gambling policy, and online teaching and learning.

CHAPTER ONE: COMMUNICATION STUDIES

Dr. Rosalie S. Aldrich serves as Associate Professor of Communication Studies and Lead Faculty Member for Online Programs in Communication Studies at Indiana University East. Dr. Aldrich earned a Ph.D. in Communication from the University of Kentucky in addition to an M.A. in Communication from Michigan State University. She has been teaching at the university level for 11 years, including seven years online, primarily in the areas of health communication, interpersonal communication, research methods, and gender communication. Dr. Aldrich is Quality Matters Level One and Level Two certified, has taught 29 online courses, and has developed and designed eight. Dr. Aldrich has authored or co-authored numerous peer-reviewed journal articles in the areas of suicide prevention and intervention, student learning, and online teaching and learning.

Dr. Renee Kaufmann serves as Assistant Professor in the School of Information Science and Information Communication Technology at the University of Kentucky, having previously served as Assistant Professor of Communication Studies at Indiana University East. Dr. Kaufmann earned both an M.A. and Ph.D. in Communication from the University of Kentucky. She has taught at the university level for six years, including four years online, having taught seven courses online and developing and designing five, primarily in the area of communication theory. Dr. Kaufmann has authored or co-authored numerous peer-reviewed publications in the areas of instructional communication, communication technology, and interpersonal communication. She is Level One Quality Matters certified and has also earned a graduate certificate in Distance Learning Development and Implementation from the University of Kentucky.

Dr. Natalia Rybas serves as Associate Dean of the School of Humanities and Social Sciences, Chair of the Department of Communication Studies and Associate Professor of Communication Studies at Indiana University East. Dr. Rybas earned both an M.A. and Ph.D. in Communication from Bowling Green State University. She has been teaching at the university level for 14 years, including eight years online, primarily in the areas of new media and cross-cultural communication. Dr. Rybas has taught over 20 online courses and developed and designed over 10, while also earning Quality Matters Level One certification. Dr. Rybas has authored or co-authored over 10 peer-reviewed articles and chapters in the areas of critical cultural communication studies, computer-mediated communication, feminist and critical media studies, social network systems, and online teaching and learning.

CHAPTER TWO: COMPOSITION AND WRITING

Dr. Sarah Harris serves the Curriculum & Outcomes Assessment Coordinator at the College of the Sequoias. She previously served as the Writing Program

Director and Assistant Professor of English at Indiana University East. Dr. Harris earned a Ph.D. in Rhetoric Composition & the Teaching of English at the University of Arizona and an M.F.A. in Creative Writing from West Virginia University. She has 13 years of experience teaching at the university level, including three online, primarily in the areas of composition and writing studies. Dr. Harris has taught five online courses, developing and designing each, while also earning Quality Matters Level One certification. Dr. Harris has published and presented in the areas of writing program administration, retention and student success, and creative writing studies.

Tanya Perkins, M.A., serves as Assistant Professor of English and Lead Faculty Member for Online Programs in English at Indiana University East. Ms. Perkins earned an M.A. in English Studies from Western Washington University and has been teaching at the university level for five years, including three online, primarily in the areas of composition, professional writing, and fiction. She has taught four online courses, developing and designing each, while earning both Level One and Level Two Quality Matters certification and a Certificate in Online Teaching from IU East. Ms. Perkins has published and presented in the areas of service learning, the resume as autobiographical narrative, and digital composition processes.

Melissa Blankenship, M.F.A., Lecturer of English at Indiana University East, earned her M.F.A. in Creative Writing from Murray State University and has been teaching at the university level for nine years, including two online, primarily in the areas of rhetoric and composition, creative writing, and literature. Ms. Blankenship has taught nine courses online, developing and designing six, while also earning Level One Quality Matters certification.

CHAPTER THREE: ENGLISH

Dr. Edwina Helton serves as Director of Graduate Programs in English, Lead Faculty Member for Online Graduate Programs in English, and Professor of English at Indiana University East. Dr. Helton earned a Ph.D. in English from Miami (OH) University and M.A. in English from the University of Akron. She has taught at the university level for 24 years, including 14 online, primarily in the areas of rhetorical studies, minority literatures, linguistics and the history of the English language, and gender and writing. Dr. Helton has taught over 50 online courses, developing and designing over 40, while earning both Level One and Level Two Quality Matters certification and a Certificate in Online Teaching from IU East. Dr. Helton has authored or co-authored several books and numerous, peer-reviewed journal articles and chapters in the areas of teacher preparation, composition and literature pedagogy, language development, and online teaching and learning.

Dr. Margaret Thomas-Evans serves as Chair of the Department of English and Assistant Professor of English at Indiana University East. Dr. Thomas-Evans earned a Ph.D. in English from Miami (OH) University and an M.A., in English from Wright State University. She has taught at the university level for 28 years, including 13 online, primarily in the areas of technical writing and composition studies. Dr. Thomas-Evans has taught over 80 online courses, developing and designing over 10, while earning Level One Quality Matters certification. Dr. Thomas-Evans has published and presented in the areas of online teaching and learning, faculty development, and technical writing.

Dr. Steven Petersheim, Assistant Professor of English at Indiana University East, earned a Ph.D. in English at Baylor University and has taught at the university level for eight years, including four years online, primarily in the areas of American literature, ethnic literature, creative writing, composition, and film and literature. He has taught 13 online courses and developed and designed 11, while earning Level One Quality Matters certification and a Certificate in Online Teaching from IU East. Dr. Petersheim has co-edited a volume and written several peer-reviewed chapters and articles in the areas of nineteenth-century American literature, transatlantic literature and culture, environmental literature, and cultural studies.

CHAPTER FOUR: POLITICAL SCIENCE

Dr. Chera LaForge serves as Assistant Professor of Political Science at Indiana University East. Dr. LaForge earned an M.A. and Ph.D. in Political Science from the University of Illinois. She has taught eight years at the university level, including four years online, primarily in the area of American politics. In addition to earning both Level One and Level Two Quality Matters certification, Dr. LaForge has taught 21 online courses and developed and designed 10. She has also published and presented in the areas of American politics, political institutions, legislative behavior, and online teaching and learning.

Dr. Kris Rees, Assistant Professor of Political Science and Lead Faculty Member for Online Programs in Political Science at Indiana University East, earned a Ph.D. in Political Science and Central Eurasian Studies from Indiana University, in addition to an M.A. in Central Eurasian Studies, also from Indiana University. He has taught at the university level for six years, primarily in the areas of comparative politics, politics of the developing world, political philosophy, and international relations. Dr. Rees has taught eight courses online and developed and designed six, in addition to earning Level One Quality Matters certification and a Certificate in Online Teaching from IU East. Dr. Rees has published and presented in the areas of nationalism and civic identity, supranational identity building, language policy and policy implementation, and conflict and political protest.

Lilia Alexander, M.P.A., serves as an Adjunct Instructor of Political Science and Public Affairs at Indiana University East. She is a doctoral candidate in Education Policy Studies at Indiana University and also possesses an M.P.A. from the University of North Georgia. She has been teaching at the university level for four years, including four years online, primarily in the areas of public administration and policy, organizational leadership and management, and American government. Ms. Alexander has taught 15 online courses and developed and designed eight, while earning Quality Matters Level One certification and a Certificate in Online Teaching from IU East. She has published and presented in the areas of online teaching and learning and state involvement in higher education policymaking.

Dr. Ross C. Alexander serves as Vice President for Academic Affairs and Provost at the University of North Alabama. He formerly served as Dean of the School of Humanities and Social Sciences and Professor of Political Science at Indiana University East. Dr. Alexander earned a Ph.D. in Political Science from Northern Illinois University and an M.P.A. from Arizona State University. He has been teaching graduate and undergraduate courses at the university level for 18 years, including 12 years online, primarily in public administration and policy, American politics, and political theory. Dr. Alexander has taught over 50 online courses and developed and designed over 20, while also earning Quality Matters Level One certification and a certificate in Online Teaching from the University System of Georgia. Dr. Alexander has authored or co-authored over 20 peer-reviewed journal articles and book chapters in the areas of American national government, state and local government, public budgeting and finance, gambling policy, and online teaching and learning.

Dr. Stephanie Whitehead serves as Associate Professor of Criminal Justice and Director for the Center of Teaching and Learning at Indiana University East. Dr. Whitehead earned a Ph.D. in Criminal Justice from Indiana University and an M.S. in Criminal Justice from Eastern Kentucky University. She has been teaching at the university level for eight years, including five years online, primarily in the areas of policing; class, gender, race, and crime; research methods; and crime and popular culture. Dr. Whitehead has taught over 16 online courses and developed and designed six. She is Level One and Level Two Quality Matters certified and has also earned a Certificate in Online Teaching from IU East. Dr. Whitehead has authored multiple peer-reviewed articles in the area of race and policing.

Dr. M. Michaux Parker serves as Associate Dean in the School of Humanities and Social Sciences, Chair of the Department of Criminal Justice and Political Science, and Associate Professor of Criminal Justice at Indiana University East. Dr. Parker earned a Ph.D. in Criminal Justice from Michigan State University and an M.S. in Criminal Justice from North Carolina Central University. He has been teaching at the university level for 12 years, including five years online, primarily in the areas of criminal justice research and statistics. Dr. Parker has taught five classes online and developed and designed three, in addition to earning Quality Matters Level One certification. One of the foremost scholars in the field of gangs, Dr. Parker has authored or co-authored over 15 peer-reviewed articles and chapters.

Dr. Beth Trammell serves as Assistant Professor of Psychology and Lead Faculty Member for Online Programs in Psychology at Indiana University East, where she teaches courses in abnormal psychology, developmental psychology, personality theory, and behavior disorders primarily. Dr. Trammell earned a Ph.D. in School Psychology and an M.A. in Counseling Psychology from Ball State University. She has taught 13 online courses at the university level and developed and designed six, in addition to earning Quality Matters Level One and Level Two certification. Dr. Trammell has authored or co-authored numerous peer-reviewed journal articles in the areas of parenting, childhood behavioral disorders, and online teaching and learning.

Dr. Greg Dam serves as Assistant Professor of Psychology at Indiana University East. Dr. Dam earned a Ph.D. in Cognitive Neuroscience and an M.A. in Learning Sciences from Northwestern University. Dr. Dam has been teaching at the university level for six years, primarily in the areas of neuroscience. He has taught and developed or designed five online courses. Dr. Dam has earned Quality Matters Level One certification and boasts a number of peer-reviewed journal articles in the areas of voluntary movement and neuroscience.

Dr. Amanda Kraha serves as Assistant Professor of Psychology at Indiana University East, teaching courses in research methods, statistical techniques, and cognitive psychology primarily. Dr. Kraha earned a Ph.D. in Experimental Psychology from the University of North Texas. She boasts eight years of university level teaching experience, including three online. Dr. Kraha has taught 14 online courses and developed and designed three, while also earning Level One Quality Matters certification and a certificate in online teaching and learning from the University of California-Irvine. Dr. Kraha has written several peer-reviewed journal articles in the areas of cognitive psychology, human memory, and statistical analysis.

Dr. Dianne Moneypenny serves as Assistant Professor of Spanish and Lead Faculty Member for Online Programs in World Languages at Indiana University East. Dr. Moneypenny earned a Ph.D. in Hispanic Studies from the University of Kentucky and an M.A. in Spanish from the University of Louisville. She has been teaching at the university level for 13 years, including six years online, primarily in the areas of Spanish language, literature, and Hispanic culture. Dr. Moneypenny has taught over 35 online courses and has developed and designed 21. She has earned Level One and Level Two Quality Matters certification and a Certificate in Online Teaching from IU East. Dr. Moneypenny has authored and co-authored numerous, peer-reviewed articles and chapters in the areas of medieval Spain, food studies, and online teaching and learning.

Dr. Julien Simon, Associate Professor of Spanish and French, earned both an M.A. and Ph.D. in Spanish from Purdue University. He has taught for 16 years at the university level, including nine years online, primarily in the areas of Spanish and French language, literature, culture, and cinema. Dr. Simon has taught 22 online courses and developed and designed 12, in addition to earning Level One Quality Matters certification. Dr. Simon has a book and numerous peer-reviewed articles and chapters in the areas of cognitive literary studies, film studies, and teaching and learning.

CHAPTER EIGHT: HISTORY

Dr. Justin Carroll serves as Associate Professor of History and Lead Faculty Member for Online Programs in History at Indiana University East. Dr. Carroll earned a Ph.D. in History from Michigan State University and has been teaching at the university level for five years, including five years online, primarily in the areas of American history, British Empire, and Great Lakes indigenous. He has taught a dozen online courses and has developed and designed four, in addition to earning Quality Matters Level One and Level Two certification. Dr. Carroll has presented in the areas of American history, British Empire, and Great Lakes indigenous and has a book under contract with the Michigan State University Press.

Dr. Christine Nemcik serves as Assistant Professor of History and World Languages at Indiana University East. Dr. Nemcik earned an M.A. and Ph.D. in Latin American History from Indiana University and has been teaching at the university level for 11 years, including three years online, primarily in the areas of Latin American history, Spanish, American history, and Hispanic culture. She has taught over a dozen online courses, developing and designing seven, in addition to earning Level One Quality Matters certification. Dr. Nemcik has presented in the areas of Central American history and immigration.

Dr. Daron Olson serves as Chair of the Department of History, World Languages, and Philosophy and Associate Professor of History at Indiana University East. Dr. Olson earned a Ph.D. in History from Southern Illinois University and an M.A. in History from the University of North Dakota. He has been teaching at the university level for 12 years, including seven years online, primarily in the areas of modern Europe and the modern world. Dr. Olson has taught five online courses and developed and designed two, in addition to earning Quality Matters Level One certification. Dr. Olson is one of the foremost scholars in Scandinavian and Scandinavian American Studies, having written an acclaimed book published by the University of Minnesota Press.

CHAPTER NINE: FINE ARTS—DRAWING

Carrie Longley, M.F.A., serves as Chair of the Department of Fine and Performing Arts and Assistant Professor of Fine Arts at Indiana University East. Ms. Longley earned an M.F.A. in Ceramics from Indiana University and has taught at the university level for eight years, primarily in the areas of 3-D fundamentals, sculpture, and ceramics. Her work has been featured at several, national and international, juried exhibitions. As Chair, Ms. Longley has led the development of nine online courses in fine and performing arts in a variety of disciplines while also earning Level One Quality Matters certification.

Kevin Longley, M.Ed., Adjunct Instructor of Fine Arts at Indiana University East, earned an M.Ed. in Educational Leadership from Antioch University McGregor and has taught for two years at the university level, all online, and for 13 years at the high school level. An avid artist, he has taught and developed two online Drawing courses and earned Level Two Quality Matters certification.

CHAPTER 10: SOCIOLOGY, ANTHROPOLOGY, AND GEOGRAPHY

Dr. Denise Bullock serves as Chair of the Department of Sociology, Anthropology, and Geography and Associate Professor of Sociology at Indiana University East. Dr. Bullock earned a Ph.D. in Sociology from the University of Missouri and an M.A. in Sociology from the University of Houston. She has been teaching at the university level for 15 years, including two years online, primarily in the areas of social theory, interactionist theory, gender, sexualities, deviance, and media. Dr. Bullock has earned Quality Matters Level One certification, taught seven online courses, developing and designing each. Dr. Bullock boasts several publications and presentations in the areas of sexualities, queer studies, and identity.

Dr. Katherine Miller-Wolf serves as Assistant Professor of Anthropology and Lead Faculty Member for Online Programs in Anthropology and Sociology at Indiana University East. Dr. Miller-Wolf earned both an M.A. and Ph.D. in Anthropology from Arizona State University. She has taught at the university level for 10 years, including five years online, primarily in the areas of anthropology and archaeology. Dr. Miller-Wolf has taught 13 online courses and developed and designed six, in addition to earning Level One and Level Two Quality Matters certification. Dr. Miller-Wolf has authored or co-authored several peer-reviewed journal articles and chapters in bioarchaeology, social organization, kinship identity, and physical anthropology.

Dr. Wazir Mohamed serves as Associate Professor of Sociology at Indiana University East. Dr. Mohamed earned an M.A. and Ph.D. in Sociology from Binghamton University. He has taught at the university level for 14 years, including four years online, primarily in the areas of social inequality, social change, social problems, race and ethnic relations, and globalization. Dr. Mohamed has taught eight online courses, having developed and designed each, in addition to earning Level One Quality Matters certification. Dr. Mohamed has authored numerous, peer-reviewed articles and chapters in the areas of ethnic politics and social justice, the expansion of slavery, and food security.

Marc Wolf, M.A., R.P.A., serves as Visiting Lecturer of Anthropology and Geography at Indiana University East. He is a doctoral candidate in Anthropology at the Graduate Center of the City University of New York and also earned an M.A. in Archaeological Studies from Boston University. Mr. Wolf has taught at the university level for five years, including three online, having taught eight online courses and developing and designing three, primarily in the areas of native North America, Mesoamerica, archaeology, human geography, and GIS. Mr. Wolf has earned Level One Quality Matters certification and has authored and co-authored numerous, peer-reviewed publications in the areas of Maya archaeology, settlement patterns, and cultural geography.

CHAPTER 11: PHILOSOPHY

Mary A. Cooksey, M.A., serves as Program Coordinator for Philosophy and Religion, Lead Faculty Member in Online Programs in Philosophy and Religion, and Senior Lecturer of Humanities at Indiana University East. Ms. Cooksey earned an M.A. in English and an M.A. in Philosophy from Ball State University. She has been teaching at the university level for 36 years, including 10 online, primarily in the areas of philosophy and religious studies. Ms. Cooksey has taught over 40 online courses, developing and designing 20, in addition to earning both Level One and Level Two Quality Matters certification. Ms. Cooksey has published and presented in the areas of biomedical ethics, feminist philosophy, and the scholarship of teaching and learning.

Dr. Parul Khurana serves as Associate Professor of Biology at Indiana University East. Dr. Khurana earned a Ph.D. in Plant Cell Biology from Purdue University. She has taught at the university level for 12 years, including two years online, primarily in the areas of botany, cell and developmental biology, and genetics. Dr. Khurana has taught three online courses, having designed and developed each, in addition to earning Level One Quality Matters certification. Dr. Khurana has authored and co-authored numerous, peer-reviewed journal articles in the areas of plant cell biology and online teaching and learning.

Dr. Neil Sabine serves as Dean of the School of Natural Sciences and Mathematics and Professor of Biology at Indiana University East. Dr. Sabine earned a Ph.D. in Zoology from Brigham Young University and an M.A. in Biology from Southern Illinois University. He has been teaching at the university level for 31 years, including eight years online, primarily in the areas of biology, zoology, and animal behavior. Dr. Sabine has taught over a dozen online courses and developed and designed eight, in addition to earning Level One Quality Matters certification. Dr. Sabine has published and presented in the areas of animal behavior and online teaching and learning.

CHAPTER 13: MATHEMATICS

Dr. Young Hwan You serves as an Associate Professor of Mathematics at Indiana University East. He earned a Ph.D. in Mathematics from Purdue University and has taught at the university level for 13 years, including four years online, primarily in the areas of calculus, finite mathematics, statistics, linear algebra, and numerical analysis. Dr. You has taught 27 courses online and has developed and designed nine, in addition to earning Level One Quality Matters certification. Dr. You has authored or co-authored numerous, peer-reviewed articles in the areas of complex variables, partial differential equations, optics, and online teaching and learning.

Dr. Josh Beal, Assistant Professor of Mathematics at Indiana University East, earned a Ph.D. in Mathematics from Ohio University. He has taught at the university level for 11 years, including two years online, primarily in the areas of probability, analysis, and math finance. He has taught nine online courses and developed and designed five. Dr. Beal has published and presented in the areas of stochastic processes and optimization and has also earned Level One Quality Matters certification.

CHAPTER 14: EDUCATION

Dr. Jamie Buffington-Adams, Assistant Professor of Education at Indiana University East, earned a Ph.D. in Literacy, Culture, and Language Education from Indiana University and an M.A. in Language Education from Indiana University Purdue University Indianapolis (IUPUI). She has taught at the university level for six years and has taught online the entire time, teaching over 25 online courses and developing and designing nine, primarily in the areas of education foundations, teaching methods, and special education. Dr. Buffington-Adams has earned Level One and Level Two Quality Matters certification and a Certificate in Online Teaching from IU East. She has co-written a book and authored or co-authored numerous, peer-reviewed chapters and articles in the areas of marginalized and disenfranchised youth, curriculum studies, and disability studies.

Dr. Denice Honaker serves as Assistant Professor of Education at Indiana University East and earned an Ed.D. in Curriculum Studies and Early Childhood and Literacy Education and an M.S. in Elementary Education from Indiana University. She has taught at the university level for seven years, including two years online, primarily in the areas of early childhood and elementary education. Dr. Honaker has taught five online courses, developing and designing each, in addition to earning Level One Quality Matters certification. Dr. Honaker has published and presented in the areas of early childhood education, family literacy, and teacher preparation.

Dr. Jerry Wilde serves as Dean of the School of Education and Professor of Education at Indiana University East. Dr. Wilde earned a Ph.D. in Educational

Psychology from Marquette University and has taught at the university level for 20 years, including 12 online, primarily in the areas of educational psychology, adolescent development, and multicultural education. He has taught 25 online courses and developed or designed five, in addition to earning Level One Quality Matters certification. Dr. Wilde has written numerous books and authored or co-authored several, peer-reviewed journal articles in the area of cognitive behavioral interventions with children and adolescents.

CHAPTER 15: ECONOMICS AND FINANCE

Dr. Oi Lin Cheung, Associate Professor of Finance at Indiana University East, earned an M.S. and Ph.D. in Financial Economics from the University of New Orleans and an M.B.A. from the University of Macau. She has taught at the university level for 14 years, including six years online, primarily in the area of finance. Dr. Cheung has taught over 30 online courses and has developed and designed five, while earning Level One Quality Matters certification. Dr. Cheung has authored and co-authored numerous peer-reviewed articles in the areas of management communication behavior in financial statements, ADR returns, entrepreneurship, and innovation and economic growth.

Dr. Litao Zhong serves as Director of the Business and Economic Research Center and Assistant Professor of Economics and Finance at Indiana University East. Dr. Zhong earned a Ph.D. in Economics and Finance from Southern Illinois University and an M.B.A. from Baldwin-Wallace University. He has taught at the university level for nine years, including eight online, primarily in the areas of economics, managerial economics, and international finance. Dr. Zhong has taught over 30 courses online and has developed and designed seven, while earning Quality Matters Level One certification and a Certificate in Online Teaching from IU East. Dr. Zhong has authored or co-authored numerous peer-reviewed journal articles in the areas of international economics and regional economics.

Dr. Paula Kerler Baumann, Associate Professor of Nursing at Indiana University East, earned a Ph.D. in Nursing at Indiana University and an M.B.A. from Ball State University. She has been teaching at the university level for 12 years, including four online, primarily in the areas of legal and ethical issues in nursing, professionalism, quality and safety in health care, and health policy. Dr. Baumann has taught 12 online courses, developing and designing five, while earning Level One Quality Matters certification. Dr. Baumann has published and presented in the areas of team-based learning, innovation behaviors of nursing, and nurse residency programs to improve transition to practice.

Dr. Tonya Breymier serves as Associate Dean of the School of Nursing and Health Sciences and Assistant Professor of Nursing at Indiana University East. Dr. Breymier earned a Ph.D. in Human Services from Capella University and an M.S. in Nursing Education from Ball State University. Dr. Breymier has taught at the university level for 11 years, online all 11, primarily in the areas of graduate nursing education. She has taught over a dozen online courses and developed and designed four, while earning Level One Quality Matters certification and Certified Online Instructor credentialing from LERN. Dr. Breymier has published and presented in the areas of simulation and experiential learning.

Dr. Karen Clark serves as Dean of the School of Nursing and Health Sciences and Associate Professor of Nursing at Indiana University East. Dr. Clark earned an Ed.D. in Adult and Community Education and a M.S. in Nursing from Ball State University. She has taught at the university level for 30 years, including six online, primarily in the areas of community health, nursing research and evidence-based practice, and complementary and alternative therapies. Dr. Clark has taught 20 online courses and developed and designed three, in addition to earning Quality Matters Level One certification. Dr. Clark published and presented in the areas of RN to B.S.N. education and the scholarship of teaching and learning.